The Savor of the Sea

The Savor of the Sea

A Complete Seafood
Cookbook by

Dan Morris
& Matilda Moore

Illustrations by Peter Landa

The Macmillan Company : New York
Collier-Macmillan, Ltd. : London

This book is dedicated to all the people of the world who eat fish, either through choice or through necessity, and to all the people who do not eat fish, but will, we hope, learn to do so sometime. In other words, we dedicate this book to all mankind.

Contents

Our thanks to many people (and we wish that we could name them all) but particularly to Ed Moore for his specialties and Inez Morris for her creative cookery, for her methods of testing (which proved to be mighty tasty!), and for her organization of content. And, after her, our thanks to all the people of all the embassies around the world who favored us with recipes; to Mrs. Emily M. Robinson, of the United States Department of Agriculture's Extension Service; to Francis Anderson, of the United States Bureau of Commercial Fisheries' Consumer and Marketing Division; to John Von Glahn, of the Fishery Council at famed Fulton Fish Market; to Chet Brown, the lobsterman of Booth Bay, Maine, and Point Lookout, Long Island; and our heartfelt thanks to all the boys at Paddy's Clam House in New York.

Part One
Fish and Shellfish

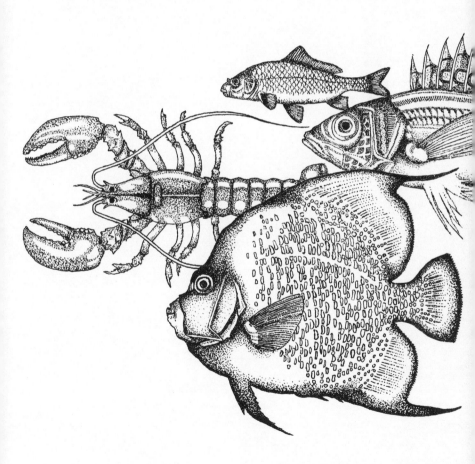

For the purposes of this book, we will speak of all animals with scales and fins that live in the water as FISH.

We will speak of the two classifications of animals with outer shells that live in the water, that is, the crustaceans and the mollusks collectively, as SHELLFISH.

The crustaceans are: lobsters, crabs, shrimp, prawns and crayfish. The mollusks are: oysters, clams, scallops and mussels.

I

Good Health Begins
in the Kitchen

Good health begins in the kitchen and that is what this cook-book is about—good health and good food.

The food we eat has a great deal to do with the kind of lives we live. If we eat a properly balanced diet, we have a better chance of living a properly balanced life. We'll have more energy, a better outlook and a better chance of coping with the daily problems of our lives.

Fish has a highly important place in that properly balanced diet. Nutritionists and doctors say fish should have a major place in our diets. They differ only on how often we should eat it. Some say once a day, some say four times a week and some say five fish meals each week.

"We recommend," says Dr. Fredrick J. Stare, chairman of the Harvard University Department of Nutrition, "that fish be included in diet four times a week. Seafoods fulfill the modern conception of good nutrition. They are high in the protein that contains the important amino acids, high in mineral content, low in fats—and those fats that fish do have are of the polyunsaturated type."

The late Dr. Norman Joliffe, author of the book *Reduce and Stay Reduced*, director of the New York City Health Department's Bureau of Nutrition, and maître d' of New York's Anti-Coronary Club, advised men over thirty to eat as the Japanese eat.

Dr. Emil Conason, coauthor of *Eat Well and Live Longer*, tells of a study of three groups of Japanese men: one group lived in Japan, another in Hawaii, and the third in Los Angeles. They ate in accordance with local practices and the study showed that heart disease was four times greater in Hawaii than in Japan and ten times greater in Los Angeles than in Japan. Fish is the dietary mainstay in Japan; animal fats are practically unknown there. The closer they came to our mainland, the worse their eating habits became.

Dr. Ancek Keyes, author of *Diet and the Epidemiology of Coronary Heart Disease*, sums it up this way: "Though alike in so many ways, Japanese in Japan, in Hawaii and in California differ in their diets, in their serum cholesterol concentration and in their proclivity to develop coronary heart disease."

Experts think so highly of fish as a health food that you'll find it on virtually every diet, whatever the reason behind the diet.

The United States Department of the Interior, which keeps track of our eating habits, says:

Fishery products are excellent sources of highly digestible protein. In addition, many contain fat, mineral matter and vitamins. Fish and shellfish can be included in the diet with full confidence that they supply high quality food.

Proteins build and repair body tissues. About one-third of the protein consumed daily should come from animal sources to balance the less efficient proteins of cereals and vegetables. An average serving of fish or shellfish supplies enough animal protein to satisfy this daily requirement. Fishery proteins are from 85 to 95 percent digestible and contain all of the so-called essential amino acids. Protein comprises about 18 percent by weight of the edible portions. These values are about equal to those of meat.

Minerals are essential for the performance of certain functions of the body and the maintenance of teeth and bones. In general, the mineral content of fish is similar to that of beef, although the iodine content is much greater in fish. The edible portions of most fish are satisfactory sources of magnesium, phosphorous, iron, copper, and iodine. Shellfish are particularly rich in these minerals. The flesh of both saltwater and freshwater fish are quite low in salt content.

Vitamins are important for growth and the maintenance of general well-being. Fat fish, like salmon and mackerel, are excellent sources of both vitamins A and D, an average serving supplying about 10 percent of the daily allowance of vitamin A and all of the vitamin D required. An average serving of either lean or fat fish will supply about 10 percent of the thiamine, 15 percent of the riboflavin and 50 percent of the niacin needed each day.

Fats are used by the body for flesh and energy. The fat content of fishery products varies with the kinds of fish and the season of the year. Very lean fish may contain only 0.5 percent fat, while fat fish may average 20 percent or more. Either fat or lean fish can be used in diets since the amount of fat and calories can be adjusted through choice of cooking methods and type of sauce used. Research has shown that the nutritional properties of fish flesh are approximately equal for all species.

Those are the basic arguments for eating fish regularly. This cookbook is meant to provide you with good recipes and tell you how to cook fish correctly in order to bring out its naturally delicious flavor.

II

The Market Forms of
Fish and Shellfish

*Shrimp are sold
in the following five ways:*

1. FRESH and whole (with heads on). Shrimp are sold this way around New Orleans and, less often, around other shrimp-harvesting centers.
2. FRESH OR FROZEN. Headless, with or without shells.
3. FRESH OR FROZEN COOKED. Generally peeled, cleaned and deveined.
4. FROZEN AND BREADED. Peeled, deveined and coated with bread crumbs or cornmeal.
5. CANNED. Ultraclean, processed in natural juices for fresh taste and fresh-cooked texture.

Fresh shrimp have a mild odor and the meat is firm. The color of the shell may be light pink, tan or grayish green. Sold raw, they are called green shrimp, but the term has nothing to do with color. When cooked, the shell turns pink and the meat acquires an opaque white to reddish tint.

Shrimp are sold according to size, with the larger ones bringing the higher prices. They are often graded by the number of headless shrimp to the pound and may be described by such general terms as jumbo, large, medium and small.

The largest size runs under fifteen shrimp per pound; the smallest size runs over sixty shrimp per pound. Jumbo shrimp, while costing more, take less time to peel and devein. Smaller shrimp cost less but take longer to prepare.

Figure 1 Market Forms of Shellfish. In Shell (clockwise): lobster, clams, crab, oysters.

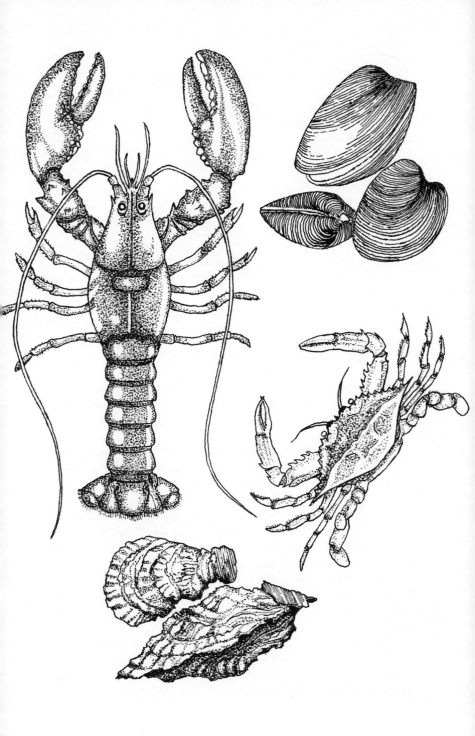

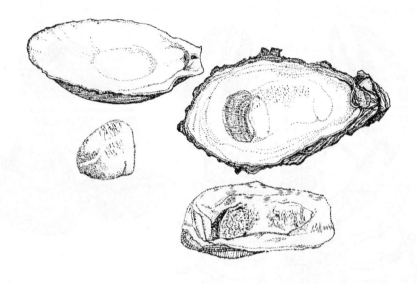

Figure 2 Shucked: Scallop shell (left top) and meat (left bottom); Oyster shell (right top) and meat (right bottom).

PRAWNS are best described as edible shrimplike crustaceans. Flavor and food value are just about the same. Recipes are interchangeable.

LOBSTERS are the most popular crustacean in America. There actually are two kinds of lobsters, the northern lobster and the spiny lobster, also called the rock lobster or crayfish.

NORTHERN LOBSTER, through modern methods of handling and transportation, is available in every state of the Union. It is caught from Labrador to North Carolina, with the bulk of the catch coming from the Maine and Massachusetts coasts.

When buying live lobsters, make sure the lobster's legs are moving and that the tail curls up under the body when the lobster is picked up. It should perform thus right up to cooking time.

When the lobster is taken from the ocean, its shell is a dark bluish green, which quickly turns to red during cooking.

Live market-sized lobsters usually weigh from one to three pounds and are graded in four sizes:

1. CHICKEN: three-quarters of a pound to a pound.
2. QUARTERS: one and one-quarter to one and one-half pounds.
3. LARGE: one and one-half to two and one-half pounds.
4. JUMBO: over two and one-half pounds.

Whole lobsters, cooked in the shell, are also marketed. They should have a seashore odor and they should be bright red in color. Straighten out the tail of a cooked lobster and it should spring right back to a curl when you let it go.

Cooked lobster meat is available either fresh, frozen or canned. Frozen lobster meat can be purchased in six-, fourteen- and sixteen-ounce cans. The fourteen-ounce size is the most popular one.

SPINY (ROCK) LOBSTER can be easily distinguished from the northern lobster by the absence of large, heavy claws and by

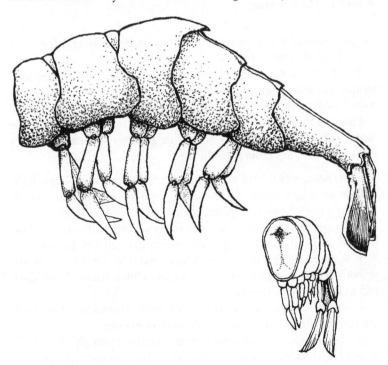

Figure 3   Headless.

Figure 4 Cooked Meat.

the presence of many prominent spines on its body and legs and by its long, slender antennae.

The rock lobster ranges through most of the world's tropical, temperate and subtropical waters and, in the United States, is found most commonly in Florida and Southern California waters.

Frozen lobster tails vary in weight from four ounces to more than a pound. Their color is no test of goodness because it varies from one breeding ground to the next.

1. FLORIDA, CUBA, THE BAHAMAS: smooth shell with large light yellow or white spots on the first segment of the tail, which generally has a brownish-green color.

2. WESTERN AUSTRALIA: tails are fairly smooth with small white dots on most of the tail segments which are reddish brown.

3. SOUTHERN CALIFORNIA AND WEST COAST OF MEXICO: tails are smooth without either spots or stripes. Color varies from dark red to brown and orange.

4. SOUTH AFRICA, NEW ZEALAND, EASTERN AUSTRALIA: tail shells are rough with no spots; brownish maroon in color.

5. MEDITERRANEAN AND SOUTHWEST EUROPE: rough shell with a number of white spots and streaks; color is a reddish tan.

Live spiny lobsters are available in some parts of California and Florida. They should be alive at time of cooking. When cooked, the shell turns red and the meat is white with tinges of red.

Whole, cooked spiny lobsters are available in some areas, but the cooked meat is more often marketed in cans.

CRABS have a distinctive flavor, tenderness and high food value that make them one of America's most popular shellfish. Four main kinds are captured in our marine waters. Hard-shell crabs are sold live within comparatively short distances of their feeding grounds. Soft-shell crabs are shipped with special care for hundreds of miles. Soft-shell crabs are molting blue crabs taken just after they have shed their hard shells and before the new armor has formed. State laws prohibit the sale of soft-shell Dungeness crabs.

1. BLUE OR HARD CRABS: East and Gulf coasts
2. DUNGENESS CRABS: Pacific coast, Alaska to Mexico
3. KING CRABS: North Pacific, off Alaska
4. ROCK CRABS: New England and California coasts

There are two crab species that are purely of local importance.

STONE CRABS: Florida
TANNER CRABS: Alaska

When bought live, crabs should show leg movement. Cooked, they should be bright red and should have no disagreeable odor. By lifting the lid under their body section slightly it is possible to smell any strong odor.

Cooked crab meat found in the stores comes from all four of the main varieties.

Blue crab meat is packed in four ways:

1. LUMP MEAT—whole lumps of white meat from the large body muscles
2. FLAKE MEAT—small pieces of the body's white meat
3. FLAKE AND LUMP—a combination of the two
4. CLAW MEAT—brownish-tinted meat from the claws

New England rock crab meat is sold in only one grade and is brownish in color.

Dungeness crab meat comes both from the claws and the body. The body meat is white; the claw or leg meat is reddish.

King crab meat is taken mainly from the legs, then frozen and packed for distribution around the world. The entire leg section, cooked and frozen and still in the shell, also is marketed.

Soft-shell crabs can be purchased either live or frozen.

Canned crab meat is usually packed in five-, six-and-a-half- and thirteen-ounce containers.

SCALLOPS, although they have two shells just like clams or oysters, are marketed only as dressed meat. It is a pity, because their shells are among the handsomest to come from the sea.

Unlike clams and oysters, scallops swim freely over the ocean floor in a constant forage for food. They obtain locomotion by snapping their two shells together and all this exercise develops an oversized muscle called the adductor muscle or the eye. That is the part of the scallop that is marketed in the United States. In Europe, people eat the entire scallop.

There are two varieties, the large sea scallop and the smaller bay scallop. Both have saucer-shaped shells. The sea scallop's shell can grow to as much as eight inches in diameter; the bay scallop's shell grows to about four inches. It is the shell of the bay scallop that has a scalloped edge; while the sea scallop does not. Nor does a sea scallop shell have the grooves that distinguish the bay dweller.

The sea scallop, whose eye may be as large across as two inches, is taken from the deep water off the northern and Middle Atlantic States.

The eye of the bay scallop attains a diameter of only about one-half inch. They are gathered in the inshore bays and estuaries from New England to the Gulf of Mexico and they have made Long Island's Peconic Bay famous.

Scallops are marketed all year but are at their best when taken from November to April. Fresh scallops are a light cream color, sometimes varying to a delicate pink. They're packed and iced at sea and are sold in the markets either in fresh or frozen form. Fresh scallops and frozen scallops when thawed should have a sweetish odor. When bought in packages, they should be practically free of liquid.

Both the bay and the sea scallop have lean, light, firm meat and a sweet flavor. Both contain high levels of well-balanced protein, very little fat and many of the essential minerals and vitamins.

OYSTERS have been enjoyed as a food for an unrecorded length of time. Indians were eating them long before America was discovered. The ancient Greeks and Romans served oysters at their banquets. Today, in the United States alone, about one hundred million pounds of oysters are sent to market every year.

Oysters combine flavor with ease of preparation, whether they're going to be eaten cooked or raw, and have more health-giving qualities than any other shellfish.

An average serving of six oysters will supply more than the daily allowance of iron and copper, about one-half of the iodine and about one-tenth of the needed protein, calcium, magnesium, phosphorous, vitamin A, thiamine, riboflavin and niacin. Few foods are better balanced nutritionally, the only thing they lack is calories.

Oysters may be purchased in three forms:

1. SHELL OYSTERS: they must be live when purchased. Their shells must be tightly closed. Stored at about 32° F. they'll keep very well. Gaping shells that do not close when handled indicate that the oysters are dead and not to be eaten.

2. SHUCKED OYSTERS: shucked means they've been removed from their shells and you're buying only the meat—there is no waste, every bit of meat is edible. Shucked oysters should be plump and have a natural creamy color with clear liquor and without any shell particles.

Fresh shucked oysters are usually sold in pint or quart containers, either metal or waxed. Properly iced or refrigerated, they will remain fresh for a week to ten days.

Frozen shucked oysters should not be thawed until ready to be used. Once thawed, they should never be refrozen.

3. CANNED OYSTERS: packed on the Atlantic and Gulf coasts, canned oysters generally are sold in No. One picnic cans. The drained weight is seven and one-half ounces. Packed on the Pacific coast, the drained weight is usually five or eight ounces.

The story about oysters being safe to eat only in months that contain the letter "R" is purely an old wives' tale. Oysters are safe to eat in any of the twelve months of the year.

There are two reasons for the "R" legend coming into being. The first goes back to the days before ice and electric refrigeration. Oysters, which need refrigeration, could not be eaten in the warm months, May, June, July and August.

The second reason still applies but it has to do only with the tastiness of the oyster. When the sea is warm, oysters pump tremendous amounts of water through their systems in order to take in and to rid themselves of the creatures and plants that comprise their diet. As a result they become thinner and less tasty. In the cold-water months when oysters have less work to do, they again become plump and tasty.

CLAMS abound in hundreds of species in American waters but we eat only a few and the market varieties sold on the East coast are not the same as those sold on the West coast. Each locality has different names for the same clam and, in some cases, the same name for different clams. The most popular marketed species on the Atlantic coast are the hard clam, the soft clam and the surf clam.

In New England and parts of Long Island, the hard (hard-shell) clam is called quahog. In the Middle Atlantic States and on south, a hard clam is called simply "clam."

Dealers call the smaller hard clams either littlenecks or cherrystones. They call the larger hard-shells chowders. The small ones are usually served raw on the half shell, the chowders are used primarily for chowders and soups.

The larger soft clams are known as in-shells and the smaller sizes are known as steamers.

The most common market clams on the Pacific coast are littleneck, butter, pismo and razor. But the Pacific's littleneck clam is not the Atlantic's littleneck. They're two different species.

The famed pismo clam comes from Pismo Beach in California. The delicious razor clam comes from Long Beach in Washington.

All clams may be bought in three ways: shelled, shucked or canned.

1. SHELL: these are generally sold by the dozen or by the pound. Make sure they are alive. With hard clams, gaping shells that do not close when handled mean the clam is dead and not to be used.

With other varieties, there should be some constriction of the neck or siphon when the clam is touched. Fresh shell clams will remain alive for several days if kept in the refrigerator at about 32° F.

2. SHUCKED: means the clam meat has been taken from the shell. Usually they are sold by the pint or quart in metal or wax containers. Shucked clams should be plump, with clear liquor, and free from shell particles. Properly handled and refrigerated or iced, they will remain fresh and edible for a week to ten days.

Shucked clams also are available the year around in quick-frozen packages. They should not be thawed until ready for use and should never be refrozen.

3. CANNED: hard, soft, razor, surf and pismo clams come whole or minced or as chowder in containers varying in size from three and one-half ounces to four pounds. Clam juice, broth and nectar are also available in bottles or cans.

MUSSELS are probably the most overlooked shellfish in American waters. They are flavorful and healthy when prepared according to European chefs' and housewives' recipes.

In buying, follow the same criteria that you would for clams or oysters. Make sure they're alive. In other words, make sure the shells are tightly closed.

How Much Fish to Buy

No one but the housewife herself knows how much her own family will eat, but the following may help you decide whether to double a recipe or cut it in half.

Fish servings generally are based on one-third to one-half pound of cooked fish per person. These quantities assume dinner

Figure 5 Whole or Round Fish.

Figure 6 Drawn Fish.

Figure 7 Dressed Fish.

Figure 8 Steaks.

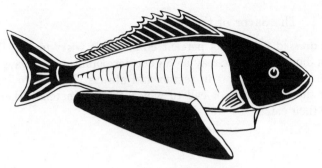

Figure 9 Fillets.

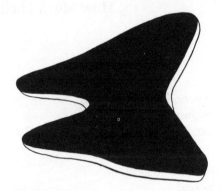

Figure 10 Butterfly Fillets.

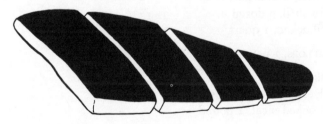

Figure 11 Fish Sticks.

will include other courses. They will not be enough for a family with healthy appetites sitting down to a one-plate meal.

To provide the amount suggested above, buy one-third pound per person of fresh or frozen fillets, sticks or steaks. Buy one-half pound per person of fresh or frozen dressed fish and one pound per person of fresh or frozen whole fish.

Since fillets are 100 percent edible, steaks are 85 percent edible and dressed fish are 45 percent edible, it is wiser to buy fillets even though the price may be higher per pound. It is always best to buy the fish that is in season and always cheapest to buy it near the main ports of call to which the commercial fisherman take their catch.

How Much Shellfish to Buy

To serve six people

CRABS
Live, 6 to 12 pounds; 18 to 36 crabs
Cooked, 1 pound
Dungeness, cooked, 4 to 6 pounds; 3 to 6 crabs

LOBSTERS
Live, 4 to 6 pounds; 6 lobsters
Cooked, 1 pound

OYSTERS AND CLAMS
In shell, 3 dozen
Shucked, 1 quart

SCALLOPS, 1 pound

SHRIMP
Headless, 1½ pounds
Cooked meat, 1 pound

MUSSELS
In shell, 4 pounds

III

When and Where to Buy Fish and Shellfish

Fish have their seasons, too, and wherever the piscatorial weather takes them is where the price of fish is cheapest, because they are caught that much closer to the market. This section tells you when, where, and what fish to buy in order to take advantage of price. The list is broken down by main ports of call to which commercial fishermen bring their catch. All you need do is check the ports closest to you, since that is your retail fish vendor's source of supply.

The numbers listed after each fish is your key to the best buys. The lowest number is the month of the lowest prices, and so on. The omitted months are the more expensive or the not-available months. The breakdown is only for fresh fish and shellfish, not for frozen seafood.

Maine

	Jan.	Feb.	Mar.	Apr.	May	June	July	Aug.	Sept.	Oct.	Nov.	Dec.
COD			4	3	1	2						
CUSK			3	4	1	2	5		6			
FLOUNDER												
Blackback			5		2	3			4			1
Dab				1	2	3						
Gray sole				6	1	3	2	4	5			
Yellowtail					4				5	3	2	1

	Jan.	Feb.	Mar.	Apr.	May	June	July	Aug.	Sept.	Oct.	Nov.	Dec.
HADDOCK						3	4	2	1			
HAKE												
Red						1	2	4	3			
White						2	1	3	4			
HALIBUT			3	2	1							
MACKEREL						1	2		3			
OCEAN PERCH				5	4	1	2	3	6			
POLLOCK					2	1		3				
SMELT	3	6		4						1	2	5
TUNA							1					
WHITING						2	1					
WOLF FISH			4	3	1	2						
CLAMS												
Hard-shell					4		2	1	3			
Soft-shell			4	2	1			3	5			
LOBSTER							3	1	2	4		
SEA MUSSELS		4	1	2	3							
SEA SCALLOPS							1	2	3		4	5

Massachusetts

	Jan.	Feb.	Mar.	Apr.	May	June	July	Aug.	Sept.	Oct.	Nov.	Dec.
COD				2	1	3						
CUSK				2	3	4	5	1	6		8	7
FLOUNDER												
Blackback						1	2	6	4	3	5	
Dab	2				4	1	3					
Fluke		3	1	2		5				4		
Gray sole		2			1	4						3
Lemon sole					2	1	4	6	3	5		
Yellowtail							1	2	5	3	4	
HADDOCK		8	2	1		3	6	4	7			
HAKE												
Red	5				4			2	1	3		
White						4	5	6	2	1	3	
HALIBUT			3	1	2	4						
MACKEREL						1	4		2	3		
OCEAN PERCH						1	4		2	3		
POLLOCK	1	4									3	2
SCUP (porgy)		2			3	1	4					
SWORDFISH							3	1		2		
WHITING						6	2	1	3	4	5	
WOLF FISH			4	3	1	2	5					
SEA SCALLOPS					5	2	7	4	1	3	6	

New York City

	Jan.	Feb.	Mar.	Apr.	May	June	July	Aug.	Sept.	Oct.	Nov.	Dec.
BLUEFISH					1			4	3	2		
BUTTERFISH	1	3	2			4			5			
COD	1	6	2	3	4							5
CROAKER			3	2		5	4	1	6			
EELS					2	3			4			1
FLOUNDER												
Blackback					1	2	3	6	4	5	8	7
Dab	1		4	3	2							
Fluke		5	1	2		3	6	4				
Gray sole		2		1	3	5						4
Lemon sole					5	1	4		3	2		6
Yellowtail			4				3	6		1	5	2
HADDOCK		3	1	2		4						
HAKE												
Red	3	2	1									
White						6	4	5	2	1	3	
HALIBUT					4	1	2	3				
HERRING												
Sardine				4	3	1	8	5	6	2	7	
Sea, large	1	4	3	2								5
KING MACKEREL	1	2	4					5				3
MACKEREL	5	4		3		1			6			2
MULLET	5							4	3	1	2	6
POLLOCK	1							6	4	5	3	2
SALMON												
Chinook (king)					3	2	1	4				
Chum (fall)											1	
Silver (cohoe)								3	1	2		
SCUP (porgy)			3		1	2	4		5			
SEA BASS		2		4	5	1	3					
SEA TROUT												
Gray					5	4		3	2	1		
Spotted											2	1
SHAD			3	1	2							
SMELT		5	4							2	3	1
RED SNAPPER	3				2					4		1
SPANISH MACKEREL	1	3									4	2
SPOT								3	1	2		
STRIPED BASS		1	3	2						5	4	
SWELLFISH		4		2	1	3						
SWORDFISH							2	1	3			

	Jan.	Feb.	Mar.	Apr.	May	June	July	Aug.	Sept.	Oct.	Nov.	Dec.
TILEFISH			2	1								
TUNA							2	3	1			
WHITING						3	2	5	4	6	1	
CLAMS												
Hard-shell				3		5	1	2	4	6		7
Soft-shell		3	5		6	1	2		4	7		
CRAB MEAT				5	6	2	1	3	4	7		
CRABS												
Hard-shell					6	4	3	1	2	5		
Soft-shell					1	2	3	4				
LOBSTERS					2	4	3	5	6	7		1
LOBSTER MEAT					3	4		1	2			
MUSSELS (bay)					4	2	6	7	3	5		1
OYSTERS												
In shell	2	5	6							1	4	3
Shucked	3									2	4	1
SEA SCALLOPS				7	5	2	1	3	6	4		
SHRIMP	4				6	1	2		3	5		
SQUID			2		3	1	4					

Maryland

Ocean City

	Jan.	Feb.	Mar.	Apr.	May	June	July	Aug.	Sept.	Oct.	Nov.	Dec.
CROAKER								3	2	1		
FLUKE, FLOUNDER						2	3	1			4	
MACKEREL		2	4	3								1
SCUP (porgy)				2	1	5				4	3	
SEA BASS					5	2	1	3	4			
SEA TROUT						2			4	1	3	

Cambridge

	Jan.	Feb.	Mar.	Apr.	May	June	July	Aug.	Sept.	Oct.	Nov.	Dec.
CROAKER					1	2	5	4	3			
SHAD			3	1	2							
STRIPED BASS		3	2	1								4
WHITE PERCH	5	3	1	2	4							
CRAB MEAT						5	3	1	2	4		
OYSTERS (shucked)	3	4								5	2	1

	Jan.	Feb.	Mar.	Apr.	May	June	July	Aug.	Sept.	Oct.	Nov.	Dec.

Crisfield

	Jan.	Feb.	Mar.	Apr.	May	June	July	Aug.	Sept.	Oct.	Nov.	Dec.
CRAB MEAT					5	3	1	2	4	6		
CRABS												
Hard-shell						3	4	2	1			
Soft-shell						3	2	1	4			
OYSTERS (shucked)	4									2	3	1

Virginia

Eastern Shore

	Jan.	Feb.	Mar.	Apr.	May	June	July	Aug.	Sept.	Oct.	Nov.	Dec.
CROAKER							3	2	1			
FLUKE, FLOUNDER						3	1	2				
MACKEREL			3	4	1							2
SEA TROUT					2	1	3					
SPOT							3	2	1			
CRAB MEAT					4	1	2	5	3			
OYSTERS (shucked)	4									2	3	1

Hampton Roads

	Jan.	Feb.	Mar.	Apr.	May	June	July	Aug.	Sept.	Oct.	Nov.	Dec.
BUTTERFISH	2	5		1		3	6		4			
CROAKER						2	3	1	4			
FLUKE, FLOUNDER	1	3	5	2								4
KING WHITING								2				1
MACKEREL				1								
SCUP (porgy)	5	3	2	1								4
SEA TROUT						5	6	2	1	3		4
SHAD			1	2								
SPOT								2	1	3		
STRIPED BASS			1	3						4	2	
CRAB MEAT				5	6		2	1	3	4		
OYSTERS (shucked)	4	7	6						5	1	3	2
SQUID												1

Lower Northern Neck

	Jan.	Feb.	Mar.	Apr.	May	June	July	Aug.	Sept.	Oct.	Nov.	Dec.
CROAKER						2	1	3				
SEA TROUT					2	1						

	Jan.	Feb.	Mar.	Apr.	May	June	July	Aug.	Sept.	Oct.	Nov.	Dec.
SHAD			2	1	3							
SPOT							2	1	3			
STRIPED BASS			2	1								
CRAB MEAT						2	1	3	4	5		
OYSTERS (shucked)	1	2	5								4	3

North Carolina

	Jan.	Feb.	Mar.	Apr.	May	June	July	Aug.	Sept.	Oct.	Nov.	Dec.
BLUEFISH						2			3	1		
BUTTERFISH	1					3	4	2				
CROAKER			2	3								1
FLUKE, FLOUNDER	2											1
KING WHITING	1	4		5							2	3
MULLET									2	1		
SEA TROUT												
Gray										3	2	1
Spotted									3	1	2	
SHAD	4	2	1	3								
SPANISH MACKEREL						1	3	2				
SPOT									1	2	3	
SHRIMP						1	2	3		4		

Gulf States

	Jan.	Feb.	Mar.	Apr.	May	June	July	Aug.	Sept.	Oct.	Nov.	Dec.
DRUM (Red)	2	3		6						4	5	1
GROUPER		2	5		1	3			4			
KING WHITING	4		3	1	2							
MULLET	2					4	6	3	5	1		
SEA TROUT												
(spotted)	2			4	1					6	5	3
SNAPPER (red)	2	6		4	1	3						5
CATFISH			5	3	1	2	4	6		7		
CRABS												
Hard-shell				4	1	2	3	5				
CRAB MEAT				4	1	2	3	5				
OYSTERS	1	2	3	4								
SHRIMP						5		3	2	1	4	

California

	Jan.	Feb.	Mar.	Apr.	May	June	July	Aug.	Sept.	Oct.	Nov.	Dec.
BARRACUDA		3	2			1	4			5		
FLOUNDER												
Sand Dab			2	4	7		5	1	3	6		
Sole						2	4	1	5	3		
Other		6	4					1	2	3	5	
HALIBUT												
California		4	2	3			1					
Other	3				1	2						
KINGFISH		3	2	6	4	5					1	
LINGCOD						5	4	1	3	2		
PERCH		3	2	1				4				
POMPANO	4		1	2					6	3	5	
ROCKBASS	3	6			5	2	4				1	
ROCKFISH			6	8	5	4	2	3	1	7		
SABLEFISH				3	5	2	4		1	6		
SALMON					4	3	1	5	2			
SEA BASS												
Black								3		1	2	
White						4	6	3	2	1	5	
SHAD				2	1							
SMELT				6		3	4	1	2	5		
SWORDFISH							2	1	3			
CARP		3	1	5			2		4			
CATFISH				5					3	2	1	4
ABALONE				1		3			4	6	5	2
CRABS	1	3		2							5	4
LOBSTERS (spiny)	2									3	1	
SHRIMP							3	1	2	4		
SQUID						1	2	3				

Seattle

	Jan.	Feb.	Mar.	Apr.	May	June	July	Aug.	Sept.	Oct.	Nov.	Dec.
COD		5	1	2	3					4	6	
FLOUNDER		1	6	4	2	7	5				3	
HALIBUT					2	3	1	4				

	Jan.	Feb.	Mar.	Apr.	May	June	July	Aug.	Sept.	Oct.	Nov.	Dec.
LINGCOD		2	1	3	4	5						6
ROCKFISH	5	4	2	1	3				6	7		
SABLEFISH									2	1	3	
SALMON												
Chinook (king)					5	4	2	1	3			
Chum (fall)										2	1	
Silver (cohoe)							4	1	2	3		
SMELT						2	1	4	3			
CRAB MEAT	2	3	5	1	4					6		
OYSTERS (shucked)	1	3	4	6						5	7	2

Chicago

	Jan.	Feb.	Mar.	Apr.	May	June	July	Aug.	Sept.	Oct.	Nov.	Dec.
HALIBUT					2	1						
MACKEREL		1	5	3		2				4		
SALMON												
Chinook (king)					2	1	3	4				
Silver (cohoe)							3		2	1		
SNAPPER (red)				6	5	1		7	3	4	2	
BLUE PIKE			1								2	3
BUFFALO FISH			5	2	4	3	1	6				
BULLHEAD	5		4	1	3				6	2		
CARP		3	6	1	2	4						5
CATFISH				1	3	2				5	4	
CHUB		6				5	2	1	4	3		
LAKE HERRING	1	4		3				5		2		
LAKE TROUT				6	4	5	3	2	1	7		
PICKEREL		5	2			1			4	3		
SAUGER	1	2				6			5	3		4
SHEEPSHEAD			4	1	2	3						
SMELT	4	2	1	3								
SUCKER			5	2		3				4	1	
WHITEFISH					3	1	2	4				
YELLOW PERCH				3	4		1	2		5		6
YELLOW PIKE					3	1	5	2	6	7		4
CLAMS												
Hard-shell						2	1	3	4	5		
LOBSTERS	1	6			3	2			7	4		5
OYSTERS												
In shell	4	6	2							5	3	1
Shucked	2									4	3	1
SCALLOPS					2		3		4			1

IV

Regional Names of
Most Popular Fish

Fish have many colloquial and regional names; in fact, some fish are known by two or three different names in the same state.

When you see a recipe later on in this book for, let's say, sea trout, you'll know that we mean weakfish, shad trout, common weakfish, gray weakfish, tiderunner, gator trout, squeteague, squit, summer trout, sun trout, silver sea trout, or spotted squeteague. The name you'll know it by depends on where you live. The only name which does not change with locale is the Latin name that marine scientists have given each fish. In this chapter we'll give: (1) the most common market name, and whether the fish is fat or lean; (2) the scientific name; and (3) all the regional names we know of.

	Latin Name	Regional Names
ALBACORE (fat)	*Germo alalunga*	Long-finned tuna, abrego
GREAT BARRACUDA (fat)	*Sphyraena barracuda*	Barracuda, sea tiger, becuna, picuda, saltwater pike
CALIFORNIA BARRACUDA (fat)	*Sphyraena argentea*	Scooter, snake, scoot, barry, log barracuda, Pacific barracuda
BUTTERFISH (fat)	*Poronotus triacanthus*	Harvestfish
BLUEFISH (lean)	*Pomatomus saltatrix*	Tailor, skipjack, fatback, snapping mackerel. Small ones are called snappers.
BLUE RUNNER (lean)	*Caranx crysos*	Jack crevalle, crevalle, hardtail jack, green jack

	Latin Name	Regional Names
CHUB (fat)	*Leucichthys species*	Longjaw, blackfin, bluefin
COD (lean)	*Gadus callarias*	Atlantic cod, grouper, black snapper, common cod. Young ones are called scrod.
CROAKER (lean)	*Micropogon undulatus*	Texas croaker, hardhead, chut, golden croaker, corvina, roncadina, crocus
DAB (lean)	*Hippoglossoides platessoides*	Sea dab
BLACK DRUM (lean)	*Pogonias cromis*	Gray drum, sea drum, oyster drum, oyster cracker, channel bass, barbed drum, big drum, striped drum, drumfish
RED DRUM (lean)	*Sciaenops ocellatus*	Channel bass, redfish, spot-tail, puppy drum
FLOUNDER (lean)	*Pseudopleuronectes americanus*	Winter flounder, flatfish, sand dab, blackback
FLUKE (lean)	*Paralichthys dentatus*	Summer flounder, plaice, northern flounder, doormat
RED HAKE (lean)	*Urophysis chuss*	Mud hake
WHITE HAKE (lean)	*Urophysis tenuis*	Common hake, squirrel hake
LITTLE TUNA (fat)	*Euthynnus alleteratus*	False albacore, skipjack, spotted bonito
LAKE HERRING (lean)	*Leucichthys artedi*	Bluefin, cisco
KING MACKEREL (fat)	*Scomberomorus cavalla*	Kingfish, silver cero, black salmon, cavalla
KING WHITING (lean)	*Menticirrhus species*	Kingfish, ground mullet, whiting, gulf king whiting, surf whiting, southern whiting, sand whiting, silver whiting

	Latin Name	Regional Names
MACKEREL (fat)	*Scomber scrombrus*	Boston mackerel, Atlantic mackerel, common mackerel, spike, tinker
SPANISH MACKEREL (fat)	*Scomberomorous maculatus*	Sierra mackerel, cero, spotted mackerel
PACIFIC MACKEREL (fat)	*Pneumatophorus diego*	Greenjack, greenback, zebra, striped mackerel
OCEAN PERCH (lean)	*Sebastes marinus*	Rosefish
WHITE PERCH (lean)	*Morone americana*	Bluenose, gray, black perch
YELLOW PERCH (lean)	*Stizostedion vitreum vitreum*	Pike perch
PICKEREL (lean)	*Esox reticulatus and E. lucius*	Jack, grass pike
POLLOCK (lean)	*Pollachius virena*	Boston bluefish, pollack, silver cod, green cod, queddy salmon, sea salmon
POMPANO (fat)	*Trachinotus carolinus*	Permit, great pompano, golden pompano, Carolina permi
ROCKFISH (lean)	*Sebastodes species*	Rock cod, red cod, snapper; black, blue, vermillion and orange rockfish; black sea bass, priestfish, neri, barracho, rasher, chilipepper, quillback, bolina, butterball, roosterfish, gopher, kelp rockfish, gallo, chefra, sand bass, red rock, spotted rock. And so the list of rockfish aliases go—until there's one hundred or more. The important thing to remember is that you can cook them all, using

	Latin Name	Regional Names
ROCKFISH (*Cont.*)		just about any recipe but particularly the bass recipes, and they'll all taste grand.
SABLEFISH (fat)	*Anoplopoma fimbria*	Black cod
SCUP (lean)	*Stenotomus chrysops*	Porgy, fair maid, northern porgy
SEA BASS (lean)	*Centropristes striatus*	Common sea bass, rock bass, bluefish, blackwill, hannahill, humpback
WHITE SEA BASS (lean)	*Cynoscion nobilis*	Sea trout, weakfish, king croaker, white croaker
BLACK SEA BASS (lean)	*Stereolepis gigas*	Giant sea bass, California sea bass, jewfish, black rockfish
STRIPED BASS (lean)	*Roccus saxatilis*	Striper, rockfish, greenhead, squidhound, rock bass
ATLANTIC SALMON (fat)	*Salmo salar salar*	Kennebec salmon, New England or Maine salmon, silver salmon
CHINOOK SALMON (fat)	*Oncorhynchus tshawytscha*	Tyee, king salmon, tule, quinnat, spring salmon
CHUM SALMON (fat)	*O. keta*	Fall salmon, hayho, calico, dog salmon
PINK SALMON (fat)	*O. cerbuscha*	Humpback, haddo
SILVER SALMON (fat)	*O. kisutch*	Cohoe, silverside, skowitz, hooknose
SEA TROUT (lean)	*Cynoscion family*	Weakfish; shad, sun, summer, gator, spotted, gray, sand, speckled, white and silver trout; gray, spotted, southern, sand and silver weakfish; squeteague, squit, tiderunner

	Latin Name	Regional Names
SHEEPSHEAD (lean)	*Archosargus probatocephalus*	Sargo, sea bream, convict fish, prison fish
SNAPPER FAMILY (lean)	*Lutjanus family*	Red, Pensacola, Lane, mangrove, mutton, Caribbean, green, gray, black, dog, spotted and Cuban snapper; pargo, muttonfish, lawyer, caji, redtail, jocu and Cubera
SWELLFISH (lean)	*Spheroides maculatus*	Blowfish, globefish, swell toad, puffer
SMELT (fat)	*Osmerus mordax*	Winterfish, frostfish
PACIFIC SOLE (lean)	*Pleuronectidae species*	Rex, petrale, sand dover, English sole
GRAY SOLE (lean)	*Glyptocephalus cynoglossus*	Witch flounder
SWORDFISH (lean)	*Xiphias gladius*	Broadbill
SAUGER (lean)	*Stizestedion*	Sand pike
SHEEPSHEAD (lean)	*Aplodinotus grunniens*	Freshwater drum, gaspergou
WOLF FISH (lean)	*Anarichas lupas*	Ocean catfish
YELLOWTAIL (lean)	*Limanda ferruginea*	Yellowtail flounder, rusty dab

There you have them, the regional names that the most popular marketed fish are known by. If we included all the fish caught and cooked by sports fishermen that don't often go to market, we'd need a book just for names. However, don't be surprised if you find recipes for a lot of them in this book. Fluke, alias summer flounder, for instance. And, if you like the recipe but can't find the fish, just go ahead and cook the fish you have. You'll find that 98 percent of all fish recipes are interchangeable.

V

Proper Care of
Fish and Shellfish

The best possible time to eat fish is immediately after it comes from the water. The next best thing is to handle it properly, refrigerate it properly and, if frozen, thaw it properly. There is no other way of preserving good quality and taste.

Causes of Spoilage

There are three primary causes of breakdown in quality: bacterial action; oxidation of the oil or fat in the flesh; enzymic action in the flesh.

1. Bacterial action contaminates fishery products when there is poor sanitation in handling and high temperature after fish have been removed from the water. It is almost entirely arrested when fish are frozen and stored at very low temperatures. It can be considered practically eliminated so long as the fish are kept in this condition.

2. Oxidation of the oil or fat can cause spoilage of frozen fish even at low freezer temperatures if not properly packaged. You'll know oxidation has set in if you detect any yellow discoloration on the surface of the skin or on the flesh in areas exposed to air. Oxidation can be retarded greatly by glazing the fish with a thin coating of ice or by wrapping it in moisture- and vaporproof paper.

3. Enzymes are substances in the flesh that both build up and tear down body tissues while normal life processes are going on. Common to all forms of animal life, these reactions are controlled

automatically as long as life is maintained. Although the temperatures at which fish are stored have a definite effect on the speed of the digestive reaction of the enzymes after death, the enzymic action cannot be completely stopped by handling and storage. No matter how well you handle, package or store fish, enzymic action that sets in after death cannot be stopped completely. But, if the storage conditions are good, the temperatures low enough and the fish properly packaged, the enzymic action has no important effect on the quality.

Since fish come to the consumer in a variety of ways—one of the main consumers being the person who goes out and catches his own, it follows that there must be a variety of ways of caring for fish.

Handling and storing
your own catch

SALTWATER: Nothing can be tastier than fresh-caught fish, and a few simple precautions taken on the beach or in your boat are all that is necessary to preserve their fine flavor.

If you've never caught a saltwater fish and you'd like to try, we'd like to suggest that you get yourself a copy of *A Family Guide to Saltwater Fishing* * by Dan Morris.

1. If you want to keep your fish alive, pin them through both lips with a stringer made just for this purpose. Every tackle shop sells them. Tie the free end of the stringer to a post, an oarlock or a boat cleat and let the fish frisk deep enough in the water to be below the sun's rays. Or, if the fish are small enough, put them in a gunny sack tied to the boat in the same way.

Don't ever thread a stringer through a fish's mouth and gills. The stringer will keep its mouth open and the fish will swallow water and drown.

2. If you can't keep your catch alive then give them a preliminary cleaning immediately to (a) keep the flesh from drying out if the sun is hot; (b) to keep deterioration from setting in; (c) to allow the blood to drain out naturally, because a bled fish is a better-tasting fish.

* Collier Books, 95¢.

Simply cut his belly open, starting back at the anus and slicing forward. Leave his head on but remove the innards. Use your knife tip to scrape away most of the blood along the spine, your fingernail to remove what's left. (The reason for not removing the head is simple: it will keep the flesh on the "neck" end from overcooking. If you don't want to serve a fish head and all, just remove the head after you've finished cooking.)

After cleaning your fish, put it in a gunny sack or wrap it in seaweed. Then bury it in the sand (making sure you're above the tide line so that it won't be washed away), dangle it in the water or keep dousing it with seawater to keep it moist.

Anything else in the way of cleaning—scaling, washing, finning, filleting, skinning or steaking—can wait until you get home.

FRESHWATER: You'll find few if any recipes for freshwater fish in this cookbook, not because they're not good to eat—they are—but because most of the recipes in this book can be used for any freshwater fish you catch. There are few basic recipes that apply only to freshwater fish. Most freshwater fish recipes concentrate on the sauces. All you need do when you want to cook freshwater fish is select a recipe in this book that seems appropriate and a sauce to go with it and substitute the freshwater fish for the one the recipe calls for.

If you are a freshwater fisherman, and you can become one by reading Ed Moore's book *Fresh Water Fishing,** there's a different procedure to follow after you've caught and cleaned your catch in the same way you would clean a saltwater catch.

1. Make sure you have a well-ventilated creel, because air circulating around your catch helps retain the flavor.

2. Collect a mess of twigs—preferably willow twigs—cool dry swamp grass or hay.

3. Line the bottom of the creel with an ample layer of grass or twigs.

4. Place some grass or twigs inside the dressed fish.

5. Finally, put a layer of fish on top of the layer of twigs or grass inside your creel. Cover that layer of fish with another

* Collier Books, 95¢.

layer of grass or twigs and keep building layer upon layer in the same way.

One important word of reminder: never wash your cleaned catch, whether it's saltwater fish or freshwater fish, until you're ready to cook it, because water weakens the flesh and hastens deterioration. Wipe it dry before placing it in your creel. If you want to keep your freshwater fish alive, do as you would with a saltwater fish.

If you prefer, you can buy a basket that's specially made for freshwater fish. Most freshwater tackle shops have them. Just drop the fish in the basket as you catch them and lower the basket into the water.

Handling and storing
fresh fish
bought in the market

To make sure that fresh fish retains its flavor, keep it constantly refrigerated below 40° F. and preferably at freezing point, 32° F. Fresh fish can be kept for a week to ten days in this way and still be edible. For the fish to be tastiest when served, make two days of cold storage your limit.

Handling and storing
fresh shellfish

When storing fresh shellfish, maintain the temperature at or close to 32° F. A few degrees higher can cause considerable loss of quality in a very few hours.

Handling and storing
frozen fish and shellfish

Keep it frozen solidly until ready for use. Once it's thawed, don't refreeze it. Fish will keep a long, long time if wrapped in a moisture- and vaporproof paper or if glazed and stored at no more than zero ° F. Improperly packaged, there will be a gradual loss of moisture and the fish will shrink and dry out. But, since you don't know what happened to the fish before you bought it, keep frozen fish only about a month if you have your own freezer; only about a week if you keep it in a refrigerator's freezer compartment.

Thawing frozen fish and shellfish

If additional cooking time is allowed, you can cook frozen fish, fillets and steaks immediately after taking them from the freezer. But they'll be much easier to bread or stuff or fry if you thaw them out first. You have no choice if the fish is frozen either in the whole or round. Then you have to thaw them before you can clean them.

1. The best way and the recommended way is to defrost fish by placing them in your refrigerator and letting them remain there until pliable enough to handle. At 40° F., it will take about eighteen hours for a one-pound fillet to thaw.

2. The fastest way to defrost a whole or drawn fish without spoiling it is to cover it with cold running water. How long the thawing process takes depends on the size and the shape of the fish.

3. Steaks or fillets will thaw out in about 30 minutes if immersed in cold running water. Keep them in the freezer package while defrosting.

4. The worst way to thaw fish is by leaving it out of the refrigerator at room temperature. In fact, we recommend that you not do it. Room temperature thawing may be a time-saver, but the thinner parts of the fish will thaw more quickly than the thicker parts and spoilage can set in.

5. Whole or drawn fish can also be thawed by being embedded in crushed ice. But it's inconvenient, messy and very slow.

6. Give frozen shellfish the same treatment you would any other frozen fish, but, in this case, it is best to thaw before cooking because shellfish should be cooked quickly and heat cannot quickly penetrate anything that is frozen.

VI

Cleaning Your Fish

Earlier, we told you what to do down on the beach or alongside the pond to keep your catch wholesome and tender until you got home.

When you reach home with a full stringer there is more to be done to make your fish ready for either the stove or the refrigerator. The more thorough cleaning, which means removing the fins and scraping away the scales, comes at this time. We'll start from scratch, assuming you didn't do any preliminary cleaning on the beach.

The tools to use

You'll need two tools for cleaning a fish, a good knife and a scaler. Every tackle shop in the country sells scalers and you needn't spend much more than a quarter. If necessary, you can even scale a fish with the edge of a spoon.

Any good kitchen knife will do for eviscerating a fish but they are not so suitable for filleting. The best way to buy a good fillet knife and know it's good is to ask your butcher to buy it for you. The blade should be thin, narrow and razor sharp. Stainless steel looks the best but doesn't hold its edge so well.

There are three main steps in cleaning: finning, scaling and eviscerating, or gutting. Which order you take them in probably doesn't make a great deal of difference. But we've found that it works best to first scale, then fin and finally gut. That is the order we will follow here. Figure 12 will show you where to find things.

Scaling

Lay the fish on its side on a cleaning board and work the scaler from tail to head. Some people find it gives them enough anchorage to hold the fish by the head while scaling. We find it simpler to pin the tail to the board with an icepick and hold onto the handle. Then the fish can't slip and the scaling goes that much faster. Be sure to work as close as possible to the fins.

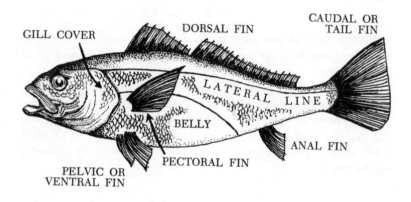

Figure 12 A fish and its fins.

Finning

You'll need the fillet knife's sharp point for this operation. Place the fish on its side and slash all the way from head to tail close on both sides of the dorsal fin but not so close that you'll slice through bone. Then press the dorsal firmly between your thumb and the side of the knife and pull. Out will come the fin, every bone intact. Repeat the operation on the fish's bottom side and cut a circle around the pectoral fins on the sides.

Eviscerating

Place the fish on its side and slice the belly open by starting back at the anus and cutting forward to the gill covers. Then the innards will come out easily. You'll find the kidney alongside

A

B

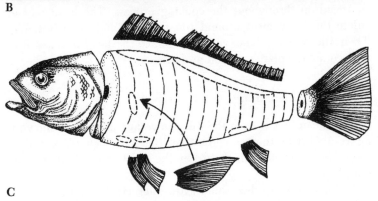

C

FINNING AND STEAKING A FISH

Figure 13A Cut closely along both sides of fins, penetrating no deeper than necessary to remove bones with fin.

Figure 13B Lift out fin with fingers, or use the side of the knife and fingers for a better grip.

Figure 13C Cut steaks.

the spine. Remove it with your fingernail or with gentle application of the point of the knife. Scrape away the blood flecks with your knife, wipe the fish with a clean cloth or absorbent paper and the chore is done—except for the head and the liver, if you like liver.

The liver is the healthiest part of the fish to eat and it tastes just like what it is—liver. You'll recognize it when you see it. Removing it from the rest of the innards takes no great knowledge and you cook it as you would chicken livers.

As for the head, there's a reason for keeping it on and for taking it off. If you're going to pan fry, for instance, you might just as well make the removal of the head part of the cleaning process. In fact, it will make the eviscerating that much simpler.

The best time to cut off the head is after slitting and before removing the innards. Slice down behind the gills, cutting through the spine and following the gill cover's vee shape. Most of the innards will come out with the head. If the fish is too big to slice through the spine, just cut the flesh all around it then place the head over the edge of the table and snap.

If you're going to bake, stuff or broil your fish it's best to leave the head on throughout the cooking process. The head will insulate the body meat around the neckline and keep it tender. Then, the cooking done, you can remove the head or leave it on to decorate the platter, as you prefer.

Steaking and chunking

Steaks can be cut from the fish you've just dressed as shown in figure 13C. Cut them no less than one-half inch thick and no more than one inch thick to get the most flavor and delicacy out of them.

As for chunking, dice some extra-thick steaks, from 2 to 4 or 5 inches thick, and your fish is chunked. That size is fine for simmering in a soup, flaking into a salad, or breaking into a chowder or a stew.

Filleting

This is the most complicated part of dressing a fish for cooking, but the little bit of skill that filleting requires is made up for by the work that it eliminates. You do not have to clean a fish that you are going to fillet.

Just lay the fish on its side on the cleaning board, slice gently through the flesh until the knife blade touches but does not penetrate the spine. Turn the blade flat against the spine and work it the length of the fish to separate the meat from the bone.

With one side filleted, flop the fish over and fillet the other. Just discard the waste and the job is done. Fins, head, innards, still intact, are all part of the waste.

People who don't have to worry about food budgets (that includes the fine chefs) start behind the gills and slice down to the tail because this kind of cut makes it easier for them to fillet a fish without including the less-tasty belly meat.

Those who have to count their food pennies or answer to the cash register (that includes most fish vendors) start behind the tail and slice toward the head, thus more easily including the belly meat as part of the fillet.

Skinning

Whether or not to skin a fish is a matter of taste. If you like a more gamy flavor, leave the skin on. If you like your fish delicately done, take the skin off. While it adds work to the cleaning process, it does away with the need for scaling. To skin a whole, dressed fish, use your knife to peel enough of the skin away from the flesh to provide you with a firm grip and then pull steadily from head to tail. If the flesh should start clinging to the skin, use your knife again and work gently through the trouble spot. If the fish is big and tough or if you have trouble getting a grip on the skin, use a pair of pliers to help you with the pulling.

To skin a fish fillet, place the fillet skin down on your cleaning board, slice gently through an end of the flesh until you can grip a bit of skin firmly, turn the blade flat, cut with one hand and pull with the other, putting slightly more emphasis on the pulling than on the cutting.

A WORD ABOUT WATER

We give this brief paragraph a capital-letter, boldface title because it is important:

Don't wash your fish after it's dressed or filleted UNTIL you're ready to cook it. Water hastens the breakdown of the flesh and deterioration sets in. This means less delicacy, less flavor. Refrigerate the fish until cooking time and THEN wash it. And there's only one right way to wash it and that is NOT by holding it under running water.

The thing to do is to dip your cleaned fish quickly in cold salted water and immediately dry it as much as possible with a towel, damp cloth or absorbent paper. If you're working with fillets or steaks you can simplify the drying by placing them on absorbent paper and letting them drain.

VII

The Basics of
Cooking Fish

How Long to Cook

The most important thing to remember in fish cookery is that all fish and most shellfish are tender before they are cooked. The cooking process is not a tenderizing process, as it is with other foods, but a flavor developer and a coagulant. The flesh of the fish or shellfish loses its transparency in a short time when it is exposed to heat; the moment it turns opaque it is virtually done. Additional cooking only toughens and dries out the meat.

The proper direction for testing doneness in fish cookery is, "When the fish flakes easily at the touch of a fork it is done." "Flaking easily" means that the flesh separates or falls easily into its natural divisions.

Always test in the thickest part, which will naturally take the longest time to cook. Don't gouge, but poke gently with your fork. If the first fish you test this way is full of tine marks, it will still taste much better than if you had overcooked it. But once you have done it a couple of times, no one will even suspect that you'd touched the fish.

A visual method of testing doneness is to check the translucent or transparent quality of the flesh. As we said above, it will change to an opaque or clouded color, usually white, cream, or pink, but will retain its moist appearance. The moment the meat looks dry or shrinks, it is overdone. Sauces should be prepared in advance so that the fish can be served the moment it is done.

Here are a few anecdotes and quotations from the experts.

Francis Anderson runs the consumer and marketing development end of the United States Bureau of Commercial Fisheries in and around New York. He has two mainstay props for his cooking demonstrations to professional cooks. One is a raw fish, the other is a pre-cooked meat or poultry dinner wrapped in a package labeled "just heat and serve."

Mr. Anderson places his two props on the table in front of him and starts from scratch to prepare a seafood platter and to "just heat and serve" the pre-cooked dinner. The idea is to see which one comes out of the oven ready to eat first.

The fish always wins and Mr. Anderson has made his point: that a fish doesn't call for much cooking time, that even seconds count and that it doesn't take many seconds to overcook it. He says, "A fish is like an egg. Cooking makes it tough."

Mrs. Emily M. Robinson, a home economist and nutritionist on Long Island for the Extension Service Association, works with housewives and mothers. Two of the Association's sponsors are the United States Department of Agriculture and the New York State College of Home Economics at Cornell University.

"Fish," she tells her classes, "must be cooked just long enough to coagulate the protein and no longer."

Like Mr. Anderson, Mrs. Robinson also believes in realistic demonstrations. Her props are two fish of the same species, size and shape. She prepares them for baking, puts them side-by-side in the same baking pan and slips it into the oven. After a short time, she takes the pan out of the oven. Both Mrs. Robinson and the class agree that the fish are undercooked.

"How much longer should they be cooked?" she asks. No matter how often she asks the question, the answer invariably is the same:

"Five minutes."

"No," says Mrs. Robinson, "thirty seconds!"

Back into the oven goes the baking pan. In exactly thirty seconds she takes just one fish out of the pan and out of the oven and quickly shuts the door on the other.

Mrs. Robinson picks up her fork and probes ever so gently at the half-a-minute fish. It flakes nicely and she gives everybody a nibble. The verdict is "delicious."

Meanwhile, the timer keeps clicking and finally there's the bell. The five minutes are up. Mrs. Robinson opens the oven, takes out the second fish and puts it beside the first. Mrs. Robinson tries flaking it with her fork. No flakes. And when Mrs. Robinson offers to give someone a taste there are no takers.

Mrs. Robinson has made her point too. Don't ever overcook a fish. But she doesn't stop there.

"The most important thing to use in fish cooking," she says, "is a fork. It is better than any timer ever made. A fish won't fall like a cake when you open the oven door. So open it often and poke gently with your fork. When the fish flakes it is done, no matter what the recipe says.

"If the recipe you're following calls for fifteen minutes of cooking time, start using your fork at seven minutes. And heed the fork, not the recipe. When the fish flakes, it is done."

Mrs. Robinson has some very good reasons for saying that. Not only because most people are inclined to overcook, but also because when a recipe calls for a three-pound fish, there is no way for the recipe to know if it is a long, thin three-pound fish or a short, fat three-pound fish.

Neither Mrs. Robinson nor Mr. Anderson nor anyone who knows anything about fish cooking can say it often enough. Don't overcook.

The Fishery Council, which has its base in New York's famous Fulton Fish Market and speaks for just about every commercial fisherman and fish dealer in New York and New England and a few more states besides, prepared a fine little booklet entitled *Fish 'n' Tips*.

When John Von Glahn, the Fishery Council's executive secretary, talks cooking to anyone, he picks up a copy of *Fish 'n' Tips* and points to these big and boldface words:

Fish is cooked to develop flavor—not to make it tender.
Fish flesh is naturally tender. Cooking coagulates the excellent protein and develops flavor at the same time. Overcooking dries and toughens fish.

Fats and Oils

No matter what fish they are meant for, fish recipes basically will work just as well with any other fish. Any recipe that calls for a particular fat fish will give just as delicious results if used with any other fat fish. Any lean fish recipe will give the same delicious results no matter which lean fish is used.

You can apply a fat fish recipe to a lean fish, but you must be more liberal with the butter, bacon, or oil in the basting. If using a lean recipe for fat fish, be less liberal with the fats you add.

The biological difference between fat fish and lean fish as far as the cook is concerned simply is that the oils that lean fish contain are concentrated in the liver; the oils that fat fish contain are distributed all over its body. Therefore the fat fish needs less lubrication in cooking.

Just as you must guard against overcooking, you also must guard against overlubricating. Any more oil or fat than you'll need to keep the fish from sticking or from toughening will only add grease to the fish.

What fats and oils to use

There was a time when butter brought out the best in fish. That is still true, but health and weight-conscious cooks are substituting vegetable oils now. They are polyunsaturated, just as the fat in fish is polyunsaturated, and they make the perfect medium for fish cookery. By way of an aside, there is one oil that possesses even greater polyunsaturation than any vegetable oil you can mention—fish oil!

There are many of them to choose from: safflower, corn, cottonseed, sunflower and soya are leading in essential fatty acid content. After them come the nut oils. Trailing well along to the rear but still in the ranks of the polyunsaturated comes olive oil.

The first group, then, are the oils in which you should do your fish cooking. Whether deep frying or pan frying, you and your family probably will be better off for it. That doesn't mean you should never use butter or olive oil; it only means that you should use them sparingly. You can always spike your vegetable oil with butter before cooking.

Mix one part butter with four parts vegetable oil, or put five ripe olives in one pint of vegetable oil. You will have the flavor you like and remember from cooking with all butter.

A vitamin-fortified margarine also makes a good butter substitute. The concentrated vitamins provide a uniformity of vitamin content that doesn't vary with the seasons of the year.

Fats or oils are used in most kinds of fish cooking. Most of all in deep frying; the least in baking, broiling, boiling or poaching and not at all in steaming. How much you use will have its effect on the ultimate flavor of the fish.

The adjective "well-greased" does not mean heavily greased, it means properly greased. If a recipe calls for a well-greased dish, make sure that every speck of the dish is covered with just enough of a film of oil to prevent sticking and no more.

The amounts you need for different cooking methods are as follows:

DEEP FRYING: The deep pot must contain enough oil to cover the fish but it should not be more than half full. The fat or oil should be heated to 350°–375° F. before cooking begins.

PAN FRYING: No more than one-eighth to one-quarter inch of oil or melted fat, which includes butter, in a heavy frying pan.

BAKING: The baking pan must be greased but just enough to prevent sticking and no more. The fish should be brushed with oil, melted butter or melted margarine.

BROILING: The broiling pan should be preheated and lightly greased. Brush the fish with oil or melted butter or margarine.

PLANKED FISH: If you use a hardwood plank, oil it well and place it in a cold oven to heat thoroughly as the oven preheats. If you use a metal or glass oven platter, grease it lightly before putting it into the oven. Brush the fish with oil or melted butter or margarine.

OUTDOOR COOKING: Grease the wire grill well.

DIET COOKING: There are two ways of diet frying. The first and the most common way is pan frying. Simple. Grease your pan with just two tablespoons of corn oil.

The second way—and it is a way that is highly recommended

both by Mrs. Robinson and the New York State College of Home Economics at Cornell University—is to bake fillets at a high temperature. This is called oven frying.

A Cornell Extension Bulletin telling how to oven fry says:

"Baking at a high temperature gives the crisp crust and browned flavor of pan-fried fish yet uses less fat, takes much less attention and causes fewer cooking odors."

(Directions for oven frying will be found on page 253.)

The Liquids to Use

In simmering, steaming, poaching or water-broiling fish, or in making soups and chowders, the only liquid you need to bring out the flavor is plain water. The flavor of the fish can be changed to your taste by substituting some other liquid for water: milk, cream, wine, even beer. The most popular substitute is court bouillon. (Recipes for court bouillon begin on page 153.)

Marinating Fish

When marinating fish, be sure to use a glass bowl and not a metal container of any kind.

Cleaning Fish Dishes and Utensils

Rub dishes and utensils that have been used for fish with slightly moistened salt and wash off with hot water before using soap.

Avoiding Fish Smell
in the House

It is the smoke from overheated oil used in cooking fish that causes an unpleasant odor. Don't let the oil reach the smoking stage and you will both improve the flavor of your fish and prevent cooking odors.

Temperatures

There is no best temperature for cooking fish, but there is a best time for using each temperature. A low or moderate cooking temperature is usually suggested because less watching is necessary, but occasionally a high temperature is an advantage, for instance to ensure crispness. Oven frying is another good example. Low temperature is best for cooking thick pieces of fish and hard-frozen fish to ensure even heat penetration. The lower the temperature, the longer the time. But your fork is still your best guide.

Slow oven	250° to 350° F.
Moderate oven	350° to 400° F.
Quick or hot oven	400° to 450° F.
Very hot oven	450° to 550° F.

While the time given with any recipe is only approximate because it is nothing more than a guide to fork-testing time (start using your fork at half the given cooking time), temperatures should be exactly as those called for in the recipe. For your guidance if you are not following a recipe:

Pan frying	350° F.
Deep frying	350° to 375° F.

Oven frying	500° F.
Baking	350° to 375° F.
Broiling	350° F.
Planked (baked)	400° F.
Water broiling	550° F.

The same Cornell extension bulletin that we mentioned earlier contains exact information on the basics of every kind of fish cooking. The Fishery Council's *Fish 'n' Tips* also contains explicit directions for basic fish cookery. We picked out the best of each, put the final results to the test and came up with the recommendations preceding the recipes for each basic cooking method in Part Three of this book. Follow those directions—with just that one admonition which we can't repeat often enough: Use your fork and not your clock. Start checking for flakiness at half the given recipe time. When the fish flakes, stop cooking and start serving. Test for doneness at the thickest part of the fish.

VIII

Cleaning and Cooking
Your Shellfish

A word of caution about shellfish

People catch fish all their lives and never land one that is poisonous. Except in very rare instances, fish move around too much to imbibe enough of anything toxic to be dangerous. But that doesn't hold for shellfish. They are sedentary in their ways, with the exception of sea scallops, and so they are susceptible to pollution and contamination in the water.

If you intend to gather your own clams, oysters, crabs, or mussels, confine your search to waters that are certified safe for swimming by the local health department. Such certification is your guarantee that the water is unpolluted. If the water is unpolluted, so will be the shellfish that live in it. As for mussels, those gathered along the Pacific coast should not be eaten. It has been found that they contain a highly toxic matter.

The methods of cleaning and cooking shellfish overlap a good deal. Some are cooked before cleaning, some are cleaned and then cooked and others are cleaned and eaten without cooking. To make it easier for you, we are putting both cleaning and basic cooking instructions under the individual shellfish name. Further cooking instructions that are necessary will be found in individual recipes. Further information about the shellfish itself and how much is needed to feed six people is given under the individual name in Chapter 3, *When and Where To Buy Fish and Shellfish.*

Shellfish is good to eat and it is easy to cook, but, like anything else, it is better cooked and better eaten when it is fresh. Frozen shellfish is inclined to toughness when it's cooked.

Some cooks suggest cooking frozen shellfish longer to make it

51

more tender, but that is not so. There is something about the texture of unthawed crustaceans and mollusks that makes the outside meat rubbery while the heat is trying to get through to the inner meat. Buy fresh shellfish whenever possible, but if only frozen shellfish is available, thaw it thoroughly before cooking.

Unless the recipe says otherwise, in preparing all shellfish dishes the shellfish meats should be added at the very last minute just before the cooking heat is turned off. These delicate meats need only be heated through to be cooked. Any additional heat will toughen them. If you want the delicious shellfish flavor to permeate the other ingredients, use the broth in which oysters, clams or mussels were steamed open, having followed our directions to be sure they are clean, and add the broth to your sauce or soup.

Clams

A clam pumps seawater through itself in great quantities and the plankton (minute matter) it contains feeds the clam. Inevitably the clam pumps in sand, a little of which remains in the shell. The easiest way to remove this sand before preparing and cooking the clams is with cornmeal.

Purging of sand

Cover your fresh clams with an ample amount of fresh cold water from the tap, spike it with salt, and add a plentiful supply of cornmeal. Let the clams stand in a cool place overnight. The clams will do the cleaning job. In the morning, the sand will be pumped out, replaced by digestible cornmeal.

If you want to hasten the purging process, add pepper to the water with the salt and the cornmeal. The clams will pump faster and an eight-hour job will be done in three.

Once the clams are purged of sand, there comes the more

difficult chore of opening them. There are two combinations for opening a clam. With one you need muscle power, with the other you need water power.

Opening clams

First scrub the shells thoroughly and throw out any that are gaping or broken. Next thing, assuming you are going to save your strength, is to put the clams in a small amount of boiling water. Cover, and steam them for about 5 to 10 minutes. That should open the shells sufficiently to permit you to insert a knife blade and twist in order to pry the shells apart. The other way of opening hard-shell clams is more difficult but preserves the taste. (Fig. 14A, B, C and D.)

Hold the clam in the palm of one hand with the hinge against the palm. Insert a slender, short but strong and sharp knife blade between the two halves of the shell and cut around the clam, twisting the blade slightly to pry the halves apart.

Removing flesh from shell

From there on, whether you use method one or two, the remaining task of cutting both top and bottom muscles free from the shell halves is the same. Insert the blade between muscle and shell and work it around in a circle. The flesh will come free.

Oysters

Opening oysters

You don't have to purge oysters of sand. All you have to do is wash the shells, open them, and eat the oysters. There is a hard way and an easy way. (Fig. 15A, B, C and D.)

The hard way is to use only a knife and strength and dexterity.

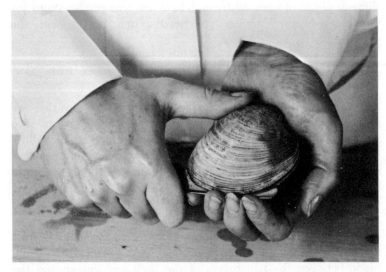

Figure 14A Hold clam thus and insert knife blade as shown.

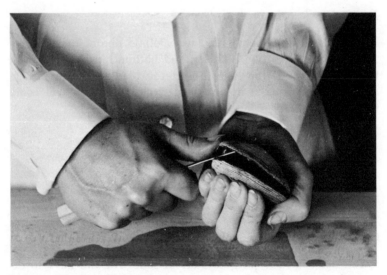

Figure 14B Cut the muscle.

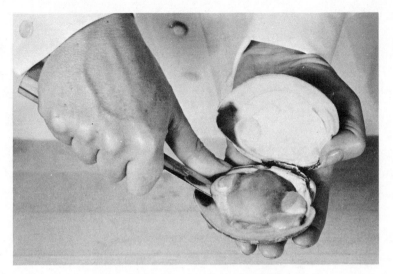

Figure 14C Cut the clam meat away from the shell.

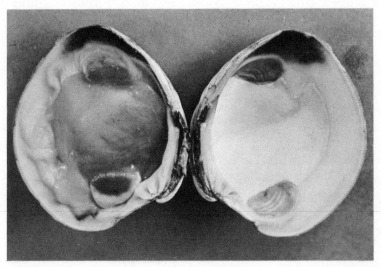

Figure 14D Presto! Clam on the half shell.

Figure 15A Tap gently with a hammer to "bill" the oyster.

Figure 15B Insert tip of knife blade.

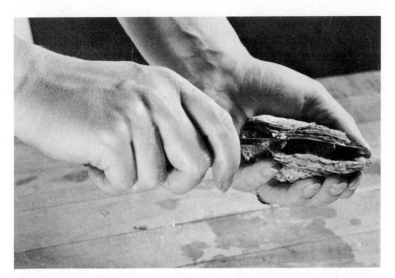

Figure 15C Cut oyster muscle.

Figure 15D Cut oyster meat from the shell.

The easy way is to use a hammer first. Whether you choose the easy way or the hard way, the first thing to do is to wash and rinse the oysters thoroughly in cold water. Then place the oyster on a table, flat shell up, and hold it firmly with one hand. Pick up the knife with the other hand and force the blade between the shells at or near the thin end. Insert the blade until you feel something fairly resistant. That is the large adductor or eye muscle by which the oyster is attached to both upper and lower shells. Cut that muscle close to the flat upper shell and the shells will come apart.

That will leave the oyster still attached to the deep lower shell. Insert the knife between what's left of the adductor muscle and the shell and work the blade around until the oyster is free. Leave it right there if you're going to serve oysters raw on the half shell. If you're going to cook the oysters, drop the meat onto a dish or into a container.

The easy way is to pick up your hammer and knock off the thin edge, or "bill," of the shells. Chip off only enough to insert the blade. The rest is simple. You can, if you like, buy a specially made oyster knife and the shucking will be even easier.

After the oyster is shucked, look it over carefully and remove any pieces of shell that may cling to the meat. These chips can be dangerous.

Cleaning oysters to cook and eat in the shell

If the liquid in which oysters are cooked in the shell is to be used—for cooking, as a broth, or as a bouillabaisse-type soup—they must be scrubbed with a good stiff brush under running water. Continue scrubbing until every bit of sand and dirt that may be caked on the shell is washed away. After cooking, strain the liquid through a double thickness of cheesecloth.

Three ways to cook oysters in the unopened shell

Once the shells are thoroughly cleaned, oysters can be cooked unopened in three different ways:

In a soup: see bouillabaisse recipes in Boiled Fish Section beginning on page 152.

Roasted: place on a baking sheet and roast in hot oven, 450° F., for about 15 minutes or until the shells begin to open. Serve on the half shell with melted butter, lemon, and seasoning.

Steamed in a pressure cooker: count six oysters per person or thirty-six for six people. Leave them in their shells but wash the shells thoroughly. Place in a pressure cooker and steam for 2 minutes at cooking pressure. *Cool cooker at once.* Serve in shells with melted butter, lemon, and seasoning.

Oyster stews

Oyster stews are always best cooked over water. This means the stew pan should be placed in a larger pan that contains the water, as a double boiler. Never boil or overcook.

Frying and other methods of cooking oysters

The most common way to cook oysters if not eaten raw is to pan fry or oven fry them. The basic procedures are identical with those used for scallops, page 60. Any variations will be described in the individual recipes. Whichever method you choose, all you need do is cook the oysters only until the edges curl and they are heated through. Do not cook longer. Fried oysters need about 1 minute of cooking on each side. If oven frying, the oven should be preheated to 500° F.

Oysters may be baked, broiled, pan roasted, deep fried or barbecued.

Mussels

Mussels are both a delicacy and a mainstay in many countries, so much so that they are cultivated and provided with ropes to cling to and grow on. We reap them only wild and clinging to rocks.

Mussels can be cooked either in the shell or shucked, but wild or cultivated, they must be cleaned before they can provide the base for any number of recipes.

Cleaning mussels

Wash them well in cold running water, meanwhile scrubbing with a stiff brush. Besides doing away with the mud, this step also will remove much of the beardlike appendages that are attached to the mussels' inner meat. After the scrubbing, allow the mussels to stand for 2 hours covered with water. Then discard any that float.

Opening mussels

Because mussel shells are comparatively thin, not much skill is needed to open them. Working over a pan to catch and save the liquid, insert a sharp, strong knife tip between the shells in the bearded area and run the blade around the edge, moving toward the broad end first. Remove the meat and cut away any whiskers that may be left.

Steaming mussels open

Place the mussels in a pot containing about an inch of boiling salted water. Cover, return the water to a boil and let the steam do its job. And that job is done the moment the shells open, no more than 3 minutes. Remove the mussels from the shell, trim away the beard, and use as the recipes require.

If the recipe calls for mussel liquid, strain it through a double thickness of cheesecloth and taste-test as you add it to your sauce.

Scallops

Whether fresh or frozen, scallops should be washed well before using and looked over for bits of shell and sand. Thaw the frozen ones before cooking.

Up to now, deep frying, broiling and, sautéeing have been the most popular ways of preparing scallops in the United States. But we are discovering at last that there are many other ways of serving scallops. They can be used in cocktails, appetizers, bird stuffings, soups, and salads. Either sea or bay scallops may be used in the recipes in this book.

Scallops have two shells, just like clams or oysters, but they are marketed only as dressed meat. (See "Buying Shellfish," page 19, for further information about scallops.)

Methods of Cooking Scallops

BROILING: Dip the scallops in melted butter or French dressing. Roll in fine bread crumbs if desired. Follow the directions given earlier for broiling fish, limiting the entire cooking time to 5 to 7 minutes at the most.

SIMMERING: Place each pound of scallops in a quart of boiling salted water, using two tablespoons salt to the quart. Cover and return to the boiling point. Simmer for 3 to 4 minutes. Drain. This will be your base for many cooked scallop recipes.

SAUTÉEING OR PAN FRYING:

1. Sprinkle with salt and pepper if desired.
2. Dip also, if desired, into egg beaten with a little milk. Then dip into fine dry bread or cracker crumbs, cornmeal or flour. Let stand for 2 to 3 minutes to dry.
3. Place the scallops in a heavy frying pan containing no more than ⅛ inch of fat or oil. Do not let the fat smoke.
4. Using moderate heat, fry until brown on one side, then turn and brown on the other. Total cooking time should be from 4 to 8 minutes, depending on the size, and absolutely no longer.
5. Drain on absorbent paper.

OVEN FRYING (BAKING):

1. Dip the scallops in a cup of milk to which a half-teaspoon salt has been added. Roll in fine dry bread crumbs. A cup of crumbs may be spiked with a teaspoon of paprika, if desired.

2. Place the scallops on a well-greased baking dish and brush with melted butter, margarine or oil.

3. Bake in a very hot oven, 500° F., for no more than 6 to 8 minutes. The high temperature insures crispness, not sogginess, uses less fat, takes less attention and causes fewer cooking odors.

NOTE: If you don't want your scallops breaded just eliminate step 1, start with the second step and sprinkle with salt.

DEEP FRYING: Scallops need only 2 to 3 minutes in hot deep fat, 350°–375° F. in a French fryer, even less if they brown sooner. When they are brown they are done. Drain on absorbent paper.

POACHING: Poach small scallops just 3 to 4 minutes. Cut large scallops in two and poach for the same length of time. They may be poached in court bouillon or salted water. Poached scallops usually are served with a sauce. This method is highly recommended for bay scallops.

NOTE: Further instructions will be found in the individual recipes and in the general cooking information preceding the fried fish and shellfish recipes.

Lobster

There are three ways to clean lobsters. One way is to clean them before you cook them. A second way is to clean them after you cook them.

If the lobsters are going to be baked or broiled you have no choice but to clean them before you cook them. If you're going to boil them or steam them the cleaning comes after the cooking. That is where the third way comes in.

You may either clean them the conventional restaurant and cookbook way or you may clean them—shell might be a more proper word for it—the Maine way.

Chet Brown and his brother Ed are Down East lobstermen —Boothbay is their home—who couldn't see hiding their lobsters under a bushel. So they became wholesalers who not only serve the finest hotels, restaurants, airlines and foreign embassies in and around New York but also serve some foreign countries.

Chet runs the distribution end from a base in Point Lookout, Long Island, and it was Chet who first told us about the Maine way of steaming and cleaning, or shelling, lobsters.

Cleaning before cooking

First kill the lobster by severing the spinal cord. Do it by inserting a knife tip between the tail shell and body and cutting. Split lengthwise and remove the stomach and intestinal vein. The stomach is the small sac between the eyes and roughly just back of the head. The stomach will lift out very easily and the vein should come with it. If it doesn't, lift it out with a fork or toothpick. Crack the large claws with a nutcracker or hammer. The lobster is ready for baking, stuffing, or broiling. (Fig. 16A, B, C, and D.)

Cleaning after cooking

THE CONVENTIONAL WAY: After the lobster is boiled or steamed, lay it on its back, split the body down the middle lengthwise. Remove the stomach and whatever is left of the vein. Do not discard the coral roe or the cream-textured green fat, the tomalley, or liver. The lobster is ready for serving. (Fig. 16B, C and E.)

THE MAINE WAY: As you can see from the accompanying diagrams, the chief instrument needed in shelling a lobster the Maine way is a pair of hands. It doesn't seem fastidious, but actually it makes for easier and neater eating. Just to prove how highly Down Easters think of this method, the diagrams were provided by the Maine Department of Sea and Shore Fisheries.

After you've taken the lobster from the pot and cooled it just enough to handle, follow the diagrams on pages 66 and 67.

1. Twist off the large claws at the point where they join the body.

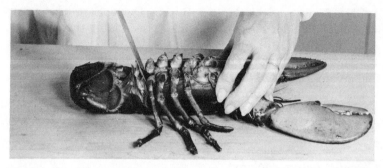

Figure 16A Place lobster on its back (hard shell down) and kill by cutting between tail shell and body.

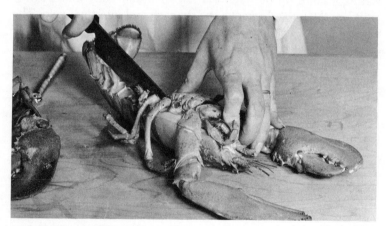

Figure 16B Split lengthwise.

Figure 16C Lift stomach (the small sac between the eyes) gently. The intestinal vein should come out with it. If it does not, finish the job with fingers, fork or toothpick.

Figure 16D Brush the lobster meat with melted butter and it is ready for cooking.

Figure 16E Although not an actual part of the cleaning process, this is as good a place as any to show you how to crack a lobster claw.

(Follow only steps A, B, C and D to clean before cooking; follow only steps B, C and E to clean after cooking.)

THE MAINE WAY OF CLEANING A COOKED LOBSTER

DRAWINGS COURTESY OF THE MAINE DEPARTMENT OF SEA
AND SHORE FISHERIES

1. Twist off the claws at body juncture.

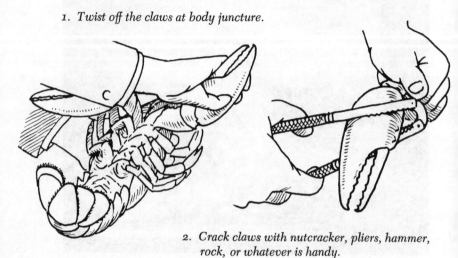

*2. Crack claws with nutcracker, pliers, hammer,
rock, or whatever is handy.*

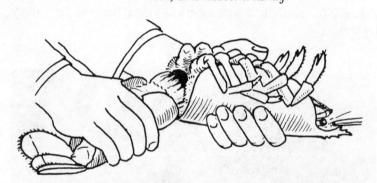

3. Separate tail from body by arching back until it cracks.

*4. Snap off the flippers
by bending back.*

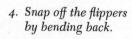

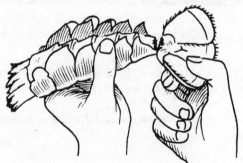

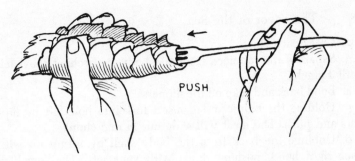

5. *Insert fork in smaller hole left by flippers and push meat out in one chunk.*

6. *Unhinge the back meat from the body thus. The "tomalley" is delicious eating, so don't discard it in this process. It is the liver and turns green in the cooking.*

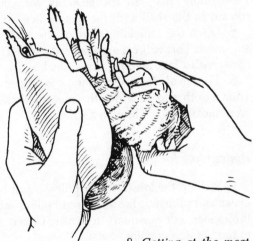

8. *Getting at the meat of the small claws is like sipping soda through a straw.*

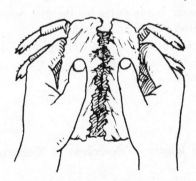

7. *Grasp remaining part of body thus and split sideways.*

2. Crack each claw.

3. Separate the tailpiece from the body by arching the back until it cracks.

4. Bend back and snap off the flippers.

5. Holding the tailpiece flat, insert fork into hole left by flippers and push. The meat will slide out in one chunk.

6. Unhinge the back from the body shell by lifting up with your right hand, pushing down with your left. The tomalley, which many people consider the best of all, will remain in the shell. Spoon it into a serving dish or eat it from the shell. (Step 6, incidentally, does all the cleaning for you. The stomach will remain in the shell with the head when you unhinge the back.)

7. Open the remaining part of the body by cracking it apart sideways. This will expose many morsels. They're too small to be eaten with a fork but fingers are ideal.

8. The small claws also contain excellent eating. Put an end in your mouth and suck out the meat and the juice just as if you were sucking cider through a straw.

Boiling live lobster

1. Pick up the lobster by gripping it just behind the large front claws and plunge it headfirst into boiling salted water, about one tablespoon salt per quart, to cover. Cover, and reheat the water to the simmering point.

2. Allow the lobster to simmer five minutes for the first pound and one minute for each quarter-pound thereafter.

3. When those exact times are up, immediately plunge the lobster into cold water.

4. Drain, rinse, clean and serve.

Broiling

1. Kill, split and clean the lobster as described in "Cleaning before cooking," page 63.

2. Place the lobster on the broiler rack, meat side up and spread it as flat and open as possible.

3. Brush with melted butter, margarine or oil. Sprinkle with

salt and pepper. Paprika, minced parsley and garlic powder are optional extras.

4. Broil about four inches from source of heat for 10 to 12 minutes, or until lightly browned.

Steaming

If you've never been way Down East in Maine, you've probably never heard of steaming lobster. But once you've tried it, don't be surprised if you never want lobster done any other way. It's simple to do and good to eat.

1. Put about an inch of water in a deep pot, one that has a tight-fitting lid.
2. Put a wire rack into the pot, making sure it will remain above the water level.
3. Heat the water until it starts to steam heavily.
4. Put the lobster on the rack, put the lid back on the pot.
5. Let it steam for 20 minutes. No more, no less.
6. Drain, rinse, shell the Maine way, page 63, and serve.

Boiling tails

1. Thaw the tails if they're frozen.
2. Insert skewers lengthwise through the meat to prevent curling if you plan to serve the tails in the shell.
3. Plunge into enough boiling salted water (about one tablespoon of salt per quart) to cover.
4. Quickly bring the water to the simmering point and allow to simmer just one minute longer than the ounce weight of the largest tail.
5. Drain, rinse and cut away the under shell.
6. Serve with melted butter.

Broiling poached lobster tails

Don't be alarmed when we suggest that lobster tails ought to be poached before they are broiled. Straight broiling will dry and coarsen lobster tail meat and loss of flavor will result. So we suggest that you poach before you broil in order to retain that delicate flavor.

It was the Fishery Council that first declared "it is best to poach the tails for five minutes before sliding under the broiler for another 5 to 6 minutes."

1. Thaw thoroughly and split or remove the under shell with heavy kitchen shears.

2. Bend tails firmly backward until they crack.

3. Place them on backs in shallow pan and add salted water, about one teaspoon salt per pint, to just below level of exposed meat.

4. Bring the water to the simmering point. Cover and poach for 5 minutes.

5. Remove lobster tails from poaching pan and place on backs in broiling pan. If shells have curled a bit, bend them flat once more.

6. Spread generously with butter or margarine. Add about one-quarter inch of poaching liquid to the pan for added moisture.

7. Set pan so tails are three to four inches below source of heat.

8. The tails are done perfectly when shell edges char and the meat is a delicate brown. Three- to six-ounce tails should take 5 to 6 minutes; larger tails should take 7 to 8 minutes.

Stock made from shell

A very fine broth for use in lobster soups and sauces can be made from the shell after the meat has been removed. The more bits of flesh left clinging to the shell the better. Crack the shell and boil for 15 minutes in water with salt, celery, carrots and onion. This broth will add delicious flavor to creamed dishes made with leftover lobster meat, so don't discard lobster shells.

Crabs

Crab and lobster meat is easily interchanged for many recipes, particularly if the meat is to be flaked.

Hard-shell

Hard-shell crabs should be cooked before they're cleaned. Drop the crab headfirst into fast-boiling salted water. Cover, bring back to a boil and boil for 5 minutes. Then simmer for 15 minutes more. Remove from pot and drain. Now to clean:

1. Break off the tail.
2. Grip the body of the crab with your left hand, keeping the large claws to the right (reverse everything if you're lefthanded), and snap off the large claws.
3. Pull off the top shell with the right hand.
4. Break off or cut off the legs.
5. Scrape off the gills and discard the digestive and other organs located in the center part of the body.

Slice away the top of the right side of the inner skeleton, starting near the front. Remove any meat on this slice; then, beginning with the right back fin pocket, remove the meat from the lower part with a circular motion of the knife. Remove the meat in the other pockets by inserting the knife underneath and prying upward. Cut the top from the left side of the inner skeleton and remove the meat in the same way as you did the right.

To get at the meat inside the claws, you'll have to break the shell by cracking each segment of each claw with a sharp blow of the knife handle. If that won't do, use a hammer. Remove the meat by grasping it with the fingers of one hand while pulling out the tendon with the other. If necessary, pry the meat out of the shell with a knife.

Make certain that you discard all the material that clings to the upper shell and that you have yanked out the orange waxy matter and spongy white substance between the halves of the body at each side.

There are two basic ways of cooking crabs—boiling and frying. The boiling method usually provides the crab meat base for broiling, baking, and cocktails. Boiled crabs are good just as they come from the pot. Here's a basic recipe for boiling enough crabs to serve six people. You'll need 24 live quarter-pound hard-shell crabs.

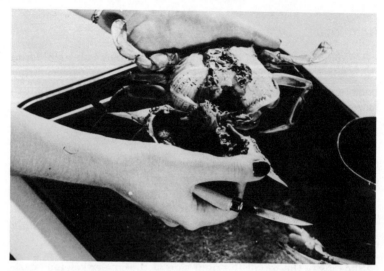

Figure 18A After crab is cooked, grip body with left hand keeping large claws to the right, then snap them off. Next, pull off the top shell with right hand and either cut or break off the legs.

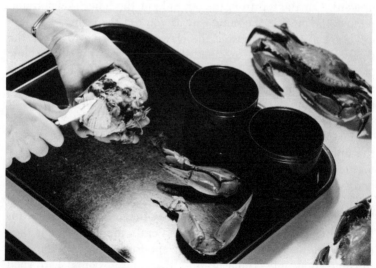

Figure 18B Scrape off the gills.

Figure 18C Use a knife to remove the digestive and other organs located in center part of body.

Figure 18D Slice off the top of the right side of the inner skeleton, starting near the front. Remove meat on this slice, then, starting at right rear fin pocket, remove meat from lower part with U-shaped turn of the knife.

1. Wash the crabs thoroughly in cold running water, making sure that all the sand is removed.
2. Place them in 8 quarts boiling water, spiked with ½ cup salt.
3. Cover and bring back to a boil. Simmer for 15 minutes.
4. Drain. Crack the claws and legs.
5. Serve hot with melted butter or margarine. Or chill and serve with mayonnaise or salad dressing.

Soft-shell

Blue crabs that have just shed their old, hard, shells are best suited for frying and there are two methods—pan frying and deep frying. They're called soft-shell crabs because their new outer shell is still only paper thin, and it need not be removed.

Usually they'll come from your market already cleaned and prepared for cooking. But if you have caught your own, follow these directions: (Fig. 19A and 19B)

1. Cut away the apronlike segment that folds under the body from the rear.
2. Cut away the face by cutting at a point back of the eyes.
3. Using your fingers, lift each point at the sides.
4. Clean out the gills.
5. Wash thoroughly in cold salted water and dry on absorbent paper.

Everything that's left is ready for the pan. To cook them for six people:

Pan frying

Dip 12 crabs in your favorite batter or dip in egg and crumbs. Place in a heavy frying pan that contains about ⅛ to ¼ inch hot but not smoking fat. Fry over moderate heat until brown on one side. Turn carefully with a spatula and brown on the other side. Total cooking time should be no more than 8 to 10 minutes. Drain on absorbent paper and serve.

Figure 19A   Use shears to cut away the face, just back of the eyes.

Figure 19B   Use fingers or shears to remove the apron and spongy parts (gills, stomach, intestines) under the points of the body covering.

Deep frying

Roll 12 crabs in your favorite batter or dip in egg and crumbs. Place in a frying basket in hot deep fat, 350°–375° F., and cook them 3 to 4 minutes or until brown. Drain on absorbent paper and serve.

Shrimp and Prawns

Shrimp may be shelled and cleaned and then simmered, or simmered first and then shelled and cleaned. If the broth is to be used, they should be peeled and cleaned before cooking and the liquid strained through a double thickness of cheesecloth. Prepare

COOKING SHRIMP BEFORE PEELING

Figure 20A Wash in collander, then place in boiling water.

Figure 20B   Remove the shells thus.

Figure 20C   Make shallow cut to get at sand vein, then lift it out with toothpick or point of paring knife.

this way also to add to a soup or broth and cook only a few minutes longer.

Cooking before shelling

1. Wash the shrimp and place in enough boiling salted water to cover. Use 4 tablespoons salt to 6 cups water for each pound of shrimp.

2. Cover the pan and bring the water back to simmer. Never boil shrimp. Water has only small beads on the surface and no steam when simmering; in other words it's just on the verge of boiling.

3. Simmer only about 3 to 5 minutes or until the shells turn pink.

4. Drain, rinse and shell. Make a shallow lengthwise cut down the back of each shrimp and remove the sand vein. A toothpick or the tip of a paring knife is an ideal tool. Wash and chill.

COOKING SHRIMP AFTER SHELLING

Figure 21A Peel shrimp thus.

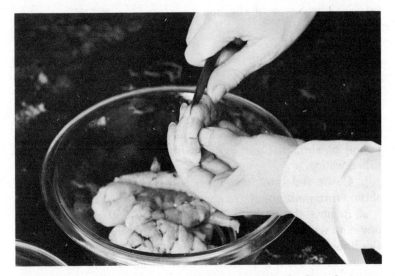

Figure 21B Make shallow cut lengthwise down back and remove sand vein.

Figure 21C Wash and place in boiling water.

Cooking after shelling

1. Remove shell, make a shallow cut lengthwise down the back and remove the sand vein. Wash off.
2. Place the shrimp in enough boiling salted water to cover. Use 2 tablespoons salt to 6 cups water, or less to taste, for each pound of shrimp. Court bouillon may be used instead of the salted water.
3. Cover and bring water back to simmer. Simmer until the shrimp turn pink, about 3 to 4 minutes.
4. Remove shrimp from the liquid with a slotted spoon so that any sand will remain in the liquid instead of on the shrimp. Strain the liquid through a double thickness of cheesecloth. If shrimp are not to be eaten immediately, store them with the stock in the refrigerator in a tightly covered dish.

Shrimp stock

Substitute liquid from shrimp cooked this way for part of the liquid in sauces and soups. The liquor from canned shrimp can also be used this way.

Deep frying

Deep frying shrimp is very simple. Shell, clean and roll in your favorite batter. Place in fryer basket in hot deep fat, 350°–375° F., for 2 to 3 minutes. When the shrimp are golden brown, drain on absorbent paper and serve.

Pan frying

Pan frying is even simpler. Shell, clean, wash, drain and fry in butter or oil until lightly brown, 6 to 8 minutes at the most. Shrimp are ready to be eaten or added to any number of recipes.

IX

The Clambake
and Other Outdoor
Cooking Methods

Every year more and more Americans are moving out-of-doors for their family meals and entertaining. For them the yard or patio, the terrace or poolside is taking the place of the indoor dining room. Further from home, camping is becoming one of the vacationing family's favorite occupations, walking and hiking are returning to popularity and boating and bicycling are coming back into their own.

There is one thing that every advocate of outdoor living has in common, whether it is due to the activity or the fresh air, they all get hungry. As a result food and cooking become a major part of the outing. From a one-day cookout to an elaborate camping trip or a backyard supper, they all include food cooked under conditions that are different from the home kitchen.

This chapter deals with the plans and preparations for outdoor meals. Cooking outdoors calls for a fire and building a good fire is an art that calls for knowledge. Some smart patio or galley may be equipped with gas or electricity, but when these utilities are not available, outdoor cooking means cooking with wood or charcoal.

There are many ways of cooking out-of-doors. Charcoal grill, outdoor fireplace, reflector oven, campfire, dutch oven, firehole or (for an old-fashioned seaside clambake) pit cooking. Which kind of cooking you choose depends on convenience and location—where you are going, how you are getting there and what will be available after you get there.

As far as the outdoor chef is concerned, all those methods have one thing in common—the cooking must be done over or in the coals or embers and not over or in the flame of the fire, except for the clambake. Then the cooking is done neither over the coals nor in the coals, it is done on red-hot stones.

Since this is a seafood cookbook, we'll try to describe all of the ways of having a clambake in detail.

Clambake Pit

Pit cooking has its advocates among outdoorsmen from the High Sierra to Cape Cod but nowhere is it practiced as generally as along the shores of New England and Long Island when it's clambake time. Clambake time is any time, mostly in the summer. A clambake is a way of steaming clams, lobster, corn, fish and fancy's fixin's the way the Indians did.

The coastal Indians dug a pit rather than built a fireplace in which to do their cooking for a very practical reason, it was easy for them to scoop a hole in the sand and if they didn't feel like digging with their hands, a clamshell was the only tool they needed.

Since a pit is nothing more than an oven with the door on top, since the ocean and the bays were the coastal Indians' main

Figure 22 Stone clambake pit. Dig a hole about 30 inches square and line all sides and bottom with stones about the size of a football.

source of food supply and since the clam is the easiest of all edible saltwater creatures to gather, the clambake was the inevitable result.

A clambake pit can be any size, shape or dimension you want, big enough to handle food for a tribe, small enough for cooking just for two.

Building and cooking
in a deep clambake pit

We describe a clambake feast for twelve people.

1. Dig a pit about thirty inches square and thirty inches deep.
2. Put a party to work collecting enough stones to line the bottom and all four sides of the pit, about six inches thick.
3. Set the stones in place so that they'll stay. (Fig. 22)

Collect enough driftwood to keep a roaring fire going in the pit for about four hours. The stones have to be sizzling hot. During those four hours you can mix work and pleasure, swimming, clamming, fishing, sunning, but most of all collecting lots and lots of seaweed. Keep the seaweed wet until the four hours are up and the stones are red hot. Then it's time to start cooking.

What you cook is up to you. You can have a three-, four- or five-course bake. Each course goes into the pit in layers sandwiched between seaweed, the food that takes the longest to cook goes closest to the bottom.

If you are going to have potatoes, lobster, chicken, fish, steamer clams and corn, they go into the pit in that order:

1. Remove all the coals from the pit. Sweep the stones as free of cinders as possible without wasting time and heat. A live green branch is the only broom to use. A regular broom will burn or, if you soak it, will take away precious heat.
2. Lay at least a three-inch layer of wet seaweed over every inch of the bottom stones.
3. Place your potatoes, scrubbed and still in their jackets, on top of the seaweed.
4. A thin layer, about a quarter-inch, of seaweed goes on top of the potatoes.
5. In go your lobsters, one for each person, and live of course.

6. Another thin layer of seaweed.

7. Add your chicken cut into serving pieces.

8. Another thin layer of seaweed.

9. Follow with your fish, cleaned and whole or cut into any style or size you intend to serve.

10. Still another layer of seaweed.

11. Now add your steamer clams. Allow twelve clams per serving. Tie each serving into a cheesecloth bag. It makes for easier handling.

12. Top with another layer of seaweed.

13. Next comes your corn, husked, the silk removed, and with the inner layer of husk replaced.

14. Top it all off with a two-inch layer of wet seaweed.

15. Cover the pit tightly with canvas to prevent any steam from escaping.

16. Let it steam for an hour. Remove the canvas and eat the feast that will be waiting.

No matter how much you try not to let it happen, you are

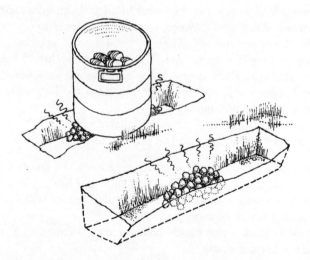

Figure 23 Stoneless pit for galvanized-can clambake. Dig a sloping trench about 12 inches deep, 12 inches wide and 30 inches long. Straddle can across the trench; feed the fire from the ends.

bound to collect some sand in the process. It can't be helped. It's the price you have to pay for the pleasure of a seaside clambake. If you think the little sand that will collect might be annoying, you can avoid some of it by wrapping foods like the chicken in aluminum foil.

Building a shallow clambake pit and how to cook in it

Through the centuries there have been many variations of the Indian-style pit. In Maine, the most popular way calls for a thick layer of hard stones about the size of a football in a circular eight- or ten-inch-deep hole. They are heated in the same way as they are in a pit. A six-inch bed of seaweed is laid down and the clams go in before the lobster. There are no seaweed layers between the food and none on top. A piece of canvas, large enough to cover all four sides as well as the top, is held down at the edges with stones.

Deep-can substitutes for clambake pits

A way that's popular in areas where no stones are available, Long Island's South Shore is such an area, calls for a thirty-gallon galvanized can. A false wire-mesh bottom is cut so that it can serve as a rack and it is propped about six inches from the bottom of the can.

The fire is inside a sloping trench twelve inches deep in the center, twelve inches wide and thirty inches long. Straddle the can atop the trench (Figure 23) and start your fire.

1. Fill the bottom of the can with five inches of water, or use half beer and half water.

2. Place your food on the wire-mesh rack in the same order used in a clambake pit.

3. Cover the can and let it alone for an hour, adding wood to the fire as needed to keep it roaring.

A family-size method that is ideal either for the backyard charcoal grill or the kitchen range calls for an oversize cooking pot with a snug-fitting cover. The steps to follow are:

1. Put one inch of salted water, preferably seawater, in the pot and heat it until it steams.

2. Plunge your lobsters into the water.

3. The clams go atop the lobsters in individual serving trays fashioned out of aluminum foil. Twelve clams to the tray.

4. Husk your corn, and add it to the pot.

5. Put the cover on the pot and let the food steam for twenty minutes.

Still another at-home clambake substitutes a five- or ten-gallon can with a tight-fitting wrap-around cover for the pot. The steps to follow are the same as those just described with two differences.

1. Do not put the can on the fire until everything is in it and the lid is on securely.

2. Punch several small holes in the cover to enable you to see the steam when it starts to escape. Start timing from that moment. Cook for 20 minutes.

Charcoal Grill

This can be of any size and shape you like. What should determine your choice is the number of people you usually cook for, whether it will be used only at home or, if you are going to take it with you, how much storage space you have in your boat, car or station wagon. Generally speaking, it need be no larger than twelve or fourteen inches in diameter and three to five inches in depth. That diameter will give you all the cooking space you need and that depth will give you all the fire pit necessary for coal cooking.

A charcoal grill is made to order for the outboard motor boating family that likes to draw up to an isolated beach for a swim and a seaside cookout. But don't depend on finding your fuel or even your tinder waiting there for you.

Charcoal, naturally, is the best thing to burn in a charcoal grill.

Carry the old-fashioned chunks or bricks with you and carry plenty of tinder and kindling along too. Canned lighter fluid is a poor substitute and it can be dangerous.

Build your fire as you would an outdoor fire but avoid any heavy wood that would burn longer than necessary to start your charcoal.

1. Place a sizable heap of tinder on top of the air vents in the bottom of the grill or, if there are no vents, pile it loosely to permit circulation. Avoid paper; it burns too fast for charcoal. Use dry twigs or thin wood shavings.

2. Next comes the kindling, piled tepee fashion around the tinder, with space on the upwind side large enough for your fingers. That's where you'll put your lighted match after the base is laid. The kindling can be short pieces of branch no more than a half-inch thick or strips of wood a quarter to a half-inch thick.

3. Heap your charcoal around the kindling, retaining the tepee shape.

4. Put a match to the tinder and see to it that the flame takes hold.

5. When the tinder and kindling are gone, spread the charcoal in a single layer around the bottom of the grill, keeping the coals as close to the center as possible without overcrowding. They should be gray hot now with flecks of red showing through.

6. Your grill is ready for cooking.

A charcoal grill is perfect for fish cookery with a barbecue touch, perfectly scrumptious for broiling fish of any size, shape or form, ideal for baking in the coals. None of them call for pots or pans but they do call for a long-handled, hinged wire grill or heavyweight aluminum foil.

For all of them there is one general rule that must be observed: wait for the flames to burn down and the coals to acquire a gray color before starting to cook. A high flame that would merely sizzle a beefsteak could ruin a fish steak.

Broiling is the simplest method of cooking fish over charcoal. Just clamp your fish inside the well-greased hinged grill, hold it at least four inches above the coals and turn and baste as need be. Don't hesitate to test for doneness with a fork. When it flakes easily it's done. Eight minutes is the most it should take.

To barbecue, all you need do is let the fish marinate in your favorite sauce for about half an hour and then broil as just described.

To bake, the fish is folded neatly into a square of aluminum foil and buried in the coals. The fork test is still the best. After about 8 minutes take the foil package out of the coals, gently open the fold and probe with your fork. If it doesn't flake easily close the fold and bake some more until it does. You'll find that aluminum cools quickly enough to handle, but it's still good to wear gloves. (Many recipes for the outdoor charcoal grill will be found in the "Broiling" section, beginning on page 223.)

The Camp Fireplace

The biggest enemy of a cooking fire in the outdoors is size. A fire doesn't have to be big to be good. In fact, it should be just large enough to do the job and no larger. That means the fireplace doesn't have to be big either.

The simplest and, to us, handiest of all one-day or weekend camp fireplaces is made merely by placing a pair of three- to six-foot rows of flat stones side by side but not parallel, as shown in Figure 24. They should be placed in line with the wind to ensure continual draft, about ten to fourteen inches apart on the upwind end, about five inches apart on the narrow or downwind end. Start your fire in the wide end, rake down coals and cook in the narrow end.

If no suitable stones can be found, which is entirely possible if the campsite is a sand beach beside the sea, the thing to do is to find two lengths of log or driftwood to use as substitutes (Figure 25). Square off the top of each with your camp ax so they can serve as your "stove-top" area. The logs should be as green, fresh, and thick as possible. The drier they are, the thicker they should be because eventually they are going to smoke, scorch and burn. But that's good, too, because when you've finished

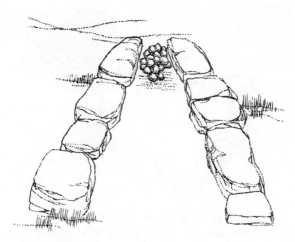

Figure 24 One-day camp fireplace. Lay down two rows of flat-topped stones in V-shape 3 to 6 feet long, in line with wind to assure continual draft. Place wide end upwind, about 10 to 14 inches wide, narrow end downwind. Build the fire there; then rake coals into narrow, or downwind end, for cooking.

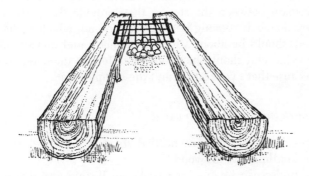

Figure 25 If flat stones are not available, green wood logs will do. Square off tops of logs to use as "stovetop" area for grill. Make narrow end about half the width of wide end.

cooking and eating and cleaning up and it's time to sit around the campfire, your wood is there and ready to roar.

A third kind of fireplace and the one that's best in a one- or two-week-or-longer campsite is shaped like a keyhole. Gather an armful of stones, about four inches in diameter, and lay them

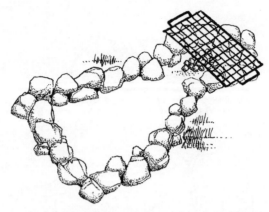

Figure 26 Keyhole camp fireplace. This shape is ideal for a one- or two-week campsite fire. Set 4-inch stones in keyhole shape, making the wide, upwind end up to three feet wide for building the camp-fire. The keyhole, the narrow downwind end, is for cooking coals. Make it about one foot wide and place the grill across it.

around in the keyhole shape shown in Figure 26 and the job is done. Keep them close together but don't fret about the gaps that remain between the stones; they provide the draft needed to keep the coals cooking hot. The round end, which is the cook-ing end, should be about a foot in diameter and downwind. The fat, upwind end should be about three feet in diameter. It's that big because that's your sit-around-the-campfire end.

Campfire fuel and how to use it

Three kinds of fuel are needed to start and feed the fire—tinder, kindling and firewood.

The tinder can be anything that's small, thin and dry such as pine needles, twigs, birch bark or wood shavings. But the easiest of all because it's the most available are the scraps of dry paper, particularly if they're waxed, that are inevitable in any camp. Just crumple them loosely and they're ready to flare.

Kindling, the middling agent between tinder and firewood, has to be large enough to hold a flame until the thick firewood starts to burn, yet small enough to be easily ignited by the tinder's hot, fast flame. Any wood that's dry and a half-inch thick will do. Dead tree branches will do. Kindling split with an ax from a solid but dry piece of wood will do even better.

Firewood, the all-important wood that provides the embers used in cooking, has to be thick enough to hold a fire yet not so thick as to be cumbersome. That means about three or four inches. As for length, about a foot or so will do. The hardwoods last longer, make the best coal beds and give off more cooking heat. They include oak, ash, hickory, elm, birch, maple, ironwood, holly, locust, dogwood and apple. Avoid spruce and fir if you can because they have a habit of popping and snapping and sending live coals shooting.

Build a campfire in the shape of a tepee. First the tinder, then the kindling and finally the firewood. Leave a small gap on the bottom of the upwind side to insert your lighted match. A good trick is to place a one-inch chunk of candle on the ground, build the tepee around it and light the candle.

The fire should be built on the widest end of the fireplace. When the wood burns to embers rake some down to the narrow end. Those are the ones you will cook on. Rake more from the large end to the cooking end as needed. A manageable piece of unlighted firewood can be your rake.

Cooking over a campfire

Place a wire rack across the sides and spanning the cooking coals. Make sure it's no less than four inches from the coals because the rack is your cooking surface and you don't want your fish to burn.

The cooking procedures now are the same as the ones you would follow on a charcoal grill. Use a hinged, long-handled grill to hold your fish for broiling. For baking wrap in heavy-weight aluminum foil and bury in the coals.

The Fire Hole in the Sand

If you're at the beach and you'd rather spend your time fishing or swimming than guarding a cooking fire, the fire hole is just the thing.

Just scoop a hollow in the sand, about sixteen inches across and about ten sloping inches deep and your fireplace is made. Build your fire in the usual way, wait for the coals, wrap your fish in heavy aluminum foil and bury it in the embers. Stay close enough to get back quickly and test for doneness with a fork. Do not go out of sight; no outdoor fire should be left unattended.

If you are planning on a top-of-stove recipe, you can use the hinged wire grill on a fire hole just as well as anywhere else. Someone will have to stay to do the turning.

If you'd like a clambake just for two you'll find that the fire hole is a versatile thing.

Just dig it about five inches deeper and line the sides and bottom with rocks (Figure 27) and you have a clambake pit in miniature. From then on follow the same steps described in the section on clambakes. Incidentally, corn husks, cabbage leaves or maple leaves can serve as substitutes for seaweed. Just soak them well in salted water, preferably seawater, and pour a quart of water on the red-hot stones after the coals have been removed.

These are the fireplaces that you can make for yourself without trouble or mechanical ability. The only store-bought one we have described so far is the charcoal grill. There are many others, such as the reflector oven, the dutch oven, the gasoline stove and the kerosene stove.

Commercial Camp Stoves

The gasoline and the kerosene stoves speak for themselves. Use them just as you would your kitchen range at home. The dutch oven, while an excellent camp cooking utensil, isn't good for fish because a dutch oven, by its very nature, calls for more cooking time than ever should be given to fish. That leaves only the reflector oven to be described.

Light and easily carried reflector ovens made of aluminum are available in all camp-outfitting stores. Open and in use as shown in Figure 28 they're perfect for casserole cooking, for baking

Figure 27 The firehole. The perfect "fireplace" for beach-party cooking. Just scoop a hole in the sand, about 16 inches across and 10 inches deep; slope sides.

such things as clam pies and for broiling your catch. They are easy to use and the most important thing to remember is to keep them shining bright. Otherwise there's nothing to reflect and your cooking is ruined before it begins.

1. With a reflector, the cooking is done with the flame and not with the coals. So build your fire with a large slab of stone or a mound of rocks as a background from which the heat can bounce off.

2. Place the oven on the opposite side of the flames, close enough to get the full benefit of the reflected heat rays bouncing off the aluminum but not too close to overcook or burn.

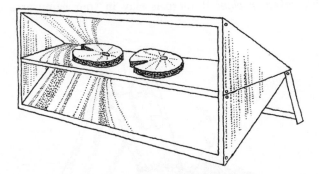

Figure 28 Reflector Oven. Buy an easily carried, collapsible reflector oven. Or make your own with cardboard and aluminum foil, or by cutting up a galvanized can. They are good for all sorts of outdoor cooking, but especially for casseroles. Place cooking pot on the shelf, build a flaming fire in front of the oven, and the reflected heat does the rest.

3. Place your fish on the rack, wear a pair of fire gloves to move the stove as need be and test for doneness with a fork.

4. Stay away from smoke-producing wood and use only hardwoods, free of pitch. Unless, of course, you want your fish to absorb the flavor of smoke blown into the oven.

A Few Tips for Cooking Fish Over an Open Fire

Planked fish: Preheat a hardwood board and grease it just as you would do at home. Split your fish and lay it on the greased plank, skin side down. Douse it with melted butter, margarine or vegetable oil and season it to taste. Tie it down with wire as shown in Figure 29 and prop the plank close to the flames with stones and sticks to brace it and hold it in place. Move the plank as needed for oven cooking and test for doneness with a fork. When done, draw the wire out sideways; less fish will cling to it that way.

Fish baked in clay: If there is clay in your camp area don't

Figure 29 Camp-style planked fish. With wire tie a fish steak to preheated plank, prop it up with sticks close to the fire as shown and cook.

let it go to waste. Pat a thin layer of the damp clay around a whole dressed fish until it's completely covered. (You needn't bother to scale the fish.) Allow it to dry enough to handle, then pack a heavy coating of clay around every inch of the package. Set it before the fire to dry, then bury it in hot coals. Figure on 7 minutes to the pound, then take it from the ashes and break away the clay. The skin and scales will come away with the clay.

Smoked fish: Place a section of aluminum screening large enough to hold your fish over a low fire built of wood that will give off more smoke than flame. Avoid the evergreens or other resinous woods. They're no good for smoking. Sprinkle the fire well with sassafras or whatever fragrant herbs you like. Rub your fish well with salt—or, better still, soak it overnight in a heavy salt brine—and lay it on the screen. Turn the fish and add herbs or wood chips as necessary. Keep the fire smoking well and figure on about 20 to 30 minutes to the pound of fish.

Barbecued fish, Indian style: Split a four-foot length of green tree branch, about two inches thick. Leave about one foot unsplit and whittle the end to a point. Split, clean and debone your fish (Indians of the Pacific Northwest used salmon) and place it between the two sections of the split branch. Hold the fish in place with short crosswise lengths of green twig as shown in Figure 30, first basting it well with your favorite barbecue sauce. Tie the upper end of the split branch with wire and poke the pointed end into the ground near enough to your fire to let the heat do its work. Cook the flesh side first. Turn, baste and test with a fork as often as necessary. When done, untie the wire on top and slide the fish gently sideways from the split branch. The twigs also should slide out sideways.

Putting out your campfire

An all-important word of caution is in order here—never make the mistake of thinking you've put out a campfire simply because you've buried the coals. They can smolder for days in buried vegetation and suddenly spring to life at a distance from your camp or cookout site. Burying coals in sand can be at least as dangerous, perhaps more so, because sand insulates and holds

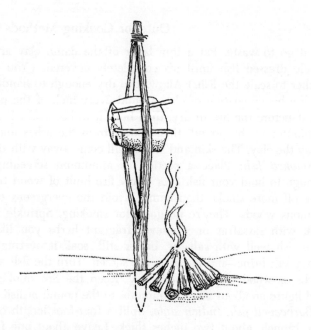

Figure 30 Camp-style "Fish Stick." The Indians of the Pacific Northwest invented this cooking method and it's a good one, especially for just-caught fish. Cut a four-foot green tree branch about two inches in diameter. Split all but about one foot of it. Whittle that end to a point. Place fish inside split, wire split end together at the top, secure fish with short lengths of green twig. Poke the branch into ground near fire as shown and start cooking.

heat. There have been cases of people digging their hands into supposedly cool sand and coming away with the skin badly burned.

The only way to put out a fire is with water—and lots and lots of it.

Part Two

Fish Sauces

I

Sauces and Their Use

Fortunately, making fish sauces can be easy, and this is a blessing because fish, more than any other food, needs a sauce.

There are many excellent sauces in this chapter for the beginner, and most of the ingredients can be found on any kitchen shelf—mayonnaise, sour cream, canned tomatoes, cocktail and chili sauces and the commercial barbecue sauces. Among the tastiest of these easy-to-make fish sauces are those based on canned or frozen cream soups. All you have to do is to heat the soup, dilute it—preferably with the liquid in which your fish was cooked—and serve. (Wherever individual taste and, of course, the recipes permit, homemade sauces should include the fish or shellfish liquids.)

There is no end to the combinations that can be made from a basic white sauce. Learn to make a smooth white sauce based on fish stock or broth, and a light hollandaise, and you can make most of the famous French fish sauces.

Fish can be basted with a sauce or simmered or baked directly in it. Cold butters can be spread on sizzling steaks or fillets just before serving. Or the fillets and steaks can be spread with sauce and baked in the oven or browned under the broiler. There are only a few ways of cooking fish, but there are many ways in which they can be changed with sauces.

It is customary to use a piquant sauce with fish that are delicate in flavor, a hot sauce with bland fish if served cold; tart sauces based on mayonnaise are served with fried fish. Many of the shellfish are simply served with the broth in which they were steamed, or with melted butter. But fish sauces, like fish recipes, are interchangeable. Individual taste and common sense are the best guides in choosing the type and amounts of sauce you'll use.

You wouldn't drown a delicately flavored baked fish in hot barbecue sauce, but you might add interest to its flavor by basting with just one or two tablespoons of the highly seasoned mixture.

Individual taste and common sense should also determine the herbs and other seasonings and how much of them you use. That's because the flavor of any particular seasoning is purely a matter of personal preference; and there's only one way to know if that taste is being satisfied—by taste-testing.

The Sauce-Making Chart, on page 143, shows you all the ingredients that can be combined with the basic sauces to suit your taste.

II

The Basics of
Sauce Making

To obtain a smooth sauce

1. Cook your sauce very slowly in the top of a double boiler, over simmering water. As you become more experienced a heavy saucepan can be used unless recipe specifies otherwise.

2. Stir constantly with a whisk or a wooden spoon until the sauce is thickened and smooth.

3. If the recipe calls for fat and starch (butter and flour), melt the fat before stirring in the starch. Add liquid gradually, stirring constantly. When you have a smooth paste, add more liquid and continue stirring until it is smoothly blended. Add remaining liquid and continue stirring and cooking slowly until sauce is thickened.

4. Use one of the new free-flowing flours that do not lump.

Correct proportions of starch, fat and liquid

Sauces can be of various thicknesses. The amount of starch and fat you mix with a cup of liquid is the deciding factor. Use half as much cornstarch as flour.

Thin sauce:	1 tbs. fat
	1 tbs. flour
	1 cup liquid
Medium sauce:	2 tbs. fat
	2 tbs. flour
	1 cup liquid

Medium thick sauce:	2 tbs. fat
	3 tbs. flour
	1 cup liquid
Thick sauce:	3 tbs. fat
	3 tbs. flour
	1 cup liquid
Very thick sauce:	4 tbs. fat
	4 tbs. flour
	1 cup liquid

Roux: white, blond and brown

Roux is the French name for a mixture of melted butter and flour that is used as the thickening agent in sauces. Roux can be made in advance and stored in the refrigerator. When preparing the sauce, put ¼ cup roux into a saucepan, add a little of the boiling liquid, fish stock, milk or bouillon, and stir with a whisk until smooth. Add remaining liquid (1 cup in all) gradually, stirring constantly over low heat until the sauce thickens.

WHITE ROUX: ½ cup butter to ½ cup flour. Melt butter, take from heat, stir in flour, return to low heat and cook, stirring constantly, until smooth.

BLOND ROUX: Prepare as white roux but let butter brown lightly before stirring in flour.

BROWN ROUX: Prepare as blond roux but let butter brown before stirring in flour. Cook roux until it is a rich brown.

You can use white or browned flour or cornstarch as the thickening agent in your sauce and the liquid can be almost anything: fish, meat, chicken or vegetable stock, cream, milk, wine, tomato, or citrus fruit juice.

If the liquid is milk, use a little less starch because milk contains solids and does not require as much thickener as water.

Browned flour

Sift flour in a thin layer onto a baking sheet. Place it in a 350° F. oven and let it brown slowly. Turn the baking sheet, shaking it lightly, every 5 minutes to brown the flour evenly. As soon as it is a golden brown, take from heat and sprinkle it onto a piece of paper to cool. Store the browned flour in a jar and use it instead of white flour in making brown sauces. You will need more browned flour than white flour, up to twice as much, depending on how dark the flour is.

The importance of well-cooked starch

Starch tastes better and is more easily digested when well cooked. Flour, which needs at least 10 minutes cooking beyond the time the sauce thickens, is the agent most commonly used. Cornstarch, which must be cooked longer, makes a clear sauce when used with water, strained broths or juice. Cook cornstarch sauce slowly in the top of a double boiler over simmering water until the sauce is smooth and clear in appearance; about 15 minutes. After it has thickened, stir it occasionally to avoid sticking.

Recooking starch-thickened sauces should be avoided because they have a tendency to become thick and pasty. Place the sauce over hot water to reheat or to keep it warm until needed, unless cooking instructions say to remove from heat and serve at once.

Adding egg to a hot sauce

1. Before adding egg yolk to a sauce, beat it and then stir it with a little of the hot sauce. Reduce heat under the sauce. As soon as it stops boiling, stir in the egg mixture and continue to stir over low heat until sauce thickens.

2. If hot lemon or tomato juice are combined with egg yolk in a sauce, remove sauce from low heat as quickly as possible

or it may curdle and become thin from the action of the acid on the egg.

3. A little egg white is sometimes stirred into a sauce just before removing it from the heat. The egg white helps to bind the oils and other liquids.

Adding hot to cold

Problems sometimes develop when there is too great a temperature difference in the sauce ingredients being combined. That is one of the reasons why cold milk or other liquids are stirred very gradually into a hot mixture. That is why a little of the hot sauce is stirred into beaten egg yolk before adding the yolk to the cooking sauce, and why some recipes call for heated or scalded liquids to be combined with the hot sauce.

NOTE: If sauce ingredients separate after cooking they can sometimes be blended together by using an electric mixer, or by beating in a little boiling water.

Making sauce from leftover seafood soup

Most leftover seafood soups make excellent sauces. If the soup is too thin, mix flour with a little water or milk to a smooth paste and stir it into the soup as you heat it in the top of a double boiler over simmering water. Continue stirring until flour cooks and sauce thickens.

FISH STOCK

When a recipe calls for fish stock, use the following or substitute the broth or court bouillon, page 153, in which the fish was simmered or poached. Reduce and strengthen broth by boiling, or add water to dilute.

Heads and bones of 2 medium or 1 large fish (do not use strongly flavored fish for a delicate sauce)

1 onion, chopped	1 bay leaf
1 carrot, chopped	2 peppercorns
1 stalk celery, chopped	1 clove
3 sprigs parsley	1 tsp. salt, or to taste
1 sprig thyme	6 cups water

Combine all ingredients and boil 30 minutes. Strain and use as a base for fish sauces.

III

Sauces: Recipes

FISH FUMET
Strong fish stock

2 lbs. fish trimmings, heads
  and bones
1 onion, chopped
6 sprigs parsley

2 tbs. butter
4 cups dry white wine, or
  to taste
salt and pepper to taste

Simmer fish trimmings, onion and parsley in butter in a covered pan 20 minutes. Add wine, cover and simmer 30 minutes longer. Season, stir well and strain. The fumet can be reduced for stronger flavor by boiling, uncovered, until reduced by one-quarter or one-half. Use as a base for sauces or as a substitute for fish stock.

FISH VELOUTÉ SAUCE

4 tbs. butter
4 tbs. flour
5 cups fish stock or fish
  fumet, page 104

½ cup chopped mushroom
  stems or peelings
  (optional)
2 peppercorns (optional)
salt to taste

Melt butter in a heavy saucepan over low heat. Add flour and stir until it starts to turn golden. Add 2 cups stock gradually, stirring constantly, until sauce thickens. Reduce heat, add remaining stock, mushrooms, peppercorns and salt and simmer 30 minutes, stirring occasionally, until sauce is reduced to 4 cups. Strain and use with any fish or shellfish or as a base for other sauces.

Fish stock or fumet may be replaced by the liquid obtained after poaching the fish for which the sauce is intended. For a stronger flavor, it can be reduced by boiling rapidly until needed for the sauce. Reduce butter and flour proportionately to the amount of liquid available.

NORMANDY SAUCE: Substitute oyster, mussel or clam liquor for the fish stock. To strained sauce add 1 cup cream, beaten with 4 egg yolks. Set over very low heat, do not let the sauce boil, and stir in salt and pepper to taste. Pour over steamed oysters, mussels or clams.

DRAWN BUTTER SAUCE

¼ cup butter	¼ tsp. white pepper, or to
3 tbs. flour	taste
½ tsp. salt	1½ cups fish stock or water
1 tsp. lemon juice	

Melt half the butter in top of double boiler over simmering water and stir in flour and seasonings until smooth. Gradually add fish stock or water and cook, stirring constantly until sauce is thickened and smooth, about 5 minutes. Cook 8 minutes longer. Stir in remaining butter, little by little and season with lemon juice.

VARIATIONS:

1. Stir in 1 beaten egg yolk and 2 tsp. minced parsley when sauce is ready to serve.
2. Stir in 1 tbs. anchovy paste with the lemon juice.
3. Stir in 2 tbs. smallest capers at the time fish stock or water is added.
4. Stir in ½ cup cooked crab meat, diced cooked shrimp or lobster meat during last 8 minutes of cooking.

Easy Cold Butter Sauces

These sauces are simple to make and have many uses. Prepared ahead of time, they can be stored in the refrigerator until they are needed. They can be melted in a bowl of steaming soup, or they can be sliced and spread on sizzling hot fish steaks and fillets the moment they are transferred from pan to serving plate. They can be heated and poured over fish as a hot butter sauce.

ALMOND BUTTER

Stir 2 tbs. ground salted almonds into 3 tbs. soft butter. Chill.

ANCHOVY BUTTER

Stir 1 tsp. anchovy paste into ¼ cup soft butter. Chill until needed. Or use 1 minced anchovy fillet for the paste.

CHILI BUTTER

Stir 1 tbs. chili sauce or catsup into ¼ cup soft butter. Chill.

CURRY-MUSHROOM BUTTER

Stir 1 tbs. ground cooked mushrooms and ¼ tsp. curry powder into ¼ cup soft butter. Chill.

DILL BUTTER

Stir 2 tsp. minced dill into ¼ cup soft butter. Chill.

GARLIC BUTTER

Stir 1 crushed garlic clove and ¼ tsp. salt into ¼ cup soft butter. Chill.

HERRING BUTTER

Stir 2 tbs. herring paste into ¼ cup soft butter. Chill.

HORSERADISH BUTTER

Stir 1 tbs. prepared or freshly grated horseradish into ¼ cup soft butter. Chill.

LEMON BUTTER

Stir 1 tsp. lemon juice and 1 tsp. grated lemon rind into ¼ cup soft butter. Chill.

LOBSTER-CORAL BUTTER

Stir 1 tbs. lobster coral (roe) and ¼ tsp. salt into ¼ cup soft butter. Chill.

MAÎTRE D'HÔTEL BUTTER

Stir 3 tbs. minced and well-dried parsley and ½ tsp. lemon juice into ¼ cup soft butter. Shape into a 1½-inch-thick roll on a piece of wax paper, roll up in the paper and chill. Slice the butter into ¼-inch-thick slices and place 1 slice on individual broiled fish steaks when they are taken from the broiler. Serve at once.

MUSTARD BUTTER

Stir 1 tbs. mild mustard into ¼ cup soft butter. Chill.

OLIVE BUTTER

Stir 2 tbs. ground ripe olives into ¼ cup soft butter. Chill.

PAPRIKA BUTTER

Stir 2 tsp. mild paprika into ¼ cup soft butter. Chill.

SARDINE BUTTER

Stir 2 tbs. sardine paste or mashed sardines into ¼ cup soft butter, add salt to taste. Chill.

SHRIMP OR LOBSTER BUTTER

1 lb. cooked shrimp or lobster shells, or shells from frozen lobster tail, meat removed	¼ cup butter ¼ cup water ¼ tsp. salt, or to taste

Crisp shells in a 250° F. oven 15 minutes. Crush them in a mortar with butter. Transfer them to a saucepan, add water and salt and simmer 15 minutes. Strain, chill the liquid and discard the shells. When liquid is cold, lift off the butter, discard the liquid and use the shrimp or lobster butter as recipes require.

Melted Butter Sauces

Among the simplest, most versatile of all sauces are those made with a melted butter base. Brush them on fish and shellfish that are to be broiled, indoors or out. Baste with them. Marinate with them. Pour them over cooked fish or use as a dip for pieces of lobster or other shellfish.

Baste less often and use less butter sauce with fat than with lean fish. See page 45.

(Margarine or oil can be substituted for butter.)

SPICY GRATED-CHEESE SAUCE

½ cup butter, melted
½ cup grated cheese
2 tbs. catsup
1 tsp. horseradish

1 tsp. lemon juice
1 tsp. prepared mustard
⅛ tsp. garlic salt
salt and pepper to taste

Combine all ingredients.

DANISH CUCUMBER-DILL SAUCE

½ cup butter, melted
½ cucumber, peeled and diced small

2 tsp. minced dill
salt and pepper to taste

Combine all ingredients.

HAWAIIAN HONEY SAUCE

½ cup butter, melted
2 tbs. white wine
2 tbs. lemon juice

1 tsp. honey
salt to taste
paprika to taste

Combine all ingredients.

LEMON-BUTTER SAUCE

¼ cup butter, melted

1 tbs. lemon juice
salt and pepper to taste

Combine all ingredients.

LEMON-ONION BUTTER

½ cup butter
1 tbs. finely chopped onion
1 tbs. lemon juice

1 tsp. finely chopped garlic
salt and pepper to taste

Cook onion and garlic in butter until soft and combine all ingredients.

LEMON-PARSLEY BUTTER   (*Maître d'hôtel*)

½ cup butter, melted
1 tbs. lemon juice

1 tbs. finely chopped parsley
salt and pepper to taste

Combine all ingredients.

PAPRIKA-BUTTER SAUCE

½ cup butter, melted
2 tbs. lemon juice
1 tsp. paprika

salt and pepper to taste
onion powder to taste

Combine all ingredients.

BARBECUE SAUCE I

½ cup butter, melted
2 tbs. lemon juice
2 tbs. powdered orange drink concentrate

2 tbs. meat stock (optional)
1 tsp. paprika
salt and pepper to taste

Combine all ingredients.

BARBECUE SAUCE II

½ cup butter, melted
2 tbs. undiluted frozen lemonade concentrate

2 tbs. catsup
½ tsp. prepared mustard
salt and pepper to taste

Combine all ingredients.

BARBECUE SAUCE III

½ cup butter
3 tbs. chopped onion
2 tbs. lemon juice
2 tbs. chopped parsley
1 garlic clove, finely
chopped

1 tsp. finely chopped
celery
1 tsp. prepared mustard
salt and pepper to taste

Cook vegetables in butter until soft and combine all ingredients.

BARBECUE SAUCE IV

½ cup butter, melted
1 tbs. lemon juice
1 tsp. vinegar
1 tsp. Worcestershire

1 tsp. prepared mustard
salt and pepper to taste
sieved hard-cooked egg
yolk (optional)

Combine all ingredients.

NOTE: Chopped cooked shellfish and shellfish liquor can be added to melted butter or oil sauces.

Canned Tomato Soup
Sauces

To a base of 1 10¾-oz. can tomato soup add:

TOMATO-CRAB MEAT SAUCE

1 10¾-oz. can condensed
tomato soup
¼ cup cream

1 cup flaked crab meat
1 tsp. mustard, or to taste

Stir all ingredients together in the top of a double boiler over boiling water. Thin with milk if desired.

TOMATO-PEA SAUCE

1 10¾-oz. can condensed
tomato soup
¼ cup cream

1 cup cooked tiny green
peas
1 tsp. minced onion

Combine as above and heat. Thin with milk if desired.

TOMATO-CUCUMBER SAUCE

1 10¾-oz. can condensed
tomato soup
¼ cup cream

½ cup peeled, minced and
drained cucumber
2 tsp. finely chopped onion

Combine as above and heat. Thin with milk if desired.

TOMATO-MUSHROOM SAUCE

1 10¾-oz. can condensed
tomato soup
¼ cup cream

1 can button mushrooms,
drained
2 tbs. finely chopped onion
2 tbs. sherry

Combine as above and heat. Thin with milk to taste.

TOMATO-CHEESE SAUCE

1 10¾-oz. can condensed
tomato soup
¼ cup cream

1 cup grated cheese
1 tsp. mustard, or to taste

Combine all ingredients and heat in the top of a double
boiler over boiling water. If sauce is too thick, stir in a little
milk or cream.

TOMATO-CURRY SAUCE

1 10¾-oz. can condensed ¼ cup cream
 tomato soup   2 tsp. curry powder

Combine ingredients, heat and dilute to desired thickness with milk.

TOMATO-CLOVE SAUCE

1 10¾-oz. can condensed 2 tsp. minced onion
 tomato soup   ½ tsp. powdered cloves
¼ cup cream   salt to taste

Combine ingredients, heat and dilute to desired thickness with milk.

TOMATO-MUSHROOM STROGANOFF SAUCE

1 10¾-oz. can condensed 1 tbs. chopped green
 tomato soup   pepper
1 4-oz. can sliced mush- 2 tbs. butter or margarine
 rooms (drain and reserve ½ cup sour cream
 liquor for other uses) 1 tsp. Worcestershire
1 tbs. chopped onion

Sauté mushrooms, onion and green pepper in butter and cook until tender. Add all other ingredients except sour cream. Simmer 5 minutes, remove from heat and stir in sour cream.

TOMATO-RELISH SAUCE

1 10¾-oz. can condensed 1 tsp. prepared mustard
 tomato soup   ½ tsp. prepared horse-
¼ cup sweet pickle relish radish

Use milk, cream, meat or fish stock for thinning to taste. Combine, heat and stir well.

Sauces Based on Canned Lobster or Mushroom Soup

Combine 1 can lobster soup or 1 10½-oz. can mushroom soup with any one of the following, heat or chill and serve. If necessary, thin with milk or cream.

ANCHOVY SAUCE

1 tsp. anchovy paste

ALMOND SAUCE

¼ cup toasted blanched almonds, chopped

CELERY SAUCE

¼ cup finely chopped celery

CHEESE SAUCE

½ cup grated Cheddar, Swiss or Parmesan cheese

CUCUMBER SAUCE

½ cup chopped peeled cucumber

1 tsp. chopped chives

EGG SAUCE (cold)

2 tbs. chopped hard-cooked egg
2 tbs. chopped celery
1 tsp. chopped chives

1 tsp. chopped green pepper
1 tsp. lemon juice

GREEN SPRING SAUCE

2 tbs. finely chopped parsley
1 tbs. lemon juice

¼ tsp. finely chopped garlic
½ tsp. vinegar
¼ tsp. powdered mustard

LEMON SAUCE (cold)

2 tbs. lemon juice
2 tsp. finely chopped chives

1 tsp. prepared mustard
½ tsp. prepared horse-radish

LOBSTER SAUCE

½ cup chopped cooked lobster meat with coral (roe) and liver

1 tbs. grated Parmesan cheese
1 tbs. sour cream
salt and pepper to taste

NEWBURG SAUCE

½ cup chopped cooked lobster meat
2 tbs. heavy cream

1 tbs. sherry
⅛ tsp. paprika
salt and pepper to taste

ONION SAUCE

2 tbs. chopped onion

¼ cup sour cream

PARSLEY SAUCE

2 tbs. finely chopped parsley

PIMIENTO SAUCE

3 tbs. chopped pimiento
1 tsp. Worcestershire

Tabasco to taste

SHRIMP SAUCE

¼ cup chopped cooked shrimp
1 tbs. chopped celery
1 tsp. chopped green onion

1 tsp. lemon juice
¼ tsp. prepared mustard
salt and pepper to taste

YELLOW SAUCE (cold)

2 chopped hard-cooked egg yolks

NOTE: Add 1 to 2 tbs. shellfish liquid and finely chopped shellfish to some of the lobster or mushroom soup sauces for a more distinctive seafood flavor.

Combination Sauces,
Based on Sour Cream, Whipped Cream
or Mayonnaise

Combine any of the following ingredients with **1 cup sour cream, whipped, or ½ cup heavy cream, whipped, or 1 cup mayonnaise.** If preferred, the sauce can be based on a combination of sour cream, whipped cream and mayonnaise combined in any proportion. Use a commercial mayonnaise or follow the recipe on page 135.

ANCHOVY SAUCE

2 tsp. anchovy paste

ALMOND SAUCE

¼ cup chopped toasted almonds

CELERY SAUCE

½ cup minced celery

CHEESE SAUCE

½ cup grated Cheddar cheese

COCKTAIL SAUCE I

2 tbs. chopped celery
2 tbs. chili sauce or catsup

1 tbs. chopped onion
curry powder to taste
salt and pepper to taste

COCKTAIL SAUCE II

1 tbs. lemon juice
½ tsp. paprika

Worcestershire to taste
salt and pepper to taste

COCKTAIL SAUCE III

½ tbs. prepared horseradish
2 tsp. chopped onion

paprika to taste
salt and pepper to taste

CUCUMBER SAUCE

½ cup peeled and chopped cucumber

1 tbs. minced chives

CURRY SAUCE

1 tbs. curry powder mixed with a little of the cream and stirred into the sauce

DILL SAUCE

1 tbs. minced dill

PARSLEY FRENCH DRESSING

¼ cup tart French dressing and 1 tbs. minced parsley

APPLE HORSERADISH

¼ cup diced apple and 2 tbs. grated horseradish

Do this at the last moment or both horseradish and apple will darken.

LOUIS SAUCE (easy)

1 tbs. chopped sweet pickle
4 tsp. chili sauce

1 tsp. lemon juice

LOUIS SAUCE (cold)

1 chopped hard-cooked egg
2 tbs. chili sauce or catsup
2 tbs. sour cream

2 tbs. chopped green pepper
½ tsp. lemon juice
salt and pepper to taste

LOUIS SAUCE (tangy)

2 tbs. chili sauce
2 tbs. chopped green onion
1 tsp. vinegar
½ tsp. prepared horseradish

½ tsp. prepared mustard
½ tsp. sugar
¼ tsp. paprika
salt and pepper to taste

PARSLEY SAUCE

2 tbs. minced parsley

RÉMOULADE SAUCE (cold)

1 tbs. tarragon vinegar (a pinch of dried tarragon can be added to any vinegar)

¼ tsp. prepared mustard
¼ tsp. finely chopped parsley

TARTAR SAUCE (cold)

1 tbs. chopped olives (optional)
1 tbs. chopped onions
1 tbs. chopped parsley

1 tbs. chopped sour pickle
½ tsp. prepared mustard
vinegar to taste

WATERCRESS-HORSERADISH SAUCE

¼ cup minced watercress
leaves and 1 tbs. grated
horseradish

WORCESTERSHIRE COMBINATION SAUCE

1 tsp. Worcestershire   1 tsp. Sauce Robert
1 tsp. A-1 Sauce

Curry Sauces

CELERY-CURRY SAUCE

Stir 2 tsp. curry powder into ¼ can cream of celery soup. Stir mixture into remaining soup. Heat and dilute with milk to taste.

MUSHROOM-CURRY SAUCE

Stir 2 tsp. curry powder into ¼ can cream of mushroom soup. Stir mixture into remaining soup. Heat and dilute with milk to taste.

CURRY WHITE SAUCE

Stir 2 tsp. curry powder into ¼ cup white sauce, page 123.

Stir mixture into ¾ cup white sauce, heat and dilute with milk to taste.

NOTE: Increase or decrease amount of curry powder according to taste.

White Sauces and Other Light Cream Sauces

BASIC WHITE SAUCE
See page 101 for thicker white sauce

2 tbs. butter	salt and pepper to taste
2 tbs. flour	(white pepper can be
1 cup milk or cream	used)

Melt butter in the top of a double boiler over boiling water. Stir in flour until thoroughly blended, gradually stir in milk and seasonings and continue stirring until sauce is thickened and smooth. Cook, stirring occasionally, 15 minutes.

VARIATIONS:

ANCHOVY SAUCE: Add 2 tsp. anchovy paste.

ALMOND SAUCE: Add ½ cup chopped toasted almonds.

CELERY SAUCE: Add ½ cup finely chopped celery.

CHEESE SAUCE: Add ½ cup grated cheese, Swiss, Cheddar or Parmesan.

CUCUMBER SAUCE: Add ½ cup chopped peeled cucumber and 2 tsp. chopped chives.

ONION SAUCE: Add ¼ cup minced onion and ½ cup sour cream.

PARSLEY SAUCE: Add ¼ cup finely chopped parsley.

WATERCRESS SAUCE: Add ½ cup minced watercress leaves.

YELLOW SAUCE: Add 4 sieved hard-cooked egg yolks.

BÉCHAMEL SAUCE

2 tbs. butter
4 tbs. flour
3 cups boiling milk

¼ tsp. salt
2 white peppercorns

Melt butter in a heavy saucepan over low heat, add flour and stir until it starts to turn golden. Stir in milk gradually with a wire whisk and continue to stir until the sauce thickens. Add seasonings and cook slowly, stirring frequently, 30 minutes. Strain and serve as a sauce or use as a base for other sauces.

VARIATIONS:

1. Add 1 tsp. minced onion to the butter and cook until soft.
2. Add 1 sprig chopped parsley and a pinch of nutmeg before serving.

MORNAY SAUCE

1 recipe béchamel sauce,
above
2 egg yolks

¼ cup cream
3 tbs. grated Swiss or
Parmesan cheese

Reduce heat under béchamel sauce so that it does not boil. Stir in yolks, beaten with cream. Add 2 tbs. cheese and stir until smooth. Pour sauce over prepared fish or shellfish, sprinkle with remaining cheese and brown under a hot broiler.

SAUCE NANTUA

1 recipe béchamel sauce, ½ cup heavy cream
  page 124   salt to taste
1 recipe shrimp or lobster
  butter, page 110

Heat béchamel sauce, stir in the shrimp or lobster butter,
add cream and bring to a boil. Season and serve with fish
or shellfish.

CREAM SAUCE

1 recipe béchamel sauce, ½ tsp. lemon juice
  page 124   salt to taste
½ cup heavy cream

Boil the béchamel sauce in an uncovered saucepan, over low
heat, until it is reduced by one-quarter, stirring occasionally.
Stir in cream, increase heat slightly and add lemon and salt.

This sauce is also a base for creamed fish and shellfish recipes.

VARIATIONS:

CAPER SAUCE I: Add 2 tbs. smallest capers.

CAPER SAUCE II: Add 2 tbs. smallest capers, 1 tbs. minced parsley
and 1 tsp. minced dill.

DILL SAUCE: Add 1 tbs. minced dill.

EGG SAUCE: Add 2 sliced hard-cooked eggs.

HORSERADISH SAUCE: Add ¼ to ½ cup freshly grated horseradish.

MUSTARD-DILL SAUCE: Add 1 tbs. prepared mustard and 2 tsp.
minced dill.

MUSTARD SAUCE: Add 1 tbs. prepared mustard and ½ tsp. dry mustard.

BERCY SAUCE

1 recipe cream sauce,
   page 125
¼ cup dry white wine
¼ cup fish stock or liquor
   from poached fish

1 shallot, chopped
1 tbs. chopped parsley
¼ cup whipped cream
   (optional)

Add wine, stock, shallot and parsley to cream sauce and stir over very low heat until sauce is warmed. Fold in whipped cream and pour over any boiled, steamed or poached fish on an ovenproof serving platter. Brown in a 400° F. oven and serve at once.

NOTE: Bottled or leftover hollandaise sauce, page 133, can be substituted for the whipped cream.

CURRY SAUCE

4 tbs. butter
1 small onion, finely
   chopped
½ bay leaf

1½ tbs. Madras curry
   powder
3 tbs. flour
1½ cups fish stock
½ cup heavy cream

Heat butter, add onion and cook until soft. Reduce heat, add bay leaf, curry powder and flour and stir until smooth. Add fish stock gradually and cook over low heat, stirring constantly, until sauce is smooth and thickened. Strain sauce, bring it back to a boil, add cream, stir well and serve over any fish or shellfish.

LOBSTER SAUCE

1 leftover boiled lobster
shell, meat removed
½ cup diced lobster meat
—use all available coral
(roe), tomalley (liver)
and fat (white sub-
stance)
1 carrot, sliced

½ onion, sliced
2 celery stalks, sliced
4 sprigs parsley
¼ cup butter
3 tbs. flour
½ cup cream
salt and pepper to taste

Break up lobster shell and boil 20 minutes in water to cover
with carrot, onion, celery and parsley. Strain off the liquid
and boil it rapidly until it is reduced to half. Melt butter in
the top of a double boiler, over boiling water. Stir in flour
until smooth. Gradually add the reduced lobster stock, stirring constantly, until sauce is thickened and smooth. Add
salt and pepper, stir in cream and simmer, stirring frequently
12 minutes over low heat. Add lobster meat, serve with fish.

VARIATIONS:

LOBSTER SAUCE WITH PASTA: Add one more cup diced lobster
meat and serve over pasta cooked *al dente*.

LOBSTER SAUCE WITH RICE: Remove meat from 1 frozen lobster
tail, substitute tail shell for leftover lobster shell, dice meat, simmer in sauce last 5 to 10 minutes of cooking, and serve in sauce
over rice.

RICH WINE SAUCE

2 tbs. butter
3 tbs. flour
½ cup dry white wine
½ cup fish or meat stock

¼ cup cream
1 egg yolk, beaten
salt and pepper to taste

Melt butter in the top of a double boiler over boiling water. Stir in flour and gradually add wine and stock. Stir until sauce is smooth and thickened. Reduce heat. Stir cream with egg yolk until smooth. When water has stopped boiling, stir creamy mixture into sauce and continue to stir for 2 minutes. Add seasonings and any suggested variations. Serve at once over cooked fish.

VARIATIONS:

CAPER SAUCE: Add 1 tbs. smallest capers.

DILL SAUCE: Add 2 tsp. minced dill.

SPINACH SAUCE: Add 1 cup well-drained cooked spinach.

MUSHROOM SAUCE: Add ½ cup sliced mushrooms, sautéed in butter and drained.

WINE SAUCE WITH MUSHROOMS

4 tbs. butter
1 4-oz. can mushrooms, sliced — drain, reserve liquor
4 tbs. flour
1 cup dry white wine

1 cup mushroom liquid, or add enough water or stock from cooked fish
2 tbs. sour cream
1 tsp. lemon juice
salt and pepper to taste

Melt butter in the top of a double boiler. Brown mushrooms lightly in it. Set over boiling water and blend in flour. When smooth, add wine and mushroom liquid, stirring constantly until thickened. Remove from heat and stir in sour cream, lemon juice and salt and pepper. Serve immediately.

VARIATION: Substitute 1 cup sliced fresh mushrooms for the

canned mushrooms and substitute 1 cup fish or meat stock for the mushroom liquid.

HOT SOUR CREAM SAUCE

½ cup diced salt pork or bacon
1 medium onion, minced
2 tbs. flour
1 cup fish stock or bouillon

2 tbs. tomato puree
1 tbs. white wine
½ tsp. paprika
1 cup sour cream

Fry diced salt pork, add minced onion and cook until lightly browned and tender. Blend in flour. Add fish stock very slowly, stirring constantly, and cook until sauce thickens. Add tomato puree, wine, paprika and sour cream and simmer gently another 5 minutes. Strain or not as you prefer.

STROGANOFF SAUCE

1 medium onion, chopped
¼ cup butter or margarine
2 tbs. flour
1 cup liquid from canned mushrooms, or add enough court bouillon or other broth

1 8-oz. can of mushrooms, drained
¼ tsp. Worcestershire
2 tbs. tomato paste or puree
½ cup sour cream
salt and pepper

In the top of a double boiler, lightly brown onion in butter. Set over boiling water and blend in flour, add mushroom liquid, stirring constantly, until sauce thickens. Add mushrooms, Worcestershire and tomato paste and continue cooking 5 minutes. Remove from heat, stir in sour cream and salt and pepper.

Brown Sauces

BROWN SAUCE I

¼ cup brown roux, page 102

¼ cup cold brown stock or bouillon

1 cup boiling brown stock or bouillon

salt and pepper to taste

Stir roux with cold stock, gradually add boiling stock and set over low heat. Simmer, stirring constantly, until the sauce thickens. Reduce heat further and let the sauce cook 10 more minutes. Add salt and pepper and serve. Bouillon cubes and boiling water can be substituted for the stock or bouillon.

BROWN SAUCE II

2 tbs. beef fat

2 tbs. flour *

1 cup fish stock, brown stock or bouillon

salt and pepper to taste

Melt the fat, stir in flour and let the mixture brown slowly over very low heat, stirring frequently. When the roux is a rich brown, add the stock gradually, stirring constantly, until the sauce is smooth and thickened. Reduce heat further and let the sauce cook 10 more minutes. Add salt and pepper and serve.

MIROTON SAUCE

1 recipe brown sauce, page 130

½ cup diced tomato

2 tbs. minced onion

1 tbs. butter

2 tsp. brown mustard

salt and pepper to taste

* Always use twice as much brown flour as white flour for a sauce.

Sauté tomato and onion in butter until they are soft, combine with remaining ingredients and heat to boiling.

MUSHROOM SAUCE

1 recipe brown sauce,
   page 130
½ cup sliced mushrooms
2 tsp. butter

1 dash mushroom essence
   (optional)
1 tbs. minced parsley
salt and pepper to taste

Sauté mushrooms in butter until they are soft, combine with remaining ingredients and heat to boiling.

BRITTANY SAUCE

1 recipe brown sauce,
   page 130
2 shallots, minced
2 tsp. butter
½ garlic clove, crushed

¼ cup white wine
1 tbs. tomato paste, or to
   taste
1 tbs. minced parsley
salt and pepper to taste

Sauté shallots in butter until they are golden, add garlic and remaining ingredients and heat to boiling. Stir well.

OYSTER SAUCE

1 recipe brown sauce,
   page 130
1 cup oysters and their
   liquor

¼ cup sliced mushrooms
2 tbs. butter
½ cup fish fumet, page 106
salt and pepper to taste

Poach oysters in their own liquor until the edges curl. Sauté mushrooms in butter 5 minutes, add oysters, liquor and remaining ingredients and heat to boiling. Stir well and serve at once.

POLONAISE SAUCE

1 recipe brown sauce,
  page 130
½ cup red wine
¼ cup slivered almonds
¼ cup raisins

¼ cup crushed ginger-
  snaps
1 tsp. vinegar
½ tsp. sugar
salt and pepper to taste

Combine all ingredients and heat until raisins are puffed. Stir well and serve.

SAILOR'S SAUCE

4 tbs. butter
1 medium onion,
  chopped
1 medium carrot,
  chopped
1 bay leaf

1½ cups fish trimmings,
  heads and bones
  water
4 cups dry white wine
2 tbs. flour
salt and pepper to taste

Melt 1 tbs. butter in pan, add onion and carrot and stir until lightly browned. Add bay leaf and fish trimmings and enough water to just cover. Simmer 15 minutes. Add wine and simmer, covered, about 1 hour, or until liquid is reduced to half. Strain and set aside. Over low heat, stir flour into remaining butter until it is lightly browned. Add 2 cups of the strained wine stock and stir until smooth. Add salt and pepper and serve.

GENEVA SAUCE

½ recipe brown sauce,
  page 130
1 carrot, sliced
1 onion, sliced
1 bay leaf
2 sprigs parsley
1 sprig thyme

2 tbs. butter
head and bones of 1
salmon or ½ lb. fish
trimmings
1 cup dry red wine
salt and pepper to taste

Simmer carrot, onion, bay leaf and herbs in butter 20 minutes, stirring occasionally. Add fish trimmings and stir well. Add wine and simmer, uncovered, until reduced to half. Strain, add brown sauce and bring to a boil. Add salt and pepper and serve.

VARIATIONS:

BROWN CAPER SAUCE: Add ½ tbs. smallest capers.

BROWN MUSHROOM SAUCE: Add 1 cup sautéed sliced mushrooms.

BROWN MUSTARD SAUCE: Add ½ tbs. mild brown mustard.

BROWN HORSERADISH SAUCE: Add ½ cup freshly grated horseradish.

BROWN RAISIN SAUCE: Add ½ cup raisins, previously soaked in the cup red wine for 1 hour.

Egg Sauces

HOLLANDAISE SAUCE

4 egg yolks	1⅓ cups butter
1 tsp. tarragon vinegar	pinch cayenne
1 tsp. water	salt to taste

Whip egg yolks with vinegar and 1 tsp. water until light and foamy. Cook in the top of a double boiler over barely boiling water. Using a wire whisk, stir in the butter bit by bit, stirring until each bit is melted and incorporated before adding the next. Add lemon juice, salt and cayenne and serve at once.

NOTE: The top of the double boiler should not touch the boiling water. The sauce is cooked in the steam.

MOUSSELINE SAUCE

> 1 recipe hollandaise
> sauce, page 133

> ½ cup cream, stiffly
> whipped

Just before serving the warm hollandaise, fold in whipped cream. Serve with poached salmon.

BÉARNAISE SAUCE

> 1 tsp. dried or minced
> fresh tarragon
> 1 tsp. dried or minced
> fresh chervil
> 1 shallot, chopped
> ¼ cup tarragon vinegar
> 3 egg yolks
> 1 cup butter, cut into 8
> pieces

> 2 sprigs tarragon, leaves
> removed and minced
> 2 sprigs fresh chervil,
> leaves removed and
> minced
> small pinch cayenne
> salt to taste

Simmer tarragon, chervil, shallot and vinegar in the top of a double boiler until reduced to about 1 tbs. Cool, add egg yolks and whip until light and foamy. Place over barely boiling water. Using a wire whisk, stir in each piece of butter, stirring until it is melted and incorporated before adding the next piece. Add salt and cayenne. Strain the sauce, or use it unstrained, and stir in the minced tarragon and chervil leaves. Serve at once.

NOTE: The top of the double boiler should not touch the boiling water. The sauce is cooked in the steam.

BÉARNAISE BUTTER: Chill leftover sauce and serve as a compound butter, spread on sizzling hot broiled fish steaks or fillets.

CHORON SAUCE

1 recipe béarnaise sauce,
  page 134
¼ cup thick tomato puree

or 2 tbs. tomato paste
salt to taste

Fold tomato puree into the finished béarnaise sauce, season
and serve.

MAYONNAISE

(A commercial mayonnaise may be substituted in any of the
recipes calling for mayonnaise.)

2 large egg yolks
1 tsp. salt, or to taste

¼ to ½ tsp. vinegar or
  lemon juice
1 cup oil

Stir egg yolks with salt and ¼ tsp. vinegar in a large shallow
bowl. Use a wooden spoon. Continue to stir while adding
oil, drop by drop. As soon as the sauce begins to thicken, add
the oil in a thin stream. If the sauce becomes too thick, add
a few more drops of vinegar.

Oil, yolks and bowl should be at the same temperature. Do
not use refrigerated egg yolks with warm oil. Everything
should be cool, neither too warm nor too cold.

RÉMOULADE SAUCE

1 cup mayonnaise
2 tsp. prepared mild
  mustard
2 small gherkins, minced

1 tbs. minced capers
1 tbs. minced parsley
½ tsp. each, minced
  chervil and tarragon
  salt and pepper to taste

Combine all ingredients and serve with cold or hot fried fish
or shellfish.

TARTAR SAUCE

1 cup mayonnaise, page 135
2 tbs. chopped onion
1 tbs. chopped dill pickle
or pickle relish, drained
1 tbs. chopped parsley

1 tbs. chopped chives
1 tbs. chopped capers
1 tsp. prepared mustard
salt and pepper to taste

Combine all ingredients and serve with fried fish or shellfish, cold fish dishes and hot broiled fish steaks.

VARIATION:

WATERCRESS SAUCE: Omit pickle and capers and substitute ¼ cup finely chopped watercress leaves.

Clear Sauces Thickened with Cornstarch

HERB SAUCE

1 cup clear stock, fish,
meat or chicken
4 tbs. butter
3 tsp. cornstarch
1 tsp. vinegar
2 tbs. minced onion
¼ garlic clove, minced

1 tbs. chopped dried
parsley
½ tbs. minced dried
tarragon
½ tsp. prepared mild
mustard
salt and pepper to taste

Heat stock thoroughly in heavy saucepan, remove from heat, add butter one tablespoon at a time. Stir. Sprinkle in cornstarch, stirring vigorously. Add vinegar, onion, garlic, parsley, tarragon and mustard. Set aside.

Reheat 15 minutes before sauce is needed by placing over very low heat and stirring frequently. When hot, add salt and pepper to taste.

ORIENTAL SAUCE

1¼ cups chicken, fish or meat stock, strained
⅓ cup brown sugar
⅓ cup pineapple juice
2½ tsp. cornstarch

2 tbs. vinegar
6 blanched almonds, slivered
2 tbs. lemon juice
soy sauce to taste

Combine chicken stock, brown sugar and pineapple juice in the top of a double boiler over boiling water. Mix cornstarch with 3 tbs. water to make a thin paste. Drizzle slowly into sauce, stirring constantly until it thickens. Add vinegar, lemon juice, soy sauce and continue cooking, stirring occasionally, about 15 minutes. Add almonds.

Chopped pineapple chunks or sautéed green pepper may be added, if desired.

PINEAPPLE-LEMON SAUCE

1 cup pineapple juice
1 tbs. lemon juice
½ tsp. grated lemon rind (optional)
¼ cup sugar

⅛ tsp. salt
¾ cup water
2½ tsp. cornstarch
3 tbs. butter

Place first six ingredients in heavy saucepan and stir. Sprinkle in cornstarch and stir until dissolved. Place over medium heat and stir frequently. When bubbles form, turn down heat and allow to cook about 10 minutes. Add butter, 1 tbs. at a time, stirring constantly 5 minutes. Set sauce aside and allow to thicken. Stir before serving.

Red Sauce

Based on catsup, chili sauce and tomatoes.

COOKED RED SAUCE   *Basic Recipe:*

½ cup catsup or chili   2 tbs. melted butter,
   sauce   margarine or oil
2 tbs. chopped onion

Sauté onion in butter, add catsup, stir and simmer gently until heated through and thoroughly blended.

VARIATIONS:

1. Add 1 tbs. grated Parmesan cheese
2. Add 1 garlic clove chopped, and 1 tsp. prepared mustard. Sauté garlic with onion and continue as above.
3. Add ¼ cup water, 2 tbs. vinegar, 1 tbs. Worcestershire, 1 tsp. prepared mustard, and 1 tsp. brown sugar. Combine all ingredients and add to basic sauce.
4. Add 2 tbs. chopped celery, 1 tbs. chopped green pepper, ½ tsp. lemon juice, ½ tsp. prepared horseradish, and ⅛ tsp. minced garlic. Sauté celery, pepper and garlic with onion and continue as above.

UNCOOKED RED SAUCE   *Basic Recipe:*

1 cup catsup or chili sauce   1 tsp. vinegar
2 tbs. drained prepared   1 tsp. Worcestershire
   horseradish   1 dash Tabasco
2 tbs. minced green onion   ½ garlic clove, crushed
   or onion   salt and pepper to taste
1 tsp. brown sugar

Combine all ingredients and serve with cold fish or shellfish, or use for barbecuing.

VARIATIONS:

1. Omit horseradish, sugar, vinegar and Worcestershire and substitute 2 tbs. dry white wine, 2 chopped ripe olives and 1 tbs. minced parsley.

2. Prepare sauce as variation, above, and substitute olive oil for wine and olives. Add 1 tsp. minced fresh or dried oregano and a dash powdered cloves.

3. Add 2 tbs. liquid smoke, or if cooking outdoors, add a few hickory chips to the fire.

MEXICAN AVOCADO AND TOMATO SAUCE

2 ripe avocados
1 medium onion, chopped
1 garlic clove, chopped
1 tbs. oil
2 tomatoes, peeled, seeded and chopped

1 tbs. chopped parsley
¼ tsp. chili powder (optional)
1 lemon, cut in wedges
salt and pepper to taste

Lightly brown onion and garlic in oil and cook until tender.
Peel avocados, mash them and combine all ingredients. Serve immediately over cooked fish steaks or fillets and garnish with lemon wedges.

CIOPPINO SAUCE

3 or 4 large ripe tomatoes chopped (peel and seed if preferred)
1 large onion, chopped
1 green pepper, seeded and chopped
1 carrot, grated
1 stalk celery, chopped
1 8-oz. can Italian tomato sauce

2 tbs. minced parsley
½ tsp. dried oregano
3 tbs. red wine (optional)
1 garlic clove, crushed
1 cup fish, meat or chicken stock (bouillon can be substituted)
1 tbs. olive oil
salt and pepper to taste

Place all ingredients in heavy pot, cover tightly and simmer slowly about 1 hour. Stir occasionally to be sure sauce is not sticking. If sauce becomes too thick, add a little stock.

Pour over fish and shellfish as directed in Cioppino recipe, page 159.

NOTE: This sauce can be used to pour over cooked whole fish, steaks or fillets, a whole fish can be baked in it, or it can be thinned with stock and used to steam or poach steaks or fillets.

CREOLE SAUCE

¼ cup chopped onion	½ tsp. salt, or to taste
½ cup chopped green pepper	¼ tsp. black pepper
1 garlic clove	1 to 1½ cups strong fish or meat stock
½ cup butter	½ cup finely sliced mushrooms
¼ cup flour	2 tbs. minced parsley
4 medium tomatoes, chopped (peel and seed if preferred)	

Sauté onion, pepper and garlic in butter until onion is golden. Remove garlic, stir in flour until blended and smooth. Add tomatoes, seasonings and 1 cup stock. Simmer 45 minutes, adding a little more stock if necessary. Add mushrooms and parsley and simmer a few minutes longer until mushrooms are tender.

VARIATIONS:

1. Add 2 tbs. chopped stuffed green olives with the mushrooms.
2. Add ½ cup chopped celery with the tomatoes.
3. Add ¼ cup diced pimiento with the pepper.

FRESH VEGETABLE SAUCE

2 large ripe tomatoes, chopped	½ green pepper, seeded and sliced (optional)
1 large onion, sliced	1 to 1½ cups chicken stock
1 carrot, sliced	1 tsp. salt
3 stalks celery, diced	1 tbs. dry wine

Place all ingredients and 1 cup stock in a heavy pot. Cover tightly and simmer 15 minutes.

Carefully place fish, fish fillets, or steaks on the vegetables. Replace cover and simmer gently 10 minutes more, or until fish flakes easily when tested with fork.

Any fish fillet or steak can be cooked on top of the vegetables in this recipe. The thicker the fish, the longer it will need to cook and the more liquid you will need to add.

When fish is tender and vegetables are soft, take out fish, press vegetables through a sieve and pour over fish.

Marinades

UNCOOKED MARINADE I

3 cups water	1 tsp. salt
1 cup vinegar	½ tsp. black pepper
2 garlic cloves, minced	pinch of cuminseed

Combine the ingredients, pour into a glass or enamel bowl. Do not use a metal container. Add fish and marinate it in refrigerator overnight.

UNCOOKED MARINADE II

3 cups red wine	6 peppercorns
1 cup oil	1 clove
2 onions, sliced	3 bay leaves
1 carrot, sliced	2 sprigs thyme
2 garlic cloves	2 sprigs parsley
1 tsp. salt	

Combine the ingredients, pour into a glass or enamel bowl. Do not use a metal container. Add fish and marinate it in refrigerator 2 to 12 hours, depending on recipe. Strain marinade and poach fish in it or use it as a base for the sauce.

COOKED MARINADE

4 cups water	1 tsp. dried thyme
1 cup vinegar	½ tsp. dried tarragon
1 large onion, chopped	1 bay leaf
1 shallot, chopped	4 sprigs parsley
1 carrot, diced	2 tsp. salt
1 garlic clove, split	4 peppercorns

Combine all ingredients in a pot and simmer 1 hour. Cool marinade and pour it into a glass or enamel bowl. Do not use a metal container. Add fish and marinate it in refrigerator 2 to 12 hours, depending on recipe. Strain marinade and poach fish in it or use it as a base for the sauce.

IV

Sauce-Making Chart

ADD ONE OR MORE TO SAUCE BASE IN COLUMN 1

SAUCE BASES Use These Sauces As They Are or in Combination with Columns 2, 3, 4, 5 (1)	For Very Delicate Flavor (2)	For Stronger, Richer, Flavor (3)	Cocktail and Barbecue for Sauces (4)	For Highly Spiced and Oriental Sauces (5)
CREAM: sour cream, thick cream, whipped cream	ALMONDS, slivered	BASIL	ANCHOVY, paste, fillets	CAYENNE
FRENCH DRESSING	CELERY, chopped, salt	BAYLEAF	CAVIAR, eggs, paste	CHILI POWDER
MAYONNAISE	CHEESE, creamed, grated, soup	CATSUP	CLOVES, whole	CORIANDER
OIL: animal fats, butter and margarine, olive and peanut oil, vegetable oils	CHERVIL (tastes like mild parsley)	DILL	GARLIC, crushed	CUMIN
SOUP (canned, frozen or leftover): celery, cheese, fish and shell-fish, mushroom, tomato	CHIVES, chopped	FRENCH DRESSING	HERRING, paste	CURRY
STOCK (unthickened): chicken, fish, meat, vegetable	CLOVES, powdered	GARLIC, powder	HORSERADISH, prepared	FENNEL
TOMATOES (canned or cooked): catsup, chili sauce, spaghetti sauce, stewed	COCONUT, milk, shredded	GREEN PEPPER, rings	LEMON, frozen concentrated lemonade	GARLIC, whole, cloves
	CREAM, heavy, sour, thin, whipped	LEMON, slices	MOLASSES	HERRING, fillets
Sauce Bases That Require Some Preparation	EGG, hard-cooked, riced, beaten white, yolk	LOBSTER, coral and liver	MUSTARD, prepared	HORSERADISH, grated
STARCH-THICKENED	GREEN PEPPER, finely chopped	MUSHROOMS	OLIVES, whole	HONEY
BROTH: chicken, fish, meat (brown sauce), vegetable	HONEY	ONION, chopped	ONION, sliced	MUSTARD, powdered
JUICE: pineapple, lemon and orange, tomato	LEMON, grated rind, juice	OYSTERS, chopped, whole	SAGE	PEPPERCORN, whole
	LOBSTER, chopped	PAPRIKA	SOY SAUCE	TARRAGON
	MARJORAM	PARSLEY, chopped, dried	TABASCO	
	MAYONNAISE	PEPPER, ground	TUMERIC	
		PICKLE, chopped	VINEGAR	
		SAFFRON	WORCESTERSHIRE	
		SALMON, smoked and chopped		
		SUGAR, brown		

MILK: white sauce	MILK	TOMATO PASTE
WINE	OLIVES, chopped	TOMATOES, sliced
	ONION, powdered	TOMATO, juice
	ORANGE, grated rind, juice	
	PIMIENTO, chopped, sliced	
	PINEAPPLE, chunks, juice	
	SALT	
	SHALLOT (mild flavor like onion)	
	SHRIMP, chopped, whole	
	STOCK, meat, fish, vegetable	
	SUGAR, white	
	THYME	
	TOMATOES, cooked, canned	
	WATER	
	WINE, dry, white, red, sherry	

1: List of sauce bases that can be used as they are or in combination with ingredients listed in columns 2, 3, 4 and 5

2: What to add for very delicate flavor

3: What to add for stronger, richer flavor

4: What to add for cocktail and barbecue sauces

5: What to add for very highly spiced and Oriental sauces

(The ingredients in all five columns are arranged alphabetically and are not meant to be read across the page.)

Part Three
Recipes

Read Part One for detailed instructions for buying, cleaning, cutting up, storing, defrosting, and otherwise preparing your fish for cooking.

I

Introduction and Instructions

Many kinds of fish are called for in the recipes that follow, but that does not mean you must have that fish. No matter what fish is suggested, any other fish can be substituted.

A red snapper recipe can also be a striped bass recipe or a yellowtail or a weakfish recipe. A bluefish recipe can be used for mackerel and salmon can be substituted for tuna. Fluke or flounder take the place of sole. Use shellfish, whole or chopped, in recipes calling for flaked fish.

Interchange the fish according to the seasons, remembering only that a fat fish recipe goes best with a fat fish and a lean fish recipe goes best with a lean fish. You can even interchange lean and fat fish recipes if you remember to baste more often with butter or oil while cooking lean fish. The chart beginning on page 27 shows which fish are fat and which are lean.

Wherever a recipe calls for a sauce but does not include the directions, you'll find them in Part Two, which begins on page 99.

We have arranged the recipes by method of cooking: Top of stove, broiler (indoors and outdoors), oven, and miscellaneous buffet and luncheon party recipes. Each method is accompanied by detailed cooking instructions. (There is additional cooking information in Cleaning and Cooking Shellfish, which begins on page 51.)

You will find seafood recipes from every corner of the world in this section. They came from United Nations missions, from consulates and embassies here in the United States, from foreign capitals and other sources.

If you find the language of some of the foreign recipes odd, it is because they are translated exactly as they were received.

They have been tested, and instructions clarified where necessary.

Before you start cooking, remember important points which were emphasized in the preceding chapters:

A fish is done when it flakes easily with a fork—start using your fork to test it at half the given cooking time!

Refrigerate cleaned fish until cooking time and *then* wash it. Just before cooking cleaned fish, douse it quickly in cold salted water and immediately dry it gently with a towel or absorbent paper. Do *not* hold it under running water.

The best way to defrost fish and shellfish is to place them in your refrigerator and let them remain there until pliable enough to handle. The worst way is to leave them out of the refrigerator at room temperature. We refer you to page 36 for more details on quick defrosting.

A chart showing the most commonly marketed fish begins on page 19.

Cooking Methods

Top of stove

　　Simmering (boiling), including stews, soups and chowders
　　Deep frying
　　Pan frying
　　Poaching
　　Seafood and eggs
　　Steaming

Broiler

　　Indoor and outdoor

Oven

　　Fillets and steaks with stuffing
　　Fillets, steaks and chunked fish baked in a sauce

Fish pies
Flaked fish and shellfish loaves
Oven fried
Shellfish, flaked cooked fish and canned fish in casserole
Shellfish-stuffed seashells
Vegetables with fish and shellfish stuffing
Whole fish baked in the oven

*Buffet, luncheon and
party recipes*

Appetizers, dips, marinated appetizers, cocktails
Salads
Sandwiches
Seafood gelatin molds
Garnishes that go with fish dishes

II

Top of Stove Recipes

General Instructions for
Simmering (Boiling) Fish

This is a method of fish cooking that generally is passed over by housewives because they think all the taste and goodness are boiled away. But where fish is concerned, the word "boil" does not even mean boil. It means simmer. Water boils at 212° F. and starts to simmer at 180° F.

Simmering is simple. Just bring your liquid to a boil and then reduce it until it just bubbles around the edges. With a properly seasoned liquid, simmered fish is tasty and the residue makes an excellent broth. It makes an excellent spaghetti sauce; it makes many things. Simmering is the best way of preparing fish for flaking into salads, sandwiches, and canapes. But, most of all, simmered fish is the first step toward a dish that calls for cream sauces. Fish also may be simmered in court bouillon, acidulated in water or fish stock, described on pages 154.

The use to which you intend to put the fish will determine the way in which it should go into the pot for cooking. It can be chunked, filleted, split, or left whole. Filleting is best for serving with a sauce. Chunking is best for making salad. Either whole or split is best for boning. All are good for flaking. (See Part One, Cleaning Your Catch, for detailed instructions on cutting up fish.)

The liquids to use

In simmering, steaming, poaching, or making soups and chowders the only liquid you need to bring out the flavor is plain water. You needn't even add salt. Zest can be added and the flavor can be fitted to your taste by substituting some other liquid for water—milk, cream, wine, or beer. For the sake of both flavor and nutrition the liquid from shellfish and canned fish should never be discarded. Whenever possible, substitute it for part of the liquid used in the recipe.

Court bouillon

Court Bouillon is the French name for the broth in which fish may be poached, steamed, or simmered. It can be prepared in advance, strained, cooled, and stored for several days in the refrigerator.

COURT BOUILLON I

2 large carrots, sliced
2 large onions, sliced
6 sprigs parsley
1 sprig thyme, or dried thyme to taste
1 bay leaf
6 peppercorns, or to taste
1 cup vinegar, or less to taste (1 to 2 tbs. may add all the zest your family will want)
6 cups water

Combine all ingredients in a large pot. Cover and simmer 3 hours. Strain through a fine sieve or three thicknesses of cheesecloth wrung out of cold water. Cool and use as the liquid in which fish is cooked. Or, if you are making a quick soup, leave the vegetables in.

COURT BOUILLON II

2 large carrots, sliced
1 large onion, sliced
2 shallots, chopped
2 sprigs parsley
1 sprig each tarragon and thyme, ½ tsp. each dry tarragon and thyme
1 bay leaf
4 peppercorns, or to taste
1 clove
12 cups water

Combine all ingredients in a large pot. Cover and simmer 2 hours. Strain through a fine sieve or three thicknesses of cheesecloth, wrung out of cold water. Use as above.

COURT BOUILLON III

1 cup dry white wine or red wine
1 carrot, sliced
1 onion, sliced
2 sprigs parsley
1 sprig thyme, or ½ tsp.
dry thyme
½ bay leaf
6 peppercorns, or to taste
1 tsp. salt, or to taste
2 cups water

Combine all ingredients in a large pot. Cover and simmer 45 minutes. Strain and use as above.

COURT BOUILLON IV

2 lbs. fish trimmings, heads and bones, or use 1 lb. halibut, with skin and bones or 1 lb. salmon, with skin and bones
1 onion, sliced
2 sprigs parsley
2 sprigs dill, or ¼ to ½ tsp. dried dill
1 sprig tarragon, or ½ tsp. dried tarragon
1½ tbs. salt
1 tbs. lemon juice
2 peppercorns
1 clove
8 cups water

Combine all ingredients in a large pot. Cover and simmer 1 hour. Strain and use as above.

ACIDULATED WATER

To each quart of water add 1½ tbs. salt and 3 tablespoons lemon juice or vinegar.

FISH STOCK

To each quart of cold water add one pound of fish trimmings —head, bones, skin and tail—and 1½ tbs. salt. Bring to a boil, turn down heat and simmer 30 minutes. Strain.

Simmered Fish, Fish Balls, Soups, Stews and Chowders Made without Milk or Cream

BLOWFISH CHOWDER WITH NOODLES

18 blowfish, cleaned
½ cup flour
½ cup oil
6 tbs. butter or margarine
2 medium onions, sliced
1 small green pepper, seeded and slivered
½ lb. mushrooms (or 2 4-oz. cans), sliced
½ cup ham, slivered
salt and pepper to taste
1¾ cups water
2 garlic cloves
1 sprig parsley, or 1 tbs. dried parsley
1 small bay leaf
¼ tsp. dried thyme
2 fresh tomatoes, cut in small wedges
1 tbs. lemon juice
2 tbs. cornstarch
⅓ cup water or dry white wine
1 pkg. noodles, cooked according to package directions

Wash blowfish in cold salted water. Dry thoroughly, dredge with flour and brown lightly in hot oil. Set aside.

Heat butter in a heavy pot, add onions, green pepper and mushrooms, sauté 5 minutes. Add ham and brown lightly. Add salt, pepper and 1¾ cups water and stir well. Add blowfish. Tie garlic, parsley, bay leaf and thyme together in cheesecloth or clean white cloth, add to pot. Cover tightly and simmer 10 minutes or until fish is tender.

Remove fish carefully, place on preheated platter and keep warm in oven. Remove herbs. Add tomato wedges and lemon juice to stew and increase heat slightly. Stir cornstarch into cold water or wine until smooth. Add it gradually, stirring constantly, and cook until broth has thickened.

Place border of hot noodles around fish. Pour vegetables and sauce over platter and serve. Serves 6.

COBIA OR HADDOCK FISH BALLS
Kristiansund Blandaball—Norway

1 lb. coalfish * or haddock
2 large potatoes, peeled and boiled
3 slices fat salt pork

½ onion, cut in thin slices and parboiled
flour
salt and pepper to taste

Put fish, potatoes and 1 slice salt pork through meat grinder three times. Cube remaining pork. Add onion to mixture and grind a fourth time. Add enough flour to produce a firm mass, season to taste. Shape into balls, press a cube of pork into each, boil the balls in salted water. Serve with melted butter or drippings. Serves 4.

BOILED COD
Kogt Torsk—Denmark

Cod is one of the most popular fish in Denmark. It is eaten from September till April.

Scrape and rinse cod thoroughly. Sprinkle with salt and let stand about 1 hour. If the fish is to be served whole, place in cold water and bring to a boil. If it is to be cut, drop the pieces into boiling water. Boil, uncovered, until it flakes when tested with a fork.

Serve fish hot with boiled potatoes and melted butter. The Danes serve separate dishes of chopped raw onions,

* Our closest fish to the coalfish is the cobia.

pickled beets, riced hard-cooked eggs, finely chopped parsley and grated raw apple.

FLOUNDER ONION SOUP

1 lb. flounder fillets, cut into small pieces
3 slices bacon, diced
8 medium onions, sliced
¼ cup butter or margarine

2 tbs. flour
2 chicken bouillon cubes
4 cups boiling water
½ cup grated cheese
salt and pepper to taste
dash paprika

Fry bacon until transparent. Add onions, butter and seasonings and cook until onions are soft. Sprinkle with flour and stir until smooth. Dissolve bouillon cubes in boiling water and add gradually to pan, stirring constantly. Add fish and simmer 10 minutes longer. Sprinkle with cheese and serve. Serves 6.

HADDOCK WITH RICE   *Ukrainian*

1 lb. haddock (or cod) fillets, cut into small pieces
2 medium onions, thinly sliced
6 tbs. butter

½ cup rice
¼ cup water
2 medium tomatoes, peeled and sliced
salt and pepper to taste

Brown onions lightly in 4 tbs. of the butter.

Boil rice until almost tender, drain. Spread half in a well-greased saucepan and pour ¼ cup water over it. Add onions and the butter in which they were cooked.

Season fish and arrange on onion slices. Top with sliced tomatoes, cover with remaining rice and add remaining butter.

Cover saucepan tightly and cook over very low heat about 10 minutes after it starts to steam, or until fish flakes. Serves 4.

Bouillabaisse

The secret of a good bouillabaisse, which comes to us from France, is the mingling of flavors of a large variety of shellfish. Visit the closest fish market, one that carries a large variety of quality fish and shellfish. Pick out an assortment, we cannot tell you what they will be; it will depend on where you live and the season. You may come home with a few flounder and mackerel fillets, a codfish steak and some salmon and, if possible, red snapper. Include some shellfish, crab or lobster meat, scallops or clams. If fresh shellfish are not available or are too expensive, use frozen or canned but be sure to strain off any broth and add it to the soup for extra flavor.

Shrimp, lobster, crab (except the claws) should be shelled and cleaned before adding to the pot. Clams and crab claws and mussels can be cooked in the soup right in their shells if thoroughly scrubbed first. Page 52, in the section on cleaning and cooking shellfish, tells how to purge clams of sand inside their shells.

Add seasonings and saffron. Bring to a boil and add fish. When it is tender, add the shellfish and cook a few minutes longer.

BOUILLABAISSE

1 1-lb. lobster, cooked
½ lb. whiting
½ lb. eel
½ lb. crab
   small shellfish in the shell, such as clams (thoroughly scrubbed and purged of sand), crab claws
4 garlic cloves, crushed
2 onions, chopped
3 tomatoes, peeled and quartered

⅔ cup olive oil (peanut oil can be substituted)
½ tsp. saffron shreds, or to taste
⅛ tsp. dried thyme
1 small bay leaf
1 tsp. monosodium glutamate
   fennel and parsley sprigs (optional)
   salt to taste
8 cups boiling water
8 pieces French bread, thickly sliced

Place garlic, onions, and tomatoes in bottom of large sauce-pan. Add oil, herbs, spices, glutamate, salt, lobster, and crab. Cover with boiling water and cook 6 minutes. Add fish and simmer 10 minutes. Put small shellfish in pot and continue simmering until their shells open. Some French chefs boil rapidly to keep the oil mixed in. (Although this may improve the flavor of the broth, the fish flesh is not as nice as when simmered.) Stir frequently.

Arrange fish on preheated platter, using opened shellfish as a border.

Place thick slices of French bread, usually toasted or dried, in soup plates and cover with soup. Serves 8.

BOUILLABAISSE   *Easy—American*

2 lbs. mixed fish	enough water to make 2 cups
½ cup chopped onion	2 cups canned tomatoes
½ cup chopped celery	salt and pepper to taste
1 garlic clove, finely chopped	¼ tsp. dried thyme
¼ cup butter, margarine or oil	1 bay leaf, crushed
broth from canned shrimp and clams—add	½ tsp. saffron
	1 7-oz. can minced clams
	1 7-oz. can shrimp
	6 slices toasted bread

Remove skin and bones from fish and cut into small pieces.

Cook onion, celery and garlic in butter until tender. Add broth, canned tomatoes, fish, seasonings and herbs. Bring to boiling point and simmer 15 minutes. Add clams and shrimp and cook another 5 minutes.

Arrange bread in individual soup bowls and cover each slice with broth and fish. Serves 6.

CRAB CIOPPINO

Cioppino, like bouillabaisse, sounds complicated, but it is actually very easy to prepare. The only difficulty may be in obtaining a sufficient variety of fish and shellfish.

1 lb. cod or other fish or combination of fish

1 lb. mixed live oysters and clams in shell (thoroughly scrubbed and prepared for cooking)

2 large crabs (cleaned and meat removed from body. Claws cracked and thoroughly scrubbed but not shelled)

4 cups hot cioppino sauce, page 139. (Canned stewed tomatoes and highly seasoned tomato paste can be substituted for cioppino sauce)

Prepare sauce as directed. Place fish and shellfish in bottom of large heavy pot. Add hot cioppino sauce and simmer very gently 15 to 20 minutes or until fish flakes easily when tested with a fork.

Place some of each kind of fish and shellfish in individual bowls and pour sauce over it.

Hot toasted and buttered French bread is usually served with cioppino and the shellfish is eaten with the hands.

FISH SOUP   *Fransk Fiskesuppe—Denmark*

½ lb. each of 3 different fish in season

1 to 1½ lbs. cooked lobster or crabs

1 lb. shrimp

1 medium onion, sliced

1 leek, sliced

2 garlic cloves, crushed

¼ lb. mushrooms, sliced

½ cup olive oil or peanut oil

6 cups boiling water

salt and pepper to taste

¼ tsp. saffron

1 bay leaf, crushed

⅛ tsp. caraway seeds

1 tbs. grated orange rind

2 large tomatoes, chopped

1 cup white wine

6 slices buttered toasted bread

chopped parsley

Lightly brown onion, leek, garlic and mushrooms in oil. Add the 3 kinds of fish, chopped tomatoes, the seasonings and herbs and orange rind to the boiling water. Simmer 10 minutes, add the browned vegetables. Simmer another 10 minutes, remove from heat and let stand 1 to 2 hours.

Cook lobster and shrimp. (See instructions, pages 62 and

76.) Cut lobster in pieces; shrimp in half. Reheat soup. Add lobster, shrimp and wine and heat at a low simmer 15 minutes.

Toast and butter bread and place in individual soup dishes. Cover with soup and fish, garnish with parsley and serve. Serves 6.

MIXED FISH BALLS   *Gefüllte Fish—Jewish*

2 lbs. carp
1 lb. mixed white fish, including fluke or flounder
2 stalks celery
1 large onion

salt and pepper to taste
2 eggs, beaten
3 carrots, sliced
grated horseradish

Chop fish finely with celery and onion. Add salt, pepper and eggs, mix well and shape into small balls.

Place bones of carp in large pot and cover with water. Wrap each fish ball individually in pieces of skin from the carp and place the balls carefully on top of the bones. Or, if you prefer, place the unwrapped fish balls on the bones and lay the skin over them. Add sliced carrots.

Bring water to a boil, turn down heat and simmer fish balls gently about 40 minutes. Allow to cool slightly, then carefully remove bones and skin from the pot. Chill the fish balls in the liquid, which will form a jelly, and serve cold with grated horseradish. Serves 8 to 10.

FISH VEGETABLE SOUP   *Psarosoupa Avgolemono*
—Greece

2 lbs. mixed white fish, cut in chunks
juice of ½ lemon
salt
3 quarts water
3 carrots, cut in chunks

2 large onions, cut in chunks
4 celery stalks with leaves, cut in chunks
½ cup olive oil
2 tbs. chopped parsley
salt and pepper to taste

EGG AND LEMON SAUCE:

4 egg yolks
4 tbs. lemon juice

3 tbs. fish stock

Rub fish chunks with lemon juice and salt. Bring water to a rapid boil, add vegetables, oil, parsley, salt and pepper. Reduce heat and boil slowly 20 to 30 minutes. Reduce heat further, add fish chunks (wrap them in cheesecloth for easier handling) and simmer 15 minutes. Remove fish and keep it hot.

Reserve 3 tbs. stock for egg and lemon sauce. Strain remaining stock and vegetables, return stock to pot and reheat. In the meantime, beat egg yolks until light, slowly beat in lemon juice and gradually stir in reserved fish stock. Turn heat very low under soup, stir in sauce, mixing well. Do not allow soup to boil after egg yolks have been added.

Divide fish between soup dishes, add soup and serve. Serves 6.

STUFFED CABBAGE SOUP

1 medium head cabbage
4 cups fish, meat or chicken stock
pinch ginger or 3 crumbled gingersnaps
1 tbs. brown sugar juice of ½ lemon
½ cup tomato paste
½ onion, finely chopped
1 stick celery, finely chopped

1 slice bacon cut in small pieces
¼ cup oil
½ cup rice cereal, crumbled, or bread crumbs
1 cup cooked fish, flaked
1 egg, beaten
1 to 2 tbs. egg white for sealing edges of cabbage rolls
4 green pepper rings
1 small carrot, sliced

Set aside 8 large outer leaves of cabbage. Cut remaining cabbage into wedges and cook in stock to which you have added ginger, sugar, lemon juice and tomato paste.

Lightly brown onion, celery and bacon in oil. Combine with crumbs, flaked fish and beaten egg. Stuff cabbage leaves with the mixture, brushing egg white on edges of leaves to seal them, fasten with wooden picks and place carefully in soup. Simmer very slowly 1 hour. Add green pepper and carrot slices during last 10 minutes. Serve stuffed cabbage in center of bowl of soup and garnish with green pepper and carrot slices. Serves 4.

FISH SOUP WITH RICE

1 lb. fish fillets, skinned and cut into small pieces
2 slices bacon, diced
1 medium onion, chopped
2 tbs. chopped green pepper

2 cups boiling water
⅓ cup uncooked rice
salt and pepper to taste
2 cups tomato juice

Fry bacon, onion and pepper until light brown. Add 2 cups boiling water, rice and salt and pepper. Cook 10 minutes, add fish and cook 10 minutes longer, or until rice and fish are tender.

Add tomato juice, reheat and serve. Serves 6.

MATZO BALL SOUP

4 eggs, beaten
⅔ cup smoked fish, finely chopped (it can be broken up easily by rubbing across a coarse grater)
1 cup matzo meal

½ cup melted butter or margarine
¼ cup water
¼ cup seltzer water
salt and pepper to taste
8 cups meat or fish stock
½ carrot and ½ green pepper sliced across

Combine eggs, fish, matzo, butter, water, seltzer and salt and pepper. Stir, and chill 20 minutes.

Heat stock to boiling point, shape matzo mixture into small

balls and drop carefully into the liquid. Cover and simmer gently 20 minutes.

Cook the carrot and green pepper slices until just tender and garnish the matzo balls with them in the individual soup dishes. Serves 6.

Simmered Fish, Fish Balls, Soups, Stews and Chowders Made without Milk or Cream

SALT COD CHOWDER   *Canada*

1 lb. dry salt cod	pork, or chopped bacon
1 cup diced raw carrots	½ cup finely diced onions
3 cups diced raw potatoes	3 cups milk
½ cup finely diced salt	¼ tsp. pepper

Soak cod 24 hours in cold water. Drain, cover with fresh cold water and simmer 30 minutes. Drain again and flake.

Simmer carrots and potatoes in water to cover until tender. Do not drain. Sauté salt pork and onions in skillet until crisp. Add to vegetables. (Melted fat can be drained off but it is usually included in the chowder.) Add flaked cod, milk and pepper. Heat, but do not boil. Serves 6.

NOTE: If fish has been packaged with fins, skin and bones, they should be removed before simmering. This same method of freshening salt cod may be followed for other recipes.

VARIATION: Add one cup cooked corn, or substitute it for carrots, and 1 cup milk.

PERCH CHOWDER WITH MUSHROOMS

1 lb. ocean perch fillets, cut into 1-inch pieces	2 10½-oz. cans condensed mushroom soup
2 tbs. chopped green pepper	1½ cups milk
¼ lb. mushrooms, sliced	2 tbs. chopped pimiento
4 tbs. butter or margarine, melted	2 tbs. sherry
	salt and pepper to taste

Sauté green pepper and mushrooms in butter until tender. Remove any skin from pieces of fillet, add to green pepper mixture and cook 5 minutes or until fish flakes easily with a fork.

Combine mushroom soup with milk and heat over low flame, stirring until smooth. Add slowly to fish, stirring constantly until chowder is hot but not boiling. Stir in pimiento, wine and salt and pepper.

Serve with noodles, rice or toast. Serves 6.

TUNA STEW STROGANOFF

2 7-oz. cans tuna, drained and broken in pieces	1 cup court bouillon, page 153, and liquid drained from mushrooms
1 medium onion, chopped	½ cup sour cream
2 8-oz. cans sliced mushrooms, drained	2 tbs. catsup
¼ cup oil drained from tuna—add melted butter if not sufficient	¼ tsp. Worcestershire
	pepper to taste
2 tbs. flour	2 cups hot cooked rice

Lightly sauté onion and mushrooms in oil, blend in flour and brown. Add bouillon and mushroom liquid gradually, stirring constantly and cook until thickened. Add sour cream, catsup, Worcestershire and pepper.

Pour sauce into top of double boiler over boiling water. Add tuna and as soon as it is heated through, serve over rice. Serves 6.

BALKAN FISH STROGANOFF

2 cups flaked cooked fish, or 2 7-oz. cans tuna
¼ lb. fresh mushrooms, sliced
¼ cup chopped green pepper
1 medium onion, chopped
1 garlic clove, very finely chopped

¼ cup butter or margarine
1 10½-oz. can condensed tomato soup
1 cup sour cream
½ cup milk
1 tbs. Worcestershire
¼ tsp. Tabasco
salt and pepper to taste

Sauté mushrooms, green pepper, onion and garlic in butter until tender.

Combine tomato soup, sour cream, milk, Worcestershire, Tabasco and salt and pepper. Mix until thoroughly blended and smooth. Add slowly to vegetable mixture, stirring constantly until just below boiling point.

Add flaked fish, heat and serve over noodles, rice or toast, Serves 6.

FISH SOUP WITH FISHBALLS   *Fiskesuppe—Norway*

2 tbs. butter or margarine
3 tbs. flour
6 cups fish stock, heated
2 tbs. sour cream
1 tbs. finely chopped

spring onion (green onion and top)
12 small fish balls, page 156
salt to taste

Melt butter in a large saucepan over low heat, stir in flour and gradually add stock. Simmer 5 minutes. Add sour cream, onion, fish balls and salt and stir until fish balls are heated through. Serves 6.

STUFFED CABBAGE IN CREAMED SOUP

Koldolmar—Scandinavia

2 cups cooked flaked fish, or 2 7-oz. cans tuna
1 cup cooked rice or bread crumbs
½ cup celery, finely chopped
1 small onion, finely chopped
1 egg, beaten
1 tbs. prepared mustard
½ tsp. horseradish
12 large cabbage leaves

2 tbs. butter, margarine or oil from canned tuna
2 chicken bouillon cubes dissolved in 2 cups boiling water, or 2 cups fish broth or court bouillon, page 153
1 tbs. brown sugar
2 tbs. flour
½ cup light cream
salt and pepper to taste

Make stuffing mixture by combining fish, rice, celery, onion, beaten egg, mustard and horseradish.

Parboil cabbage leaves in salted water about 2 minutes, just long enough to make them flexible for rolling (slitting the end of the center vein of the leaves will also help). Divide stuffing among leaves, fold over the ends and roll up. Fasten with wooden picks. In a casserole lightly brown cabbage rolls in butter. Add bouillon and brown sugar. Simmer, covered, 30 to 35 minutes. Remove cabbage rolls to preheated serving dish and remove picks. Make a smooth paste of flour and cream and stir into bouillon remaining in casserole. Add salt and pepper and stir over low heat until thickened. Pour over cabbage rolls. Serves 6.

SALMON AND FLOUNDER SOUP   *A Complete Meal*

½ lb. boned salmon, cut in chunks
½ to 1 lb. flounder fillets
1 loaf French bread
½ cup butter or margarine
1 garlic clove, crushed
1 10¾-oz. can cream of mushroom soup

½ soup can milk
1 pkg. frozen peas
6 medium shrimp, shelled and deveined
2 tbs. sour cream (optional)
salt and pepper to taste

Slice French bread almost through, spread butter mixed with garlic between slices.

Heat mushroom soup with milk, stirring until smooth. Cook frozen peas according to package directions, drain, reserving liquid, add remaining butter and set aside. Add reserved liquid to mushroom soup. Barely cover shrimp with salted water and simmer until tender, about 4 minutes. Lightly toast French bread in oven. Add salmon chunks to mushroom soup and stir until salmon is almost done.

Add flounder and liquid from cooked shrimp to soup, stir until flounder is cooked. By this time, both salmon and flounder should be broken into small pieces. Remove from heat, stir in sour cream and salt and pepper. Pour into individual preheated soup dishes. Spoon a mound of hot, cooked peas into center of each dish of soup and top with a cooked shrimp. Serve with garlic bread. Serves 6.

ROLLED FILLETS OF SOLE WITH SALMON

*Filets Van Tong Met Zalm
—Netherlands*

8 fillets of sole or flounder
½ lb. slice of salmon, cut in 8 pieces
1 cup salted water

white wine sauce, page 127
capers
mashed cooked potatoes

Place a piece of salmon at one end of each fillet, roll and fasten with wooden picks. Simmer 5 to 6 minutes in salted water, or until fish flakes easily when tested with a fork. Drain fish rolls, pour sauce over them and sprinkle with capers. Surround with a border of mashed potatoes. Serves 8.

VARIATION: Spread three cups cooked spinach in a well-greased casserole. Place the cooked fish rolls on top and cover with thick cheese sauce, page 123. Bake in 375° F. oven for 25 minutes or until brown.

Shellfish Soups, Stews and Chowders Made without Milk or Cream

MANHATTAN CLAM CHOWDER

1 pt. clams
clam liquor and enough water to make two cups
3 slices bacon or salt pork, diced
1 medium onion, chopped
½ cup chopped green pepper
2 carrots, chopped
1 cup chopped celery
2 medium potatoes, peeled and diced
¼ tsp. dried thyme
¼ tsp. sugar
salt and pepper to taste
1 1-lb. 12-oz. can tomatoes
dash cayenne

Heat bacon in saucepan, add onion, green pepper, carrots and celery and cook until almost tender. Add liquor from clams, potatoes, thyme, sugar and salt and pepper. Cook 12 to 15 minutes, or until potatoes are tender but not soft.

Chop clams and tomatoes, add them to the soup with the juice from the tomatoes. Reheat and serve. Serves 6.

LOBSTER AND PORK   *Oriental Style*

1½ lbs. uncooked lobster meat	¼ tsp. sugar
¼ lb. ground pork	1 tbs. soy sauce
1 garlic clove, minced	1 tbs. sherry
¼ cup oil, butter or margarine	2 cups water
½ cup sliced green onions	2 tsp. cornstarch
1 tsp. ginger	1 egg, lightly beaten
	4 cups hot cooked rice

Prepare lobster meat according to instructions on page 63. Cut into one-inch pieces.

Cook pork and garlic in oil until lightly brown. Add onion and lobster meat and cook over low heat until lobster is tender, about 5 minutes.

Mix ginger, sugar, soy sauce and sherry with water. Add cornstarch, stirred into 2 tbs. cold water, and stir until blended and smooth. Pour slowly into lobster mixture, stirring constantly over medium heat until thick and clear. Reduce heat, stir in beaten egg very slowly, remove from heat and serve over rice. Serves 6.

LOBSTER IN BUTTER SAUCE

4 cups uncooked lobster meat, cut into small pieces	2 tsp. Worcestershire salt, pepper and paprika to taste
¾ cup butter or margarine	6 slices hot toast
2 tbs. lemon juice	2 lemons cut into wedges
1 tsp. dry mustard, or to taste	

Prepare lobster meat according to instructions on page 62.

Place next 5 ingredients in top of double boiler over boiling water and stir until thoroughly blended and hot.

Add lobster meat and cook slowly 5 to 7 minutes or until white and tender. Serve on toast. Garnish with lemon wedges. Serves 6.

MUSSEL SPAGHETTI SAUCE *Salsa Di Vongone—Italy*

4 lbs. mussels	salt and pepper to taste
1 pkg. spaghetti	4 cups mussel liquor,
6 tbs. cooking oil	strained—add water if
2 large garlic cloves,	you do not have enough
slivered lengthwise	10 sprigs parsley, finely
½ tsp. oregano	chopped

Clean and shell mussels as directed on page 60 and chop them.

Prepare spaghetti according to package directions.

Heat oil in saucepan, add garlic and cook until reddish brown. Add oregano and salt and pepper and stir in mussel liquor. Add chopped mussels, heat through and remove from stove. Stir in parsley and immediately pour entire contents of saucepan over drained spaghetti. Serves 6.

NEAPOLITAN MUSSEL SPAGHETTI SAUCE *Italy*

4 lbs. mussels	1 cup strained mussel
6 tbs. oil	liquor—add water if you
2 large garlic cloves,	do not have enough
slivered lengthwise	½ tsp. oregano
2 6-oz. cans Italian-style	salt and pepper to taste
tomato paste	1 pkg. spaghetti
1 cup water	

Clean and remove mussels from shells as directed on page 60.

Heat oil in saucepan, add garlic and cook until reddish brown. Add tomato paste, water and strained mussel liquor. Stir in oregano and salt and pepper and simmer 30 to 45 minutes. Meantime, prepare spaghetti according to package directions. Add mussels to sauce. Cook until mussels are heated through. Pour over drained spaghetti and serve. Serves 6.

MUSSELS IN WINE SAUCE   *France*

4 lbs. mussels	⅓ cup butter or
1½ cups court bouillon,	margarine, melted
page 153	3 tbs. soft bread crumbs
2 scallions, finely	1 loaf French bread,
chopped	sliced
¾ cup white wine	2 tsp. chopped parsley

Clean mussels and steam open in court bouillon according to instructions on page 60. Do not overcook. Strain mussel liquor and reserve, remove mussels from shells and remove beards.

Boil scallions in wine until tender. Add ¾ cup reserved court bouillon. Bring back to boil and remove from heat. Add butter and bread crumbs, mix thoroughly, add mussels and as soon as they are heated through, serve over French bread. Sprinkle with chopped parsley. Serves 6.

OYSTER SAUCE WITH OKRA

1 pt. oysters	1 8½-oz. can okra
3 tbs. chopped onion	2 tbs. chopped parsley
2 tbs. butter	¼ tsp. Tabasco
3 tbs. flour	¾ tsp. salt
1 cup tomato juice	

Cook onion in butter in the top of a double boiler until tender. Over boiling water, stir flour into onion and butter, slowly add tomato juice and cook, stirring constantly, until mixture thickens.

Add okra, oysters, parsley, Tabasco and salt. Cook about 5 minutes longer, or until edges of oysters begin to curl. Serve over rice or toast. Serves 6.

SCALLOPS IN COURT BOUILLON

2 lbs. scallops	page 153
court bouillon to cover,	curry sauce, page 122

Cut large scallops in half and simmer gently in court bouillon 3 to 5 minutes. Drain and use court bouillon for the liquid in the sauce and serve over the scallops. Serves 6.

NOTE: Any other white sauce can be substituted, such as mushroom or mustard.

SCALLOP-TOMATO SOUP

1 lb. scallops	3 tbs. flour
3 cups court bouillon	¼ cup water
1 1-lb., 4-oz. can tomatoes	2 tbs. chopped parsley
¼ cup butter or margarine	

Prepare one of the court bouillons as directed on page 153. Add tomatoes, butter, and scallops. (Cut large scallops in half.)

Stir flour with water until smooth, and stir into soup. Cook 3 to 5 minutes, stirring constantly, or until mixture thickens and scallops are cooked. Sprinkle with parsley and serve. Serves 6.

CANTONESE SHRIMP SAUCE

1½ lbs. raw shrimp, shelled and deveined
¼ cup butter, margarine or oil
2 pkgs. or cubes instant beef bouillon
1 cup boiling water
2 or 3 4- to 6-oz. cans

Chinese vegetables of your choice
2 tbs. soy sauce
2 tsp. cornstarch
1 tsp. ginger
pepper and salt
3 cups hot boiled rice

Cook shrimp in butter until they turn pink, about 3 minutes.

Dissolve bouillon in boiling water, add vegetables and soy sauce. Mix cornstarch to a smooth paste with ¼ cup cold water. Gradually add to bouillon, stirring constantly, and cook until thick and clear. Add shrimp, ginger and salt and pepper.

Pour into preheated chafing dish, heat and serve over rice. Serves 4.

SHRIMP JAMBALAYA

1½ lbs. cooked, shelled and deveined shrimp
2 slices bacon, diced
3 tbs. chopped green pepper
1 medium onion, chopped
1 garlic clove, finely chopped

1 tbs. flour
salt and pepper to taste
¼ tsp. chili powder
dash paprika
pinch dried basil
2 cups canned tomatoes
½ tsp. Worcestershire
3 cups cooked rice

Fry bacon, add green pepper, onion and garlic and cook until tender. Stir flour, seasonings and basil into bacon grease in pan. Slowly add tomatoes and Worcestershire. Cook, stirring constantly, until sauce thickens. Add cooked rice and shrimp, heat and serve. Serves 6.

SHRIMP MARINARA I

1 cup small shrimp, cooked, shelled and deveined	6 tomatoes, peeled and cut in small pieces
12 large raw shrimp, shelled and deveined	½ tsp. brown sugar salt and pepper to taste
3 tbs. cooking oil	½ cup white wine
1 tsp. olive oil	½ tsp. sweet basil
3 tbs. chopped onion	¼ tsp. oregano
1 garlic clove, crushed	1 pkg. spaghetti
	½ cup grated Parmesan cheese

Combine the oils in heavy saucepan. Add onion and garlic and cook until golden brown.

Add tomatoes, sugar, salt and pepper and simmer gently 20 minutes.

Add small cooked shrimp and wine and cook 10 to 15 minutes longer. Prepare spaghetti according to package directions.

Add shrimp to sauce with sweet basil and oregano. Cook 5 minutes or until shrimp turn pink.

Serve over drained spaghetti, placing 2 of the large shrimp on each plate. Sprinkle with grated Parmesan cheese. Serves 6.

SHRIMP MARINARA II

1½ lbs. shrimp, peeled and deveined	½ bay leaf
1 large onion, chopped	1 large can Italian tomatoes
¼ cup oil	2 peppercorns
1 garlic clove, crushed or minced	2 tsp. chopped or dried oregano
½ tsp. salt	2 tbs. chopped parsley

Sauté onion in oil 4 minutes, add garlic and stir 1 minute longer. Add salt, bay leaf, tomatoes and peppercorns and simmer 1 hour. Add large shrimp and oregano and simmer 6 minutes longer. Serve over rice, and sprinkle with parsley, or serve on pasta and pass grated Parmesan cheese separately. Add ½ cup Italian red wine, if you like, for the last 6 minutes.

VARIATION:

CLAMS MARINARA: Substitute clams for shrimp.

Shellfish Soups, Stews and Chowders Made with Milk or Cream

NEW ENGLAND CLAM CHOWDER

1 pt. clams, coarsely chopped	2 cups peeled, diced potatoes
3 slices bacon or salt pork, diced	2 cups rich milk
1 medium onion, chopped	salt and pepper to taste
1 cup liquor from clams— add water if necessary	chopped parsley
	2 tbs. butter

Fry bacon and onion together until lightly browned. Add clam liquor and potatoes. Cook 10 to 15 minutes or until potatoes are nearly tender. Add clams. Cool chowder for a few minutes, return to heat, add milk in a slow stream, stirring constantly. Add salt and pepper and continue stirring until chowder is hot but not boiling.

Garnish with parsley, add a small lump of butter to each individual soup bowl and serve. Serves 6.

LOBSTER STEW

1 1¼-lb. lobster, or ¾ lb.
   cooked lobster meat
¼ cup butter or margarine,
   melted
1 qt. rich milk

¼ tsp. paprika
dash nutmeg
salt and pepper to taste
chopped parsley

Cook fresh lobster and remove meat; see instructions page 63. Cut meat into ½ inch pieces.

Melt butter in the top of a double boiler over boiling water. Add lobster and cook just long enough to heat through. Add milk in a slow stream, stirring constantly, and bring to just under boiling. Add seasonings, garnish with parsley and serve. Serves 6.

NOTE:

1. In Maine, the tomalley, the coral and the thick white substance found inside the shell are simmered in butter for a few minutes, then heated together with the lobster meat. Nutmeg is omitted.

2. To add flavor, refrigerate 5 to 6 hours, then reheat and serve.

3. This recipe can be used for other shellfish.

LOBSTER NEWBURG

¾ lb. cooked lobster meat
   cut in ½-inch pieces
¼ cup butter or margarine
2 cups light cream
2 egg yolks, beaten

salt and pepper to taste
¼ tsp. paprika
2 drops Tabasco
2 tbs. brandy (otional)
2 tbs. sherry

Melt butter in the top of a double boiler over boiling water. Stir in flour, add cream very slowly, stirring constantly, and cook until thickened and smooth. Remove top pan and cool for a few minutes.

Add cream very slowly to beaten egg yolks, stirring constantly. Return to double boiler over boiling water, add lobster meat and reheat.

Remove from heat, stir in seasonings, sherry and brandy and serve on toast. Serves 6.

NOTE:

1. The tomalley and coral can be simmered together in butter for a few minutes and added to sauce at the same time as lobster meat.

2. Cooked crab meat, scallops and shrimp can be substituted for the lobster in this recipe.

LOBSTER BISQUE

1 2-lb. lobster	1 qt. milk
2 cups court bouillon, page 153, or chicken stock	dash cayenne
	salt and pepper to taste
	paprika
4 tbs. butter	1 cup toasted croutons or
4 tbs. flour	crumbled crackers

Boil lobster according to instructions on page 68. Shell and dice meat. Set it aside with coral and tomalley. Break up claws and any shell that contains meat. Boil in court bouillon at least 20 minutes. Strain through cheesecloth and set broth aside.

Melt butter in top of a double boiler over boiling water. Blend in flour, add milk and broth, stirring constantly, until thickened and smooth. Add diced lobster meat to soup. Reheat to just under boiling and remove from heat.

Mash coral and tomalley together or rub them through a sieve, and stir into soup with cayenne and salt and pepper.

Sprinkle with paprika and serve with croutons or crumbled crackers. Serves 4 to 6.

OYSTER AND CORN CHOWDER

1 pint shucked oysters
2 cups diced potatoes
1 cup court bouillon, page 153
1 qt. milk

1 12-oz. can corn
liquor from oysters
3 tbs. butter
salt and pepper to taste
1 tbs. chopped parsley

Cook potatoes in court bouillon until tender. Slowly add milk and corn and heat just to the boiling point.

Simmer oysters in their own liquor about 5 minutes, or until edges curl. Combine with milk mixture, stir in butter and salt and pepper. Serve, garnished with parsley. Serves 6.

CURRIED OYSTERS

1 pt. shucked oysters
½ garlic clove, minced
1 tbs. minced onion
1 tbs. minced green
pepper (optional)
2 tbs. butter

3 tbs. flour
1½ cups rich milk
1 tsp. curry powder, or to
taste
salt and pepper to taste
chopped parsley

Simmer oysters in their own liquor until edges begin to curl, about 5 minutes. Drain.

In the top of a double boiler, cook garlic, onion and green pepper in butter until tender. Place over boiling water and blend in flour. Add milk in a thin stream, stirring constantly, and cook until sauce thickens. Add curry powder to ½ cup of this sauce, stirring until it is smooth. Stir it into remaining sauce. Add oysters and salt and pepper.

Garnish with parsley and serve over rice. Serves 6.

OYSTER STEW

1 pt. shucked oysters, drained	1 qt. milk
¼ cup butter or margarine, melted	salt and pepper to taste
	paprika

Melt butter in the top of a double boiler over boiling water, add oysters. Cook about 3 to 5 minutes or until edges curl. Slowly add milk, stirring constantly, and heat to the boiling point. Add salt and pepper, sprinkle with paprika and serve. Crackers or oysterettes can be crumbled into stew before removing from heat or served separately. Serves 4.

NOTE:

1. *If you prefer a thicker stew,* stir cold milk into 2 tbs. flour, add gradually to stew.

2. *For a richer stew,* substitute light cream for one half the milk. Add the cream last; heat and serve. Do not let stew boil.

3. *For a quick late-night snack,* keep canned oysters on hand and substitute for fresh ones.

4. *For a stronger oyster flavor,* substitute liquor from either fresh or canned oysters for part of the milk.

OYSTER AND CELERY STEW

1 pt. shucked oysters	1 10½-oz. can cream of celery soup
liquor from oysters	milk
¼ cup butter or margarine	salt and pepper to taste
1 10-oz. can frozen oyster stew	

Simmer oysters in their own liquor in the top of a double boiler over boiling water, until edges start to curl, 3 to 5 minutes. Remove oysters and add butter to liquor.

Combine and mix the soups, and add enough milk to

make the desired consistency. Pour very slowly into double boiler, stirring constantly, and cook to boiling point.

Add oysters and salt and pepper, reheat and serve as a soup. Reduce or omit milk and serve as a main course in patty shells. Serves 6.

NOTE: You can substitute cream of mushroom, cream of spinach or cream of Cheddar cheese soup for the cream of celery. Omit the oyster liquor, if preferred.

OYSTER TOMATO SOUP

1 pt. shucked oysters, chopped	salt and pepper to taste
	onion salt to taste
liquor from oysters	1 clove
1 qt. milk	1 10½-oz. can condensed
4 tbs. flour	tomato soup
4 tbs. butter	1 cup whipped cream

Heat oysters slowly in their liquor to just under boiling. Press through a sieve. Stir milk into flour until smooth. Melt butter in top of double boiler over boiling water, add liquor from oysters, slowly add milk, stirring constantly until soup thickens.

Add oysters, seasonings, clove and tomato soup and heat. Serve topped with whipped cream. Serves 6.

SCALLOP CHOWDER

1 lb. scallops, chopped	2 stalks celery, chopped
2 slices bacon	½ bay leaf
1 cup water	2 cups milk
1 small onion, chopped	¼ tsp. sugar
2 medium potatoes, peeled and diced	1 tbs. butter or margarine
	salt and pepper to taste
1 carrot, finely diced	2 tbs. chopped parsley

Fry bacon and onion together until lightly brown. Remove bacon, crush and set aside. Add water, vegetables and bay leaf to the onion, cover and cook 15 minutes. Add scallops, sugar, milk, stir constantly, and cook until chowder is hot. Add butter and salt and pepper and garnish with crushed bacon and parsley. Serves 6.

SHRIMP CHOWDER

¾ lb. cooked shrimp, cut into ½-inch pieces
3 slices bacon
1 medium onion, chopped
1 cup boiling water

1 medium potato, diced
2 cups milk
1 tbs. butter
salt and pepper to taste
chopped parsley

Fry bacon and onion together until light brown. Add boiling water and potato, cover and cook until potato is tender.

Add shrimp. Slowly pour in milk, stirring constantly, add butter and salt and pepper, and serve garnished with parsley. Serves 6.

SCALLOP AND MASHED POTATO SOUP

1 lb. scallops, cut in half
1 cup instant mashed potato flakes
1 cup light cream

milk to taste
2 tbs. butter
salt and pepper to taste
2 tbs. finely chopped chives

Prepare potatoes according to package directions. Add cream and enough milk to make a thin soup of the desired consistency. Stir until smooth and creamy.

Simmer scallops for 3 to 4 minutes in boiling water to cover. Drain and add to soup, add butter and salt and pepper, garnish with chopped chives and serve. Serves 6.

SHRIMP CURRY I

¾ lb. cooked shrimp, shelled and deveined
4 tbs. butter or margarine, melted
1 small onion, minced
½ small garlic clove, minced (optional)
3 tbs. flour
1 cup chicken stock or court bouillon

1 cup cream or canned milk
2 cups milk can be used instead of cream and bouillon
1 tsp. curry powder, or to taste
salt and pepper to taste

Melt butter in the top of a double boiler over boiling water, add onion and garlic and cook until soft. Blend in flour, combine stock and cream and add gradually, stirring constantly. Cook until thick and smooth. Add ½ cup sauce to curry powder and stir until smooth. Stir it back into the sauce, add shrimp, heat through and take from heat. Stir in salt and pepper and serve over rice. Serves 6.

NOTE: This recipe can be used with any shellfish.

SHRIMP CURRY II   *Ceylon*

1½ to 2 lbs. shrimp, shelled and deveined
1 medium onion, sliced
1 tsp. ground red pepper
1 pinch turmeric
2 garlic cloves
2 slices green ginger, chopped (½ tsp.

powdered ginger may be substituted)
2"-piece cinnamon
salt to taste
¾ cup milk or coconut milk
1 tbs. oil
juice of ½ lime

Combine shrimp in saucepan with half the onion slices and all the ingredients except milk, oil and lime juice. Mix well and add milk. Simmer until shrimp are nearly cooked, about 3 minutes, and remove saucepan from heat. Lightly brown remaining onions in oil and add them to the shrimp mixture. Add lime juice and heat slowly 5 minutes. Serves 4 to 6.

NOTE: Curry powder, preferably Madras, can be substituted for the spices and garlic in this recipe.

SHRIMP AND EGGPLANT SOUP *Lodeh Terong—Indonesia*

1 medium eggplant	2 tbs. butter
1 cup water	1 tbs. chopped tomato
1 tbs. chopped onion	½ tsp. sugar
1 tsp. chopped garlic	1 bay leaf
2 tbs. chopped raw shrimp	1 cup bouillon
1 tbs. chopped green pepper	1 cup milk

Peel and dice eggplant and cover with water. Sauté onion, garlic, chopped shrimp and green pepper in butter. Add the tomato, sugar, bay leaf and bouillon. Bring to a boil. Add the eggplant and water and boil gently until eggplant is just tender. Add milk, and simmer another 3 minutes, stirring occasionally. Serve hot. Serves 4 to 6.

AMERICAN VARIATION: Add 4 to 6 whole raw shrimp with the milk. Serve one shrimp in center of each bowl of soup.

Poached Fish

General instructions

Poaching fish is so simple that it lends itself to family meals. Any fish can be poached.

The poaching liquid may be milk, salted water, court bouillon or a thin starch-thickened sauce or soup. Plan to serve the fish with a sauce made from the liquid in which the fish was poached.

The only part of the poaching technique that may be difficult for the novice is handling the fish without breaking it. Large fish have to be wrapped in cheesecloth, small ones can be poached in a skillet and removed with a pancake turner.

Skillet method of poaching fish

1. Heat poaching liquid in a deep skillet, using just enough liquid to cover fish.
2. Place the fish in the liquid and adjust the heat so the liquid is just simmering.
3. Cover the skillet and simmer until the fish flakes easily with a fork, about 5 to 10 minutes.
4. Remove the fish carefully to a hot platter.
5. The poaching liquid can be strained and used just as it is as a broth, or it can be the base for a sauce to serve with the fish. A simple way to make a variety of sauces is to combine the poaching liquid with undiluted canned or frozen soup.
6. Lean fish poaches better than fat fish since it does not fall apart so easily.
7. If a starch-thickened liquid or soup is used for poaching whole fish, steaks or fillets, it must be thin enough and contain ingredients that require very little or no stirring.
8. Many of the recipes for simmering fish and making soups, stews and chowders can be adapted for the poaching method, but you will have to leave out most of the vegetables, or remove them before the fish is added. Use just enough of the liquid called for in the recipe to cover the fish.

CARP À LA POLONAISE   *Poland*

1 3-lb. carp	1 long carrot
3 cups court bouillon, or to cover, page 153	sauce polonaise, page 132
	parsley sprigs

Heat court bouillon in a long pan. Stuff carp with carrot to avoid breaking the fish and put it in hot bouillon. Simmer until fish flakes easily when tested with a fork.

Prepare a single or a double recipe sauce polonaise, using the strained liquor in which carp was poached.

Serve the carp on a hot dish, garnished with parsley. Serve the sauce separately in a sauceboat. Serves 6.

EEL POACHED IN VEGETABLE BROTH WITH CREAM

3 lbs. eel	4 tbs. butter
3 carrots	4 tbs. flour
1 medium onion	½ cup cream
salt and pepper to taste	parsley, finely chopped

Cut eel into portions and sprinkle with salt. Boil carrots with onion and salt and pepper until soft; strain and return stock to pot. Add eel and cook until soft.

Melt butter, add flour and blend, stirring constantly. Dilute to taste with stock from eel and bring to a boil. Add cream and parsley. Season to taste and add the eel. Serves 6.

POACHED COD   *Finland*

2 lbs. cod or halibut fillets	1 cup boiling water
4 tbs. butter	8 small potatoes, boiled,
4 tbs. margarine	peeled and kept hot
salt to taste	2 tbs. chopped dill

Add butter, margarine and salt to boiling water. When butter and margarine have melted, add fillets, reduce heat and simmer gently until fish is tender. Put fish and potatoes on heated platter and pour butter sauce in which fish was poached over both. Garnish with dill. Serves 6.

HALIBUT OR COD WITH SHRIMP SAUCE
Denmark

2 lbs. halibut or cod
1½ cups white wine diluted
   with equal amount
   water (should be just
   enough liquid to cover)
1 tbs. chopped onion
1 tbs. chopped celery

2 tsp. chopped parsley
2 jars Danish shrimp, or
   2 7-oz. cans domestic
   shrimp, drained
1½ cups white sauce, page
   123

Bring wine, onion, celery and parsley to a boil, add halibut and reduce heat. Poach, covered, until fish flakes easily when tested with a fork. Place on preheated platter.

Make white sauce, substituting 1 cup wine broth in which fish was poached for 1 cup liquid in recipe. Add shrimp, heat to just under boiling and pour over poached fish. Minced dill or parsley can be added before serving. Serves 4.

MACKEREL IN RED WINE
Panama

2 mackerel, cut into
   chunks
1 cup oil
6 medium onions, sliced
   ¼-inch thick

½ cup flour
½ cup red wine
½ tsp. salt
   pinch black pepper
1 tbs. capers

Heat half the oil in a skillet, add onions and cook until they start to color. With a slotted spoon transfer to a saucepan. Add remaining oil to skillet. Dredge fish chunks with flour and brown them in the oil.

Add wine, salt, pepper and capers to onions in saucepan. Heat and add mackerel. Cover and poach 5 minutes. Serve hot with poaching broth or, as they do in Panama, chill before serving. Serves 4.

SALMON POACHED IN COURT BOUILLON

2 lbs. salmon steaks
  court bouillon to cover,
  page 153

green spring sauce, page
117
1 lemon, cut into wedges

Court Bouillon can be prepared first and strained, or salmon can be placed in saucepan with all the ingredients after bouillon has cooked 20 minutes. Cover and simmer fish 5 to 7 minutes or until it flakes easily.

Serve with green Spring sauce and lemon wedges. Serves 4.

STRIPED BASS IN SAUCE POLONAISE

4 lbs. striped bass fillets
  court bouillon No. 1, to
  cover, page 153

sauce polonaise, page 132

Poach striped bass in court bouillon, just at boiling point, until fish flakes easily when tested with a fork. Remove fish from skillet to a preheated serving dish and place in a slow oven, 300° F.

Strain liquid in which fish was poached and use it in preparing sauce polonaise. If you do not want a strongly flavored sauce, substitute water for part of the poaching liquid. Pour sauce over fillets and serve. Serves 8.

Steamed Fish

Steaming fish is the only method that leaves the fish moist and does not take away any of its flavor. For this reason it is the best way to heat kippered, salted or smoked fish. It is also the best method for reheating any cooked fish.

It is simple to steam fish perfectly. Use very little water in a heavy pan or kettle, cover it tightly and steam exactly the right length of time. The general rule is to allow one minute of steaming for each ounce of weight. For fish steaks of uniform thickness, steam 5 minutes for the first half-inch of thickness and 3 additional minutes for each additional half-inch, up to 2 inches.

Steaming fish on a rack over boiling water

1. Put one and a half to two inches of water in a deep pan, pot or kettle that has a tight-fitting cover.
2. Salt fish on both sides and add all other seasonings to the water. They may be garlic, oregano, wine, parsley, celery, onion, as the recipes require.
3. Place a metal rack in the pan, making sure that it will remain above the water level. If the pot or pan you are using has no rack, use a cake rack.
4. Bring the water to a boil.
5. Make sure that your fish is no more than two inches thick. Place it on the rack over the boiling water and place a tight-fitting lid on the pan.
6. Allow 5 minutes cooking time for anything up to one-half inch of thickness. (Steamed fish is so very tender that you will find it almost impossible to handle pieces that are less than one-half-inch thick.) Continue steaming three minutes for each additional half-inch of thickness.

Steaks and fillets steamed directly on top of cooking vegetables

Cooking fish in this manner is very much the same as poaching, except that the fish is placed carefully across the vegetables instead of a rack.

Use as little liquid as possible and a heavy pan or pot with a tight-fitting lid. Don't remove the lid more than is absolutely necessary.

See vegetable sauce, cioppino and other sauce recipes, in Part Two, for suggested vegetable combinations and further cooking instructions.

Pressure cooking fish

Fish should only be pressure cooked when you want to blend the flavor quickly with vegetables and you don't care if the fish itself is overcooked and dry.

Pressure cooking shellfish

The only shellfish for which we recommend this method are oysters and clams. See Part One for general instructions for cleaning and cooking oysters and clams.

Steaming molds in a pan of water

Fish loaves or "puddings" can be pressed into an oiled mold, set in a pan or pot of water (water should come three-fourths of the way up the mold), tightly covered and simmered gently on top of the stove until done, about 1 hour for a two-pound loaf. (Aluminum foil can be placed over pudding as a lid; be sure it is pressed on tightly.)

STEAMED KIPPERED FISH DINNER

2 lbs. kippered fish	small new potatoes
fresh green peas	

Place fish on a rack over boiling water. Cover tightly and steam only long enough to heat fish through.
Lift out rack and transfer fish to a hot serving platter.
Serve with peas and potatoes boiled in their jackets. Serves 4.

FISH STEAKS AND VEGETABLES WITH SHRIMP SAUCE

1 lb, fish steaks, ¾- to 1-inch thick	1 package frozen peas and carrots
1 10½-oz. can frozen shrimp soup	1 cup boiling water
	1 tbs. wine
	salt to taste

Defrost frozen shrimp soup just enough to slice with a knife. Slice it ½-inch thick and completely cover the fish steaks with the slices.

Place frozen peas and carrots in steamer. Add boiling water, wine and salt. Return to a boil and adjust steamer rack over them. Be sure that it is above the level of the vegetables and liquid. Lay sauce-covered steaks carefully on rack, cover pot tightly and cook over moderate heat 10 minutes.

Remove fish to preheated plates and keep warm. Add the remaining shrimp soup to the vegetables, stir until it reaches the boiling point. Serve the vegetables with the fish steaks. Serves 2.

SHRIMP AND CHICKEN ORIENTAL

½ lb. fresh shrimp, shelled and deveined	2 tbs. butter
	salt to taste
1½ to 2 cups diced chicken meat that has been boiled with onion, carrot, celery and seasonings	2 cups instant rice
	1 12-oz. can drained pineapple chunks
2¼ cups chicken stock, add water if necessary	2 cups Oriental sauce, page 137

Boil chicken and vegetables until done. Strain and place stock in pot to boil. Add butter, salt and rice. Adjust rack 3 or 4 inches from bottom. Place shrimp on rack. Cover pot tightly and reduce heat to simmer 2 minutes. Turn off heat and let stand 5 minutes without removing lid, or until rice is tender.

Serve rice in mounds, top with shrimp, chicken and pine-apple and cover with hot Oriental sauce. Serves 6.

FISH STEAKS WITH TOMATO AND ONION

1 lb. fish steaks, ¾- to 1-inch thick
2 cups court bouillon, page 153

2 tomatoes, thickly sliced
2 onions, thickly sliced
salt and pepper to taste
prepared mustard

Put court bouillon in bottom of steamer or heavy pot. Place rack in pot, making sure that it is above the level of the liquid. Bring bouillon to a boil.

Season both sides of fish with salt and brush top with a little mustard. Place steaks on rack and cover them completely with overlapping slices of tomato and onion. Cover pot tightly and cook over moderate heat 16 minutes.

Strain court bouillon and serve as broth, or use as a base for a cream sauce. Serves 2.

BASIC RECIPE FOR STEAMING FISH ON VEGETABLES

1½ lbs. very fresh fillets of sole or flounder
2 large, firm tomatoes, sliced
1 large onion, sliced
½ green pepper, seeded and sliced

½ cup chicken stock (remove solidified fat by chilling)
1 tsp. salt
1 tbs. dry white wine (optional)

Place all ingredients except fish in a large, heavy pot. Cover tightly and simmer 15 minutes. If liquid is reduced to less than ¼ cup, add more stock or water. Carefully place fish fillets over the top of the vegetables so that they will be cooked by steam. Replace cover and simmer gently 10 minutes more. Test fish with a fork. If it flakes easily, transfer it to serving plates. Pour vegetables and any juice left in the pot over the individual servings of fish. Serves 4.

NOTE:

1. This recipe can be used for any fish fillets or steaks. The thicker the fish, the longer it will need to cook and the more liquid it will need.

2. The same sauce can be cooked separately from the fish. After the vegetables are soft, cook it down to the desired consistency and pour over any cooked fish, or over fish before it is baked.

VARIATIONS: Add or substitute carrots or celery for any of the vegetables. Add a few raw, cleaned and shucked shellfish to sauce when fish is put in pot.

PRESSURE-COOKED SEA BASS   *Mickey's Bass Chow*

1- to 1½-lb. sea bass	1½ cups coarsely grated raw carrots
1 1 lb. 4½-oz. can tomatoes—drain and reserve liquid	1½ cups coarsely grated raw potatoes
1 tsp. salt	1½ cups chopped celery
1 bay leaf	1½ cups water
1 large onion, chopped	1½ cups reserved tomato liquid
4 peppercorns	1 tsp. sugar
1 tbs. butter	
3 slices bacon, chopped	

Place drained tomatoes, salt, bay leaf, 1 tbs. onion, peppercorns and butter on rack in cooker. Wrap fish in cheesecloth, lay on top of tomato mixture. Cook 7 minutes with regulator at cook position. Cool immediately.

Place bacon and remaining onion in heavy pot and brown. Add all the remaining ingredients. Cover tightly and simmer 15 minutes.

Take fish out of cooker, pick meat off the bones and add to vegetables, add the other ingredients that were cooked with the fish. Stir and set aside until ready to eat, an hour or longer improves the flavor. Reheat and serve. Serves 6.

Pan Frying

Pan frying has several disadvantages. The use of frying fat masks the delicate flavor of the fish, cooking odors are noticeable and the skillet is often difficult to clean. However, pan frying is an excellent way to cook small whole fish such as smelt (fishermen call all small fish "pan fish" because they fit the frying pan). Pan frying is a poor method to choose for frozen fish containing ice crystals because the moisture freed by the melting ice causes the fat to spatter.

1. Wash fish by dipping in cold salted water. *Thoroughly dry* with towel or absorbent paper.

2. Sprinkle the fish inside and out with salt and pepper.

3. Dip it into egg beaten with a little milk or water or wine. You can also dip it into milk or court bouillon or a salad dressing without the egg. Roll the coated fish in fine dry bread or cracker crumbs, flour or flour mixed with one of the foregoing. The fish can be first dredged lightly with flour to make the egg adhere. All batters described for "deep frying" can be used for pan frying.

4. *Let fish stand for a few minutes.*

5. Fry the fish in about ⅛ to ¼ inch of moderately hot fat.

6. Fresh or frozen fish that is being pan fried or broiled

should be quickly seared to help seal in the moisture. Reduce heat immediately to moderate and finish cooking.

7. Do not let the fat smoke. It is the smoke from too-hot fat that makes a house smell of fish. The easiest way to avoid it is by never letting the fat reach the smoking point.

8. As soon as the fish is brown on one side, turn it carefully with a spatula.

9. Fry until the fish is brown on the second side and flakes easily when tested with a fork. Drain on absorbent paper.

10. Do not fry a second batch of fish in the same pan without thoroughly cleaning it.

11. Handle cooked fish as little as possible to avoid breaking.

FISH STEAKS OR FILLETS   *Basic recipe for pan frying*
any fish

2 lbs. fish fillets, steaks or sticks
1 tbs. milk or water
1 egg (use 2 eggs if fish is coated with flour)
1 cup flour (optional)
salt and pepper to taste

1 cup bread crumbs, cracker crumbs or cornmeal
butter or margarine for frying
1 lemon, cut into wedges
6 sprigs parsley

Wash fish by dipping in cold salted water. Dry with towel or absorbent paper. Beat milk or water into egg.

Dredge fish lightly with flour seasoned with salt and pepper (optional). Dip in egg mixture and roll in crumbs. Let stand for a few minutes to dry.

Heat ⅛ to ¼ inch butter or margarine in heavy frying pan until it is hot but not smoking. Place fish in pan and fry over moderate heat until a light, golden brown. Turn carefully with a spatula and brown on other side until fish flakes easily when tested with a fork, remove carefully from pan and drain on absorbent paper.

Garnish with lemon wedges and parsley. Serves 4.

FRIED SHELLFISH

Basic recipe for pan frying any shellfish

1 lb. shelled clams, oysters, scallops or shrimp
½ cup flour (optional)
1 tbs. liquid, milk, water, wine, or strained shellfish liquor

salt and pepper to taste
1 egg, beaten
1 cup fine dry bread crumbs, cracker crumbs or cornmeal
butter, margarine or oil for frying

Dip cleaned shellfish in cold salted water. Drain on absorbent paper. Dredge with flour (optional). Beat liquid and salt and pepper lightly with the egg. Dip shellfish into the mixture and roll in bread crumbs. Let stand 2 to 3 minutes.

Fry in ⅛ to ¼ inch deep butter or oil which should be hot but not smoking. When golden brown, turn and brown other side. Cooking time should be about 5 to 8 minutes in all, depending on size of fish. Large scallops can be cut in half in order to cook more quickly. Serves 2.

FISH STEAKS WITH ORIENTAL SAUCE

2 lbs. fish steaks or fillets
¼ cup flour
salt and pepper to taste
butter, margarine or oil for frying

Oriental sauce, page 137 or any sauce of your choice

Wash steaks by dipping in cold salted water. Thoroughly dry with towel or absorbent paper. Dredge fish with flour sifted with salt and pepper. Fry in ⅛ inch hot but not smoking butter or oil over moderate heat until brown. Turn carefully with a spatula and fry until brown on second side. When fish flakes easily when tested with a fork, gently remove from pan and drain on absorbent paper.

While fish steaks are cooking, prepare Oriental sauce. Serve poured over hot fish steaks. Serves 4.

FLUKE AMANDINE

2 lbs. fluke fillets
   butter or margarine for
   frying
½ cup almonds, blanched
   and slivered

½ lemon
salt and white pepper to
   taste

In ¼ inch butter or margarine that is hot but not smoking lightly brown the slivered almonds. Sprinkle fillets with lemon juice, season with salt and white pepper and fry on top of the almonds until fluke flakes easily with a fork. Serve with butter from the skillet poured over the fillets and sprinkle with the almonds. Serves 6.

NOTE: Any delicately flavored, white-meat fish or any shellfish can be substituted for the fluke.

FRIED SEAFOOD WITH FRUIT

2 lbs. fillets: flounder,
   fluke or any delicately
   flavored white-meat fish
   salt and pepper to taste
1 cup flour

½ cup butter or margarine
peach halves broiled
   with brown sugar, sliced
   chilled cranberry sauce
   or other fruit or
   preserves of your choice

Wash fillets by dipping in cold salted water. Dry with towel or absorbent paper. Sprinkle with salt and dredge with flour. Fry in ⅛ to ¼ inch butter or margarine that is hot but not smoking. When golden brown, turn fish carefully with spatula and fry until lightly browned on second side and until fish flakes easily when tested with a fork.

   Serve with fruit on preheated platter.

NOTE: This recipe appeals to children; it is a good way for them to learn to like fish.

FRIED FISH FILLETS   *Austria*

3 lbs. filleted fish: cod,
  halibut, etc.
3 medium onions, sliced
½ cup oil

3 to 4 tomatoes, peeled
  and sliced
2 lemons, sliced
salt to taste

Cut fish into strips 1 inch wide. Lightly fry onions in oil. Place fish strips, sliced tomatoes and sliced lemons on top of onions, add salt and simmer 8 to 12 minutes, or until fish flakes easily when tested with a fork. Serves 6.

FISH STICKS   *Portugal*

2 lbs. fish cut into sticks
  salt and pepper to taste
1 garlic clove, crushed
¼ cup olive oil

¼ cup wine or vinegar
1 egg, beaten
1 cup dry bread crumbs

Season sticks with salt and pepper and garlic and brush with olive oil and wine. Refrigerate 1 hour.

Dip in egg, roll in bread crumbs and fry in ⅛ inch hot but not smoking butter. Turn sticks until golden brown on both sides.

Drain on absorbent paper and serve with very thin fried potatoes (chips) and peas, spinach or lettuce. Serves 4.

SPICED FISH CUBES   *Nga Hsi Byan—Burma*

2 lbs. white fish, cubed
½ cup oil
1 medium onion, minced
  ground chillies to taste
  (chili powder may be
  substituted)

1 tsp. salt
  pinch saffron
1 garlic clove, crushed
¼ tsp. ginger
½ cup tomato sauce or
  tomato juice if thinner
  sauce is desired

Heat oil. Cook minced onions and ground chillies in it. Mix

salt, saffron, garlic and ginger. Season fish cubes with the mixture and add them to onions and chillies. Add tomato sauce, cover and simmer until fish is done, approximately 5 to 10 minutes depending on size of cubes.

Serve with rice. Serves 6.

FISH GOULASH

Austria

4 lbs. cod, tuna or mackerel	1 tbs. paprika
1 cup milk	3 medium onions, minced
1 tbs. lemon juice	2 tbs. flour
salt	1 tbs. vinegar
½ cup flour for dredging	2 cups fish stock or water
3 tbs. fat	2 tbs. tomato puree
¼ lb. salt pork	1 cup sour cream

Wash and clean fish. Soak in milk 30 minutes. Remove and dry on absorbent paper, sprinkle with lemon juice and salt. Cut fish into 1½-inch cubes. Dredge with flour and fry in hot but not smoking fat. Remove with a slotted spoon, place on serving dish and keep warm.

Dice salt pork and fry. Add paprika and stir until brown. Add onions, blend in flour and vinegar. Stir in fish stock slowly, add tomato puree and sour cream. Simmer gently 5 minutes. Strain and pour over fish. Serves 6.

COD FISH TONGUES

A Unique Delicacy

15 tongues from 10- or 12-lb. cods (The Y-shaped piece of meat between "whisker" and throat of the cod is the tongue.)	⅓ cup milk
	½ cup flour
	¼ tsp. salt
	pepper to taste (optional)
	2 cups dry bread crumbs
1 egg	oil for frying

Beat egg and milk together. Wash and drain tongues and dry on absorbent paper. Dredge with flour, dip in egg mixture and in bread crumbs. Pan fry or deep fry until tongues turn golden brown. Don't overcook or the delicacy will be lost. Serves 3 to 4.

EEL WITH MAYONNAISE SAUCE

2 eels, about 2 lbs. each,
  skinned
salt and pepper to taste
flour

5 tbs. melted butter or oil
1 cup mayonnaise
1 to 2 tbs. lemon juice

Wash eel by dipping in cold salted water, thoroughly dry and cut in 3-inch lengths.

Season with salt and pepper, dredge with flour and fry until golden brown in hot but not smoking melted butter.

Serve with a sauce made of mayonnaise mixed with lemon juice and just enough water to make a thin consistency. Serves 6.

FRIED HERRINGS AND ONION SAUCE

Stegt Sild med logsauce
—Denmark

8 medium-sized herrings,
  boned
¼ cup flour
2 eggs, beaten
½ cup bread crumbs

¼ cup butter for frying
1 cup milk
3 large onions, finely
  chopped
salt and pepper to taste

Dredge herring with half the flour, dip in egg and roll in bread crumbs. Fry in half the butter. Keep fish warm.

Melt remaining butter in a saucepan over low heat. Stir in remaining flour and slowly add milk, stirring constantly, until thickened and smooth. Add onions and salt and pepper and bring to a boil. (If desired, onions may be boiled first in a little water.)

Serve with onion sauce and boiled potatoes. Serves 4.

MACKEREL IN WINE SAUCE *Damiano's Delight—Italy*

4 lbs. mackerel, cut in
  steaks
1 cup olive oil
6 medium onions, sliced

½ cup flour
1 cup red wine
1 tbs. capers
salt and pepper to taste

Heat half the oil in frying pan. Add onions and fry lightly.
Remove with slotted spoon when almost cooked, leaving oil
in pan. Dredge steaks with flour, add remaining oil to pan
and fry steaks until brown. Combine mackerel and onions in
saucepan, add wine, capers and salt and pepper and cook 5
minutes. Transfer to serving bowl and chill. This may also be
served hot. Serves 8.

GRILLED SARDINES WITH BUTTER SAUCE   *Portugal*

1 3¾-oz. can boneless
  Portuguese sardines
2 tbs. butter

1 tbs. finely chopped
  parsley
1 tsp. lemon juice

Remove sardines carefully from can without breaking. Put
the fish on a well-heated grill and cook until golden. Pour
over them in a heated serving dish this sauce: Melt butter
and heat to a nut-brown color, add the finely chopped parsley and lemon juice.

Serve with boiled potatoes, cut barrel shape, tossed with
butter and chopped parsley. Serves 2.

SARDINE-STUFFED EGGS   *Portugal*

8 hard-cooked eggs, cut in
  half lengthwise
1 3¾-oz. can Portuguese
  sardines
1 tbs. butter, softened

1 tbs. finely chopped
  parsley
salt and pepper
2 eggs, beaten
1 cup fine bread crumbs

Remove yolks from eggs. Sieve them and mix with softened butter and parsley, season with salt and pepper.

Skin, bone and pound sardines and add to yolk mixture. Use the mixture for filling the egg whites. Reshape the eggs and brush with beaten eggs, roll in bread crumbs and fry in butter until golden. Serves 4.

FRIED SHRIMP

1 lb. raw shrimp, shelled
and deveined
butter or margarine

salt and pepper to taste
lemon wedges

Wash shrimp in cold salted water. Drain on absorbent paper.

Melt ⅛ inch butter in heavy frying pan. When it is hot but not smoking add shrimp and cook until they are pink and beginning to turn light golden brown, about 4 minutes. Turn and lightly brown the second side. Cook not more than 7 to 10 minutes, depending on size of shrimp. Very small shrimp have to be stirred several times to ensure uniform cooking.

Serve with lemon wedges. Serves 4.

HERB FRIED SHRIMP: Add 2 tbs. minced fresh herbs during last minute of cooking time.

GARLIC FRIED SHRIMP: Add 1 garlic clove, crushed, during last minute of cooking time.

Hearts of Palm

Hearts of palm are the tender and delicious terminal buds of palm trees. They are situated at the point where the fronds shoot out of the stem. In some forested regions, Indians are known to use *palmito* as their counterpart to bread. Hearts of palm are consumed either fresh or canned, the latter being the most common. Although they are sold in the markets of large cities, such as Rio de Janeiro and São Paulo, they are still regarded more as a delicacy than a staple.

SHRIMP WITH HEARTS OF PALM   *Brazil*

2 lbs. raw shrimp, peeled and deveined
1 can hearts of palm (available at better markets and gourmet shops)
2 tbs. lemon juice
1 onion, sliced
1 tomato, sliced
1 small green pepper, sliced
2 tbs. chopped parsley
¼ cup olive or salad oil
bay leaf (optional)
salt and pepper to taste
2 cups cooked rice

Sprinkle shrimp and hearts of palm with lemon juice. Cook onion, tomato, green pepper and parsley in olive oil until tender.

Add shrimp, bay leaf and seasonings and cook until shrimp turn pink. Slice and add hearts of palm and heat. Serve with rice. Serves 4.

TUNNY FISH MOUND   *Portugal*

1 can Portuguese tuna
1 small onion, finely chopped
1 tbs. butter
1 cup spinach puree
1 cup hot mashed potato, seasoned to taste
6 ripe olives

Brown onion lightly in butter. Crush the tuna with the oil from the can and add it to the onion, cooking just long enough to heat the fish. Heat spinach puree and stir in the potatoes. Add the tuna and onion, pile up on a serving dish and garnish with olives. Serves 2.

Deep Fat Frying

Fish that is to be fried in deep fat should be dipped in a batter, not because it will add a crisp crust, but because the batter forms a hard shield around the fish and prevents the hot oil from penetrating and saturating the flesh. The batters for deep fat frying, except for fritter batters, are similar to those used for pan frying.

There are two types of batter for coating: mixed and unmixed.

Mixed batter is nothing more than a mixture of raw eggs, liquid and a crusting agent. Which liquid you use and what crusting agent you use depends upon the recipe. Flour produces a different crust from bread crumbs or cornmeal.

Mixed batter

Combine all the ingredients and dip the fish into the mixture. The variety of ingredients that go into this type of batter will be found in the individual recipes.

Unmixed coating

1. Break egg or eggs into a shallow plate similar to a pie plate.
2. Add 2 tbs. water, wine, milk, beer or meat or vegetable stock. Beat with a fork and season to taste.
3. Spread crusting agent, flour, bread crumbs (plain or seasoned), cracker crumbs or corn meal, liberally on a shallow plate. If the liquid was seasoned, use a plain crusting agent.
4. Dip fish in egg. Roll in the flour, crumbs or meal, making certain fish is completely coated. The dipping and rolling may be repeated, using a spatula to transfer fish from egg to crusting agent.
5. Let batter-covered fish dry for a few minutes. It is then ready for frying.
6. Use a deep pot and lower a frying basket containing the fish into it. Much the same result can be obtained in a deep skillet without the basket but there is danger of sticking and spattering. The pot must contain enough fat or oil to cover the fish but it should not be more than half full. The fat or oil should be preheated to 350° F. to 375° F. (*If you are deep frying for the first time, you should test-fry a piece to check on heat and time.*)

Fritters

Fritters are made by combining chopped fish or shellfish with the batter and dropping by spoonfuls into hot deep fat, following the same directions as for deep frying fish.

Fritter batters usually include baking powder to make them puff up and are more varied than the batters for coating fish. The ingredients are listed in the recipes.

FRIED OYSTERS   *Basic deep-frying recipe for any shellfish*

1 qt. select shucked oysters, drained	salt and pepper to taste
2 tbs. milk, thin cream, water or wine	1 cup bread crumbs, cracker crumbs or cornmeal
2 tbs. liquor from oysters	fat or oil for deep frying
2 eggs	

Add milk and oyster liquor to eggs and beat with a fork only until well blended. Add seasoning.

Dip oysters in the egg mixture. Roll in crumbs, making sure to cover completely. Dry for a few minutes. Put in a frying basket in a single layer.

Heat fat in deep fryer to hot but not smoking, 350° F. to 375° F. Deep fryer should not be more than half full. Lower frying basket containing oysters into fat and fry until golden brown, about 2 to 3 minutes.

Drain on absorbent paper and serve with lemon wedges and tartar sauce. Serves 6.

NOTE: When deep frying sea scallops, the large ones should be cut in half.

FRIED SPINY LOBSTER TAILS: Frozen spiny lobster tails should be thawed just enough to cut shell lengthwise and remove meat in one piece. Remove dark vein, then follow instructions above for coating and frying.

OYSTER FRITTERS   *Basic fritter recipe for any shellfish*

1 pt. shucked oysters, drained and chopped	2 cups flour
1 cup milk	1 tbs. baking powder
1 tbs. butter or margarine, melted (or cooking oil)	⅛ tsp. nutmeg
2 eggs, beaten	1 tsp. salt
	white pepper to taste
	fat or oil for deep frying

Beat milk and melted butter with eggs. Sift flour, baking powder and seasonings together. Add slowly to the milk mixture, stirring until blended and smooth. Add the oysters and stir gently into the batter.

Heat fat in a deep fryer to hot but not smoking, 350° F. to 375° F. Deep fryer should not be more than half full. Drop fritter batter into the hot fat by the teaspoon or tablespoon, depending upon size desired, and fry until golden brown, about 3 minutes. Remove fritters with a slotted spoon and drain on absorbent paper before serving. Do not fry too many at one time. Serves 6.

VARIATIONS:

1. Roll fritters in dry bread crumbs before frying.
2. Add ½ cup grated celery, onion and green pepper to batter.
3. Add ½ cup finely chopped leftover cooked vegetables to batter.
4. Add ½ cup finely chopped canned fruit to batter.
5. Substitute liquid from oysters or vegetables for part of milk.

SARDINE AND POTATO FRITTERS   *Portugal*

1 3¾-oz. can Portuguese sardines	1 tbs. chopped parsley
4 large potatoes	salt to taste
pepper to taste	½ cup flour for dredging
1 hard-cooked egg, chopped	2 eggs, beaten
	¼ cup fat or oil

Boil potatoes in their jackets, about 20 minutes (do not over-cook), draw off the skins and cut into thick slices.

Skin, bone and mash sardines with a fork, season with pepper, mix with chopped egg and parsley. Use this mixture as a filling between two slices of potato. When all the sand-wiches have been made, dredge with seasoned flour, dip in egg, flour again and fry. Serve very hot with green peas or beans. Serves 4.

BUTTERFLY SHRIMP

1 lb. raw shrimp, medium or large
½ cup milk
1 egg
½ cup flour
¼ tsp. baking powder
salt and pepper to taste
fat or oil for deep frying

Shell and devein shrimp, but leave tails on. Dip in cold salted water. With sharp knife, split shrimp lengthwise down the back, without cutting through. Press shrimp out flat in shape of butterfly.

Beat milk with egg. Combine flour, baking powder and seasonings and beat in the egg mixture.

Dip shrimp in batter, cover completely and place, a few at a time, in a deep-frying basket. Heat fat in deep fryer to hot but not smoking, 350° F. to 375° F. Lower frying basket into fat and cook until golden brown, about 3 minutes. Remove from fat, drain on absorbent paper and serve at once. Serves 4.

SOLE IN BATTER   *Søtunge in Beignetdejg—Denmark*

2 lbs. fillets of sole, cut in three-inch-wide pieces
2½ cups flour
½ tsp. salt
1 cup Danish beer (Amer-ican can be substituted)
4 egg whites, stiffly beaten
fat or oil for deep frying
tartar or rémoulade sauce, page 135

Sift flour with salt and gradually add beer, stirring well. If dough is too stiff to handle, add 1 or 2 tbs. beer. Fold in egg whites and let batter stand at room temperature 5 to 6 hours. (If time is limited, batter can be used after standing 2 hours.)

Coat sole with thickened batter and place, a few pieces at a time, in a deep-frying basket. Heat fat in deep fryer to hot but not smoking, 350° F. to 375° F. Lower basket into fat and cook until golden brown, about 8 minutes.

Serve hot with tartar or rémoulade sauce. Serves 4.

DEEP-FRIED FISH FILLETS

2 lbs. fish fillets each cut into two or three pieces	1 cup flour
¾ cup milk or water	½ tsp. baking powder
1 egg	salt and pepper to taste
	fat or oil for deep frying

Dip fillets in cold salted water. Dry thoroughly with absorbent paper.

Stir milk into egg and beat lightly. Sift flour with baking powder and salt and pepper. Slowly add milk to dry ingredients, stirring until smooth.

Heat fat or oil until hot but not smoking, 350° F. to 375° F. Dip fish pieces into batter and place, a few at a time, in frying basket. Lower into hot fat and deep fry until golden brown, about 5 minutes.

Remove fish from fat, drain on absorbent paper and serve with lemon wedges and parsley. Serves 6.

VARIATIONS: Add crushed garlic, marjoram, grated onion or other seasonings to batter.

FISH STICKS IN MIXED BATTER WITH POTATO CHIPS   *Fish and Chips*

2 lbs. fish sticks	¾ cup milk or water
1 cup flour	2 medium potatoes, shaved very thin for chips
½ tsp. baking powder	
salt and pepper to taste	fat or oil for deep frying
1 egg	

Dip fish in cold salted water. Dry thoroughly with absorbent paper. Sift flour, baking powder and salt and pepper. Beat egg and milk together lightly. Beat slowly into dry ingredients until smooth.

Dredge fish sticks with flour, dip in batter, remove with fork or perforated spoon, and place one layer at a time in deep-frying basket. Lower carefully into fat that is hot but not smoking 350° F. to 375° F., and cook until golden brown, about 3 to 5 minutes.

Remove fish, drain on absorbent paper, and keep hot while frying the potato chips in the same fat.

Serve fish and chips with lemon wedges and garnish with parsley. Serves 6.

NOTE: Frozen breaded fish sticks can be fried, unthawed, one layer at a time, in deep fat or oil at the same temperature. Two packages serve 6.

Fish Cakes

CODFISH CAKES

Albondigas de Bacalao
—Dominican Republic

1½ lbs. cod, cut into eight pieces
3 medium potatoes
2 eggs, well beaten
2 tbs. diced onion
4 tbs. cooking oil

4 garlic cloves
2 tbs. chopped parsley
⅛ tsp. pepper
½ cup flour
1 cup salad oil

Soak fish in cool water 1 hour. Drain and simmer in water about 10 minutes, or until fish flakes easily. Remove from heat, drain and remove skin and bones. Grind through large blades of meat grinder.

Boil potatoes until soft, about 20 minutes, cool slightly, peel and rice, stir in eggs.

Sauté onions lightly in oil. Stir in ground fish, add chopped garlic, parsley and pepper. Take from heat and mix with potatoes. Shape into cakes, roll in flour and pan fry in hot salad oil until brown. Serve with tomato sauce, page 138. Serves 6.

SALT CODFISH CAKES SCRAPPLE STYLE

2 cups dried salt codfish
1 cup yellow cornmeal
1 cup cold water
3 cups boiling water
3 tbs. finely chopped onion
½ tsp. poultry seasoning
   pepper to taste

¼ tsp. dry mustard
salt
½ cup flour, for dredging
butter, margarine or oil
   for frying
beaten egg and bread
   crumbs (optional)

Soak fish in cold water until soft, about 24 hours, changing the water twice. Squeeze water from fish and shred.

Mix cornmeal and 1 cup cold water in a saucepan, over medium heat. Slowly add 3 cups boiling water and cook 10 minutes, stirring constantly. Add shredded cod, chopped onion and seasonings. Salt, only if necessary.

Pour mixture into an oiled loaf pan and chill. It can be stored in refrigerator for several days. Turn loaf out onto a cutting board, cut in ½-inch slices, dredge with flour and pan fry in butter or oil. Serves 6.

NOTE: Cod slices can also be dipped in beaten egg and bread crumbs before frying.

TUNA CAKES
Far East

1 6½-oz. can tuna, flaked
1 egg, beaten
1 cup cooked vegetables,
   mashed or finely
   chopped (Chinese-style
   or leftover vegetables)
1 4-oz. can mushrooms,
   drained and sliced

1 stalk celery, chopped
1 medium onion, chopped
½ cup bread crumbs
butter, margarine or oil
   for frying
tartar sauce, page 121

Combine all ingredients, shape into patties and fry on hot greased griddle until golden brown on both sides. Or fry 5 to 8 minutes in ⅛ to ¼ inch oil that is hot but not smoking.

Drain on absorbent paper, arrange on a hot platter and serve with tartar sauce. Serves 6.

FISH OR SHELLFISH CAKES

1 lb. raw fish or shellfish, chopped or ground (cooked or canned fish, flaked, can be substituted)
1 small onion, finely chopped

3 tbs. butter or margarine
¼ cup dry bread crumbs
salt and pepper to taste
1 egg, beaten
½ cup flour for dredging

Sauté chopped onion very lightly in butter. Combine fish and all ingredients except flour. Shape into 8 cakes, roll in flour and fry in ⅛ inch fat at moderate heat, about 5 to 8 minutes, turning until golden brown on all sides. Drain on absorbent paper and serve with lemon wedges or a sauce. Serves 4.

NOTE: Fish cakes can be prepared ahead, stored in refrigerator and dipped in crumb coating just before frying. Fish cakes also can be dipped in flour, beaten egg and crumbs and fried.

VARIATIONS:

1. Add celery, green pepper, carrot, either grated raw or cooked and finely chopped.

2. Add 1 cup mashed potatoes or soft bread crumbs with ¼ cup liquid—milk, water, fish or vegetable.

3. Add garlic, cayenne, Worcestershire, dry mustard or other seasonings to taste.

4. Add grated cheese to taste.

MINCED FISH FOR FISH BALLS

Fiskefars for Fiskeboller—Denmark

For each pound of minced fish use:

2 tsp. salt, or to taste
½ cup butter (scant)
2 tbs. flour

1 tsp. pepper
milk or cream to make mixture soft

Pike usually is used for this recipe but cod or haddock can be substituted. For special occasions use salmon. Clean, skin and bone the fish and scrape it with a spoon until it is a fine, smooth paste. Add salt and keep working until its own natural jellies bind the mixture.

Cream butter until light, stir in flour and pepper. Work in the fish with a wooden spoon. If you are making fish balls, work in only enough milk to bind; the mixture must not be too soft. For a ring mold, work in enough milk to soften mixture.

For making balls, drop mixture from large spoon into a well-greased frying pan, fry on all sides. If cooking ring mold, cover mold with aluminum foil and place in a pan with enough boiling water to reach half way up the mold. Simmer on top of stove until set, above 1 hour.

Fish balls are served with tomato sauce, and fish mold may be garnished with lobster or crab meat and served with hollandaise sauce.

MINCEMEAT OF RAW FISH   *Sa Ton Pa—Laos*

We include this recipe exactly as we received it from the little Asian nation because we found the directions so delightfully different, yet so easy to understand. It needs a little interpretation: where "five plants of southernwood" are called for, use tarragon. Southernwood is of the same origin as American desert sagebrush—and about sixty other species that grow in the United States. All of them are in the same family as tarragon. Parsley may be substituted for Laotian parsley, green onion leaves for shallot leaves. The fennel may be omitted if you cannot find it, but don't substitute fennel seeds. The garlic can be scalded.

1. Take some two pounds of raw fish, very fresh, and reduce it to mincemeat after having first removed all the bones. Put the mixture in a basin; do not use metal dish;

2. In half a glass of water melt a teaspoonful of salt and then add the juice of 5 or 6 lemons. Pour this acidulated water into

the basin containing the fish and leave it to soak for a quarter of an hour;

3. Take five plants of southernwood, 5 onions, the same number of cloves of garlic that have been cooked for a few moments in hot ashes, and 3 or 4 pimientoes; chop them up very finely;

4. Press out the water from the fish. Boil up the juice thus obtained with above seasonings and leave it to cool;

5. Mix this juice with the chopped-up fish and season with salt and brine according to taste. Next add the equivalent of two tablespoonfuls of aromatic herbs finely chopped up: fennel, Laotian parsley, shallot leaves.

The resulting dish is a pale pink mincemeat of fish, with green speckles from the added condiments. Sa, too, is served accompanied by a green salad and the leaves of aromatic herbs.

SEAFOOD PANCAKES AND WAFFLES

Add finely chopped or ground clams, crabs, lobster, scallops, shrimp or any white fish to pancake or waffle batter. If batter is too dry, increase liquid ingredient.

WHOLE FISH IN A PANCAKE   *Afghanistan*

4 small whole fish, dressed	salt and pepper to taste
½ cup flour	vegetable oil for frying
¾ cup cold water	1 lemon, cut into wedges

Mix flour and cold water to a thick paste, add seasonings. Dip fish into paste and fry in ¼ inch vegetable oil. Pour excess paste into pan, being sure to cover the whole pan. Turn when the paste browns. Brown second side and serve with boiled or fried potatoes. Garnish with lemon wedges. Serves 4.

Seafood and Egg
Combinations

OMELETS, SOUFFLÉS, SHIRRED AND
SCRAMBLED EGGS WITH FISH

The seafood omelet or soufflé provides the perfect means for turning a small amount of fresh, canned or leftover fish into a tempting and nutritious main course.

Instructions for making a basic
seafood omelet

Select a heavy omelet pan or frying pan that is not too large for easy handling. Its sides should be gently sloped to permit the cooking egg mixture to run up and around them and the finished omelet to slide easily from pan to plate.

Heat the frying pan over moderate heat, add butter and spread generously over bottom and up the sides of pan. Be careful not to let it become smoking hot.

Combine 6 eggs with 2 tbs. water, beer, fish or meat or vegetable stock, or use 3 eggs with 1 tbs. liquid. Milk also can be used but the omelet will be tougher. Beat for less than one minute with a fork.

Pour the batter into the pan, tilting it so the egg mixture runs a little up and around the sides, leave heat at moderate. Stir the center just a few times without breaking up the omelet. Then gently move the pan back and forth to cook omelet evenly and keep the egg loose in the pan. Very gently, using a dull knife or spatula, lift the sides a few times to permit any uncooked egg to run underneath onto the hot pan.

The omelet is done when all the egg is set. Fold the omelet in half with the spatula and invert it onto a warm platter or plate. If you prefer the top as well as the bottom to be browned, slide the omelet gently onto a preheated plate, rebutter the pan, invert it over the plate and turn the omelet back into the pan. Any extra handling or overcooking will dry out and toughen the omelet so you may prefer to set the frying pan directly under the broiler just long enough to brown the top lightly.

Adding fish to the egg:

Any cooked or canned fish or shellfish can be flaked for use in an omelet, soufflé or scrambled eggs. Boiling, poaching or steaming are very good methods of cooking raw fish that is going into an egg mixture. Shellfish can be added either cooked or raw, but if used raw, it should be cut into small pieces that will be cooked by the time the egg is done.

Fish can be added directly to the egg mixture before it is poured into the frying or baking pan or it can be folded into the finished omelet. The filling can be prepared by simply breaking the fish into small pieces, creaming it in butter, making a creamed fish or any one of the many sauces described in Part Two, beginning on page 106. If you select a sauce recipe for a filling, be sure it is one that will be almost ready before you pour the omelet mixture into the frying pan because omelets cook very quickly and must be served at once.

Soufflés

Soufflés should be baked in a baking dish set in a pan of water in a moderate oven, 350° F., just until the center is firm. This will take from 30 to 60 minutes depending on the size of baking dish and depth of mixture.

CRAB OMELET WITH CHINESE VEGETABLES

- 1 cup cooked flaked crab meat
- 1 cup mixed cooked and drained Chinese vegetables of your choice (canned vegetables can be used but the fresh ones are best if you have access to a Chinese grocery)

- 6 eggs
- 2 tbs. stock from vegetables soy sauce or salt to taste pinch of pepper
butter, margarine or oil for frying

Lightly beat eggs with vegetable stock and seasoning. Combine with all other ingredients.

Follow directions for cooking basic seafood omelet, page 214. Serves 6.

NOTE: Sautéed celery, onion and green pepper can be included with the Chinese vegetables.

HERRING PANCAKE OMELET *Bornholmer Aeggerkage*
—Denmark

6 smoked herrings, boned and filleted	butter or margarine for frying
8 eggs	1 bunch radishes
1 cup milk	3 tbs. chives, minced
salt to taste	¼ head of lettuce, cut into thin strips

Beat eggs and milk together and add salt. Melt butter in 1 large or 2 small frying pans, add the eggs and cook over low heat. Stir a little to make the omelet light and keep it from setting until just before it is done. Reduce heat. Arrange the herring fillets in a star on top of the omelet. Cut the radishes into thin slices and put between the herring pieces. Sprinkle the whole omelet with chives and lettuce. Cut the omelet into wedges, like a pie, and serve hot from the pan. Serves 6.

OYSTER OMELET

8 eggs	salt and pepper to taste
½ pt. shucked oysters	2 tbs. chopped onion
3 tbs. oyster liquor	¼ cup butter or margarine
1 tbs. chopped parsley or cooked drained spinach	1 cup undiluted cream of mushroom soup

Beat together eggs, oyster liquor, chopped parsley and salt and pepper. Melt 2 tbs. of the butter in a large frying pan, add egg mixture and cook over low heat until eggs become set.

Sauté chopped onion in remaining butter. Stir in cream of mushroom soup and heat.

Simmer oysters in remaining liquor until edges start to curl, drain, add to onion and mushroom soup and place in center of omelet. Fold omelet over filling and serve on preheated plates. Serves 6.

NOTE: You can substitute mussels or any other shellfish in this recipe. If you do, you may also want to substitute cream of shrimp or cream of Cheddar cheese soup for the mushroom soup.

SARDINE OMELET PANCAKE   *Portugal*

1 3¾-oz. can Portuguese sardines	1 tbs. butter or margarine for frying
2 cold boiled potatoes, peeled and sliced	4 eggs salt and pepper
1 medium onion, finely chopped	2 tbs. tomato sauce

Drain, skin and bone sardines and cut into small pieces.

Fry potato slices and chopped onion very lightly in butter.

Beat eggs, season with salt, pepper and add tomato sauce. Melt butter in frying pan, add half of the egg mixture and cook lightly. Cover with potato slices, onion and sardine and add remaining egg mixture.

When one side is cooked, invert the omelet onto a plate and slide it back into the pan to brown the other side. Cut in wedges and serve. Serves 4.

SHRIMP OMELET

1 4½-oz. can very small shrimp	½ tsp. salt dash pepper
6 eggs	2 tbs. cheese sauce, or very soft cheese
¼ cup liquor from can of shrimp	1 tbs. butter or margarine for frying
⅛ tsp. onion powder	

Beat together all ingredients except butter. Melt butter in frying pan, add batter and cook over moderate heat until firm. Lift up the sides while cooking to allow raw egg mixture to run under cooked layer. Do not stir. Fold and slide onto a hot platter. Serve with toast. Serves 4.

NOTE: Flaked or chopped shellfish meat can be substituted for shrimp.

FISH PANCAKE OMELET

1 cup flaked cooked fish, canned tuna or shrimp
½ medium green pepper, seeded and sliced
1 small onion, thinly sliced
1 very firm medium tomato, sliced
2 tbs. butter

6 eggs
2 tbs. water (substitute fish, meat or vegetable broth if you have it)
salt and pepper to taste
¼ lb. Cheddar cheese, thinly sliced

Lightly sauté green pepper, onion and tomato in butter. Add flaked fish.

Beat eggs, water and seasoning together with a fork and follow instructions for making seafood omelet, page 214. When omelet is almost done, spread fish and vegetable mixture carefully over it and cover with sliced cheese. Place pan under the broiler flame just long enough to melt cheese.

Cut in wedges and serve immediately on preheated plates with toast and fried potatoes. Serves 6.

NOTE: Lightly sautéed vegetables, flaked fish and sliced cheese can be stirred directly into the egg mixture before cooking if you prefer. It should then be poured into two frying pans since the omelet would be too large for one pan.

FISH IN SCRAMBLED EGG

1 cup flaked cooked fish
1 medium onion, chopped
3 tbs. butter or margarine
6 large eggs, beaten
⅓ cup milk

1 tsp. Worcestershire
salt to taste
1 tbs. lemon juice
dash cayenne
2 tbs. chopped parsley

Lightly sauté onion in butter. Combine fish and all other ingredients except parsley and pour over the onions. Cook over moderate heat, stirring occasionally to keep from sticking or burning, until egg is firm. Garnish with parsley and serve with toast. Serves 6.

NOTE: Serve with canned peach halves, broiled with brown sugar and butter, if desired.

SCRAMBLED EGGS WITH LOBSTER SAUCE

2 cups hot lobster sauce, page 127
6 eggs
¼ cup milk
salt and pepper to taste

butter or margarine for frying
3 English muffins, toasted and buttered

Combine eggs, milk and salt and pepper and beat with fork. Melt butter in the top of a double boiler. Add egg mixture and stir gently but constantly until eggs are cooked and of a creamy consistency.

Spoon scrambled eggs onto English muffin halves, pour hot lobster sauce over the eggs and serve. Serves 6.

NOTE: Undiluted frozen shrimp or oyster soup can be substituted for lobster sauce.

SHRIMP WITH SHIRRED EGGS

6 large boiled shrimp   from parboiled peppers
  butter or margarine   6 eggs
6 green pepper rings, cut   salt and pepper to taste

Butter 6 shirred egg or individual baking dishes. Place one shrimp in bottom of each. Add a green pepper ring and carefully break egg over it. Sprinkle with seasoning.

Place individual dishes on cookie sheet and bake in a 350° F. oven 8 to 10 minutes, or until white is firm. Serve in dishes or invert onto buttered toast. Serve for breakfast, lunch or late supper. Serves 6.

VARIATIONS:

1. Cooked oysters, mussels or other seafood can be substituted for shrimp.

2. Shrimp sauce or cream of shrimp soup (undiluted) can be spooned over eggs and sprinkled with grated cheese before baking.

3. Egg can be combined with 1 tsp. milk or stock and seasoning and lightly beaten with fork before pouring into individual baking dishes.

FLAKED FISH SOUFFLÉ   *Denmark*

2 cups flaked fish   5 eggs, separated
½ cup butter   salt and sugar to taste
⅔ cup flour   ¼ cup bread crumbs
1½ cups milk, heated

Melt butter in a pan and stir in flour. Add milk gradually and cook over low heat, stirring constantly, until mixture thickens. Remove from heat and stir in egg yolks. Season with a little salt and sugar and fold in egg whites, stiffly beaten.

Sprinkle a buttered baking dish with bread crumbs and

fill with alternate layers of batter and fish. Leftover vegetables also may be included in the soufflé. Set in a shallow pan of water.

Bake in a 350° F. oven 40 to 50 minutes, or until center is firm. Serves 6.

SATURDAY SOUFFLÉ

1 to 1½ cups leftover fish, flaked
½ medium onion, chopped
2 slices bacon, diced
1 can undiluted cream of mushroom soup
6 eggs, separated

½ cup grated cheese
dash nutmeg
paprika
(Do not add salt, undiluted soup is highly salted)

Start bacon frying in pan. Add onion and sauté lightly. Meantime, stir mushroom soup into beaten egg yolks, add grated cheese, onion, bacon and flaked fish.

Beat egg whites until stiff, fold into fish mixture and pour into an ungreased casserole. Set casserole in a pan containing at least 1 inch water and bake in a 350° F. oven 50 to 60 minutes, or until puffed and brown. Serves 6.

OYSTER SOUFFLÉ

1 pt. shucked oysters, drained and cut in pieces
3 tbs. flour
3 tbs. butter, melted

½ cup light cream or milk
½ cup liquor from oysters
salt and pepper to taste
dash nutmeg
3 eggs, separated

In top of a double boiler over boiling water, blend flour and melted butter. Add milk and oyster liquor very slowly, stirring constantly, and continue cooking and stirring for three minutes or until sauce thickens. Remove from heat and let cool for a few minutes.

Add beaten yolks, return to low heat, stirring constantly,

for one minute. Stir in oysters and seasonings and remove from heat.

Beat egg whites until stiff but not dry, fold lightly into the oyster mixture and pour into soufflé dish or casserole. Set in pan of water. Bake in 350° F. oven about 45 minutes or until top is brown and center of soufflé is firm. More time may be needed if deep casserole is used. Serve as a breakfast, lunch or dinner dish. Serves 4.

NOTE: Add chopped onion, garlic, celery, green pepper, sautéed in butter, or seasonings of your choice to this recipe.

III

Broiler Recipes

Broil pieces of fish that are at least one-half inch thick. Very thin pieces do not brown sufficiently in the time it takes to cook. When judging broiling time it is much more important to know when the fish is done by using your fork than by watching the clock. Since broiler ovens differ considerably in speed, the times given here are approximate. Use them only as a guide.

Broiling fillets and steaks

1. Remove the broiler pan and preheat the broiler compartment or not as the manufacturer directs. Grease only the area of the broiler pan that will be covered by the fish. Do not use a wire rack.

2. Wash fish by dipping it in a pan of cold water containing salt or lemon juice. Pat dry with absorbent paper.

3. Brush fish generously with melted butter, salad oil, French dressing, marinade or other sauce.

4. Sprinkle fish on both sides with salt and pepper.

5. Arrange fish on the broiler pan. Place fillets skin side down.

6. Insert the broiler pan in the oven so that the tops of fillets or steaks are two inches (two and one-half inches if very thick) from the heat unit.

7. Broil 8 to 12 minutes, or a few minutes longer if the fish is hard-frozen. Fillets or steaks may be turned after 3 to 5 minutes, but it is not necessary. If you do turn them, be sure the pieces are small enough to handle without breaking. Fish steaks that are turned should be broiled longer on the second side. That will give the side which will be up in serving a rich brown color. Cook only until the fish flakes easily with a fork.

Broiling split and whole fish

Any fish weighing less than four pounds may be split for broiling. Split fish cooked with the bone left in is juicier and has more
flavor. Split and whole fish are broiled the same way as fillets
and steaks with these exceptions:

1. Season inside as well as out with salt and pepper and dust
lightly with flour.

2. Split fish should be cooked two to three inches from heat
unit. Whole fish, such as flounder, should be cooked three inches
from heat, and thicker fish should be cooked four to six inches
from heat unit.

3. Place split fish skin side down and do not turn.

Broiling frozen fish

To retain flavor in frozen fillets, start cooking the moment the
outside surface loses its icy rigidity. If you complete thawing
before cooking flavorful juices will be washed away with the
melting ice. A quick searing in broiler or pan retains the flavor-
giving moisture. Lower the heat and allow a bit more cooking
time after the initial searing. Make sure you baste evenly over
the entire surface.

Hard-frozen fish should be placed three to four inches from
heat unit.

Aluminum foil in broiling

Line your pan with aluminum foil for baking and broiling:
(a) to make it easier to transfer to the platter after cooking;
(b) to avoid breaking in the transfer; (c) to use less grease;
(d) to make cleaning the broiler easier.

Low-calorie broiling

The National Fisheries Institute, dedicated to better health
through the simple means of eating more fish, recommends a
method of cooking fish called "Low-Calorie Fish Broil."

Select lean fish fillets cut thin lengthwise. The broiler pan need not be greased; the moisture from the fish will prevent sticking. Preheat the pan and arrange fish in the hot pan. Cover with a low calorie topping and broil two or three inches from the source of heat, 4 minutes if fish is thin; broil 8 minutes, turning after 3 minutes if fish is thicker than, for example, flounder. Fish is done when it flakes easily when tested with a fork.

The National Fisheries Institute suggests any of the following toppings:

Savory herb topping: Sprinkle during last three minutes of cooking with your own favorite chopped herb combination. A little grated fresh carrot may be added for color.

Paprika sauce topping: Brush with a thin layer of Worcestershire, sprinkle with paprika.

Pickle topping: Cover during last three minutes of cooking with a mixture of minced pickle, onion, salt and pepper.

Spicy topping: Spread with a thin layer of catsup or chili sauce—they have fewer calories than butter.

Part Two of this book also has some excellent suggestions for low-calorie topping.

Water broiling

This method was passed on to us by John Von Glahn, who had it passed on to him by William C. Johnston, an old "Bonnaker" fisherman who lived all his life in the tiny fishing village of Fireplace on the eastern tip of Long Island. It was passed on to Mr. Johnston through generations of his family. You'll have to try water broiling to believe that fish can be so delicious yet so simple and so fast to cook.

But before we give you the simple details of water broiling, a note about the Bonnakers. The name comes from the Indian word *Accabonac* which means "springs" and which abound in the area surrounding Fireplace. The Bonnakers have fished and farmed there for several centuries and are almost a separate ethnic group.

Water broiling the Bonnaker way makes your fish moist and

tender with a crisp golden crust. The Bonnakers believe in using only fish fillets but fish steaks and small split fish can be used. We'll only describe fillets in these directions.

1. Cut fillets one-half inch thick or a little bit thicker.

2. Place them on the rack in a shallow broiling pan and sprinkle generously with dried bread crumbs and dot with butter or margarine. Do not use cracker crumbs or cornmeal.

3. Add about an eighth to a quarter inch of water to the pan. The only liquid you need to bring out the flavor when using this method is plain water. You needn't even add salt, although you may flavor water with your favorite herbs.

If you prefer, substitute some other liquid for water: milk, cream, wine, beer or court bouillon or fish or meat stock.

4. Preheat your broiler to 550° F.

5. Slide your pan into the broiler, keeping the fillets about three or four inches from source of heat.

6. Broil only 5 minutes, less if the crust turns golden brown sooner. Adjust your timing accordingly if your fish is thicker or thinner than a half-inch and test with a fork to see when it flakes.

Just one more word in way of a footnote: The early Bonnakers, we know, had no broiling ovens, they used coals.

Outdoor broiling

Outdoor and indoor broiling recipes are easily interchangeable. We are including both in this section to give a wider selection—wherever you choose to do your cooking. If you enjoy charcoal-broiled fish and you have a porch or patio, there is no reason why you can't eat it almost every month of the year. In cold weather, cook the fish outside over coals, but serve it inside.

Unless you are using aluminum foil, be sure to grease your wire grill well when cooking over coals. Aluminum foil makes handling easier, and keeps in the juices. But it cuts down on the smoke flavor and browning. To conserve sauce, apply to fish with brush or baster.

Skewer recipes, or kabob, which are usually forgotten in the winter can be enjoyed all year. Place the skewered fish across a pan and bake in the oven.

INDIVIDUAL CLAM BAKE   *Outdoors*

2 soft-shell clams	2 pieces cheesecloth,
1 1-lb. live lobster	24 x 36 inches
1 medium baking potato	3 pieces heavy aluminum
1 medium onion	foil, 18 x 36 inches
1 ear of corn, in husk	¼ cup melted butter
	¼ lemon, cut in a wedge

Build charcoal fire and place grill 4 inches above white-hot coals. Scrub clams and potato and peel onion. Pull back corn husks carefully without detaching. Remove silk and dip ear in salted water. Fold husks back over moistened kernels. Run fresh water over lobster.

Wrap clams, lobster and other items in two thicknesses of damp cheesecloth. Lay package on two sheets of foil, pour one cupful of salted water over it and wrap securely. Wrap each individual clam bake in this manner, lay package on grill and cover with a sheet of foil.

Turn package three or four times, being very careful not to pierce foil, and cook about one hour. Open out foil carefully and use instead of platter. Serves 1.

NOTES:

1. Potatoes can be baked 30 minutes in advance. Then make up the packages and bake 30 minutes instead of one hour.

2. See instructions for cleaning lobster after cooking, page 63.

3. If preferred, lobster can be killed and cleaned, instructions page 63, before it is wrapped in foil.

CRABMEAT CASSEROLE WITH CHEESE SAUCE

2 cups crab meat	2 cups white sauce made
¼ cup grated Parmesan	with light cream, page
cheese	123
¼ cup grated Swiss cheese	4 tbs. butter
	salt and pepper to taste

Place crab meat in shallow well-greased casserole. In the top of a double boiler, stir grated cheese into white sauce. When blended, beat in butter, add salt and pepper and pour over crab meat.

Broil 3 inches from heat in medium hot broiler until browned.

Watch closely because cheese sauce burns easily. Serves 6.

STUFFED FLOUNDER   *Outdoors*

6 ¾-lb. flounders, pan-dressed
1 medium onion, chopped
½ medium green pepper, seeded and chopped
1 large stalk celery, chopped
2 slices bacon, diced
1 lb. crab meat
2 cups soft bread crumbs
3 eggs, beaten

salt and pepper to taste
1 tsp. salt
paprika
juice of ½ lemon
¾ cup butter or margarine, melted
6 squares heavy-duty aluminum foil, each one large enough to wrap one fish.

Wash whole dressed fish by dipping in cold salted water. Lay flat and cut a slit down the center, stopping at least an inch short of head and tail. Run a sharp knife, laid flat, between the rib bones and the flesh, making a pocket.

Sauté onion, pepper and celery lightly with bacon. Combine with crab meat, bread crumbs, eggs and salt and pepper. Stuff into pockets in flounders.

Add salt, paprika and lemon juice to melted butter. Turn up the sides of each piece of foil and divide the lemon-butter sauce among them. Lay a fish on each foil dish and turn to butter both sides. Wrap each fish securely in its aluminum package, double-folding the edges to seal.

Place packages on wire grill of barbecue stand about 6 inches above bed of coals which has burned down to a hot, red-gray color and is no longer flaming. Cook 20 to 30 minutes, or until fish flakes easily with a fork. Be careful not to tear package or loosen sealed edges and let steam escape. Test one fish for flaking after about 20 minutes. Serves 6.

GLAZED HALIBUT STEAKS

2 lbs. halibut steaks, cut 1 to 1½ inches thick	1¼ tbs. prepared mustard salt to taste
½ cup lemon juice	grated lemon rind to taste
½ cup brown sugar, packed	

Combine lemon juice, sugar, mustard, salt and lemon rind and set aside 15 minutes.

Wash steaks by dipping into cold salted water, dry thoroughly and arrange on preheated, well-greased broiler pan from which rack has been removed. Spread with half the lemon juice mixture and broil under medium heat 3 inches from heat unit for 3 minutes. Turn heat up to high and broil about 2 minutes longer, or until sauce turns golden brown. Turn fish carefully and repeat on other side.

If fish flakes before second side is glazed and brown, place the broiler pan closer to source of heat, but watch because sugar sauce burns quickly. Serves 6.

GRILLED MACKEREL WITH CUCUMBER SAUCE

4 small mackerel	1 medium cucumber, finely diced
salt and pepper to taste	
½ cup butter, melted	1½ tbs. minced dill, or to taste

Season fish inside and out with salt and pepper, brush with 2 tablespoons of the butter. Broil in preheated broiler, about 3 inches from heat unit, 10 minutes, or until fish is golden brown. Remove to heated plates and serve with a sauce of cucumber and dill sautéed in the remaining butter.

Garnish with lemon wedges and parsley. Serves 4.

SPLIT MACKEREL WITH MUSTARD PARSLEY SAUCE

1 3- to 4-lb. mackerel	salt and pepper to taste
2 tbs. soft butter	chopped parsley or
1 tsp. prepared mustard	parsley flakes
1 tbs. melted butter	¼ cup lemon juice

Stir butter and mustard together until smooth and chill.

Wash fish by dipping in cold salted water and split, leaving bone in. Dry thoroughly and rub inside and out with melted butter and salt and pepper.

Place fish, skin side down, on well-greased preheated broiler pan from which rack has been removed. Broil about 3 inches from heat unit approximately 10 minutes or until fish flakes easily when tested with a fork.

A minute or two before fish is done, spread with mustard butter.

Place cooked fish on very hot serving platter, add any juices left in broiling pan. Pour lemon juice over and sprinkle with parsley. Serves 6.

BROILED PERCH FILLETS   *Outdoors*

2 lbs. perch fillets	2 tbs. capers and juice
½ cup butter or margarine, melted	1 tsp. prepared mustard
½ cup catsup	1 garlic clove, finely chopped
½ cup frozen lemonade concentrate, undiluted	4 bay leaves, crushed
	salt and pepper to taste

Wash fillets by dipping in cold salted water. Dry thoroughly. Cut into serving pieces that can be handled without breaking. Combine all remaining ingredients and marinate perch 30 minutes.

Drain and arrange fish in hinged, well-greased wire grill. Fasten securely and cook about 4 inches above coals that have burned down to a hot, red-grey and are no longer flaming. Cook 4 to 7 minutes on each side, basting frequently with marinade. Fish is done when it flakes easily with a fork. Serves 6.

BROILED RED SNAPPER STEAKS

2 lbs. red snapper steaks
salt and pepper to taste
¼ cup butter or margarine, melted

¼ cup chili sauce
2 tsp. horseradish sauce
1 tbs. prepared mustard
1 cup grated cheese

Wash fish by dipping in cold salted water. Dry, and season both sides with salt and pepper. Arrange on a preheated, well-greased broiler pan from which the wire rack has been removed. Brush with butter and broil 2 inches from medium heat 8 to 12 minutes, or until fish flakes easily when tested with a fork.

Combine chili sauce, horseradish, mustard and grated cheese with any remaining butter. Spread over fish for last 2 to 3 minutes of broiling time or until cheese turns golden brown and starts to melt. Serves 6.

NOTE: If you plan to turn fish, be sure to cut it into small enough pieces to handle without breaking.

MARINATED SALMON STEAKS I   *Outdoors*

2 lbs. salmon steaks
1 cup prepared French or Italian dressing

1 tbs. lemon juice
1 tsp. paprika
salt and pepper to taste

Wash steaks by dipping in cold salted water. Dry and cut into serving portions that can be handled easily without breaking.

Marinate 30 minutes in dressing combined with lemon juice, paprika and salt and pepper. Turn after 15 minutes.

Fasten steaks securely in hinged wire grill and place on outdoor barbecue stand about 4 inches above coals that have burned down to a hot, red-grey color. Grill 5 to 8 minutes to a side or until fish flakes easily with a fork, basting several times with marinade.

Serve on heated plates. Serves 6.

MARINATED SALMON STEAKS II

2 lbs. salmon steaks	1 tbs. finely chopped onion
¼ cup orange juice	1 garlic clove, finely
2 tbs. melted butter or	chopped
salad oil	1 tsp. parsley flakes
2 tbs. chili sauce or catsup	½ tsp. grated orange rind
1 tbs. lemon juice	dried oregano to taste

Wash fish by dipping in cold salted water and cut into serving size portions that can be turned easily without breaking.

Combine all remaining ingredients and set aside at least 20 minutes at room temperature. Add salmon to sauce and marinate 30 minutes. Arrange in well-greased broiler pan and place about 3 inches from heat unit. Broil at medium heat 4 to 8 minutes, basting 2 or 3 times with marinade. Turn when lightly browned on one side and repeat the process. Total cooking time should be 8 to 16 minutes, depending on thickness of steaks. Fish is done when it flakes easily when tested with a fork. Serves 6.

MARINATED SEA SCALLOPS   *Outdoors*

1½ lbs. sea scallops	½ tsp. onion salt
¾ cup butter or	⅛ tsp. garlic salt
margarine, melted	salt and pepper to taste
juice of ½ lemon	paprika

Combine melted butter, lemon juice and seasonings, except paprika, to use as marinade and sauce.

Wash scallops by dipping in cold salted water. Dry and marinate 30 minutes. Turn 2 or 3 times so that all sides are well coated with sauce.

Arrange scallops in hinged, well-greased wire grill. Fasten securely so they can't fall out, and cook about 4 inches above coals that have burned down to a hot, red-grey and are no longer flaming. Baste with remaining sauce, sprinkle with paprika, and cook 3 to 5 minutes. Turn hinged grill and repeat on other side. Scallops are done when browned and tender. Do not overcook. Serves 6.

NOTE: Large oysters, jumbo shrimp and chunks of lobster can be cooked this way.

VARIATION: Wrap shellfish with strips of bacon before placing in grill.

FROZEN BREADED SHRIMP

2 lbs. frozen breaded
  shrimp
½ cup melted butter or
  margarine
2 tbs. lemon juice

salt and pepper to taste
1 tsp. paprika, or to taste
1 cup tartar sauce, page
  121

Defrost shrimp in the refrigerator until you can separate them with a fork without disturbing the breading. Arrange on a well-greased, preheated broiler pan, rack removed. Combine butter, juice and seasonings and brush each shrimp with the mixture.

Place pan about 3 inches from heat unit and broil until shrimp are brown, 4 to 5 minutes. Turn, brush other side with mixture and broil 3 to 4 minutes longer, or until both sides are lightly browned. Serve at once with tartar sauce as a main course, or serve as appetizers, using tomato-relish sauce, page 115, as dip. Serves 6.

MARINATED JUMBO SHRIMP   *Outdoors*

1½ lbs. raw jumbo shrimp, shelled and deveined
1 garlic clove
1 cup melted butter or margarine
juice of ½ lemon

1 tsp. onion flakes
1 tsp. dried basil
1 tsp. parsley flakes
¼ tsp. prepared mustard
salt and pepper to taste

Rub bowl with cut garlic clove. Add all remaining ingredients and set aside.

Wash shrimp by dipping in cold salted water. Dry thorroughly and place in marinade 30 minutes.

Remove shrimp from marinade and arrange them carefully in hinged, well-greased wire grill. Fasten securely so they cannot fall out. Barbecue 4 minutes on one side and 4 to 7 minutes on other side, about 4 inches above hot, red-grey coals. Baste with remaining marinade. Test with a fork and taste. Do not overcook or they will toughen.

Serve with garnish of parsley sprigs and lemon wedges. Serves 6.

NOTE: Large oysters, scallops and chunks of lobster meat can be cooked this way.

SEA BASS BARBECUED WITH WINE   *Outdoors*

2 lbs. sea bass fillets
½ onion, chopped
½ garlic clove, finely chopped
½ cup butter or margarine, melted
1 8-oz. can tomato sauce

2 tbs. cooking sherry, or to taste
½ tsp. sugar
1 tsp. Worcestershire
pinch oregano
pinch thyme
salt and pepper to taste

Sauté onion and garlic in butter until tender. Add remaining ingredients and cool.

Wash sea bass by dipping in cold salted water. Dry and marinate 30 minutes.

Arrange steaks in hinged, well-greased wire grill. Fasten securely and barbecue about 4 inches from coals that are hot, red-grey, and no longer flaming. Allow 4 to 7 minutes to a side, or until fish flakes easily when tested with a fork. Baste with remaining marinade. Serves 6.

STRIPED BASS STEAKS
BARBECUED WITH COGNAC   *Outdoors*

2 lbs. striped bass steaks	2 tbs. soy sauce
¼ cup melted butter or	salt to taste
margarine	garlic salt to taste
juice of ½ large lemon	½ cup cognac

Wash steaks by dipping in cold salted water and dry thoroughly.

Combine all remaining ingredients and marinate bass 30 minutes.

Fasten steaks securely in a hinged, well-greased wire grill. Place on barbecue about 4 inches from hot, red-grey coals. Barbecue 5 to 6 minutes on each side, or until fish flakes easily when tested with a fork. Baste with remaining marinade. Serves 6.

SMELT IN FOIL PACKAGES   *Outdoors*

3 lbs. whole smelt or any small pan fish	1 large onion, finely chopped
6 squares heavy-duty aluminum foil, 12 x 12 inches	1 tbs. chopped parsley or parsley flakes
6 strips bacon	1 tbs. lemon juice
	pinch garlic salt
	salt and pepper to taste

Follow instructions for cleaning and washing whole fish. Do not split or attempt to remove bone.

Fry bacon, onion and parsley together very lightly, (or use them raw). Remove bacon and stir in lemon juice, garlic salt and salt and pepper.

Divide smelt into 6 serving portions and place each portion in center of a piece of well-greased aluminum foil. Rub each fish with the oily onion and parsley mixture and divide what is left among the cavities. Top each portion with a slice of bacon. Wrap securely in foil, folding edges double to seal.

Place packages in bed of coals that have burned down to hot, red-grey color, in either outdoor grill or pit. Cook 15 minutes, turning several times. Be careful not to puncture packages or loosen sealed edges.

Serve immediately in the opened foil packages. Garnish with lemon wedges. Serves 6.

SWORDFISH STEAKS WITH SPINACH AND SHRIMP

Water Broiled

4 swordfish steaks
1 pkg. frozen chopped or leaf spinach, or 1 lb. fresh
  salt and pepper to taste
1 tbs. lemon juice

¼ lb. small raw shrimp, shelled and deveined
¾ cup dry bread crumbs—increase if necessary for very generous coating
6 tbs. butter or margarine

Prepare spinach according to package directions or cook fresh spinach. Drain it well. Pour ⅛ inch hot water into pre-heated broiler pan or preheated ovenware platter in which you can both broil and serve. Spread the spinach over the pan or platter. Season with salt and pepper and lemon juice. Spread shrimp over spinach.

Lay the swordfish steaks on the shrimp, top with bread crumbs and dot with butter. Broil under high heat 8 to 10 minutes or until fish flakes easily when tested with a fork. Serve from the ovenware dish. Serves 4.

NOTE: An aluminum-foil-lined broiler pan makes a satisfactory substitute for an ovenware cooking and serving platter. Fish, foil and all can be transferred to serving platter.

VARIATION: Mix 2 tablespoons grated cheese with dry bread crumbs.

SWORDFISH STEAKS WITH TOMATO SAUCE AND LEMON SLICES

4 swordfish steaks
salt and pepper to taste
⅓ cup butter or margarine, melted

¼ cup tomato paste
12 lemon slices

Season steaks with salt and pepper, brush generously with butter and broil in hot broiler about 3 minutes on one side. Turn, brush again with butter, spread with tomato paste, place a row of 3 lemon slices on each steak. Broil another 5 to 7 minutes or until fish flakes easily when tested with a fork. Serves 4.

HICKORY SMOKED FILLETS   *Outdoors*

2 lbs. fish fillets
½ cup melted butter or margarine
pinch garlic salt
2 tbs. lemon juice

1 tbs. chopped parsley or parsley flakes
1 tbs. liquid hickory smoke
salt and pepper to taste

Wash fish by dipping in cold salted water and fasten securely in hinged, well-greased wire grill. Place grill on barbecue stand about 4 inches from hot, red-grey coals. Broil 4 to 7 minutes to a side, basting frequently with sauce made by combining all remaining ingredients.

Fish is done when it flakes easily when tested with a fork. Serve on hot plates. Serves 6.

NOTE: If possible, omit liquid hickory smoke and add some hickory chips to fire, but don't put fish over fire while chips are flaming.

SARDINES WITH EGG SAUCE   *Portugal*

1 3¾-oz. can boneless Portuguese sardines	4 tbs. oil
2 tbs. melted butter	1 tbs. vinegar
¾ cup bread crumbs	salt and pepper to taste
2 hard-cooked egg yolks	½ tsp. prepared mustard

Remove sardines from can without breaking them. Brush with melted butter and cover with bread crumbs, pressing the crumbs down with a knife. Broil on a hot grill. Serve with this sauce: Sieve egg yolks, stir in salad oil little by little, add vinegar, salt and pepper and mustard and stir until smooth. Serves 2.

FISH STEAKS WITH AVOCADO SAUCE   *Mexico*

3 lbs. fish steaks	2 ripe avocados
1 medium onion, chopped	tomato puree or 2
1 garlic clove, very finely chopped	peeled, chopped tomatoes
¼ cup oil	1 tbs. chopped parsley
salt and pepper to taste	¼ tsp. chili powder

Cook onion and garlic in oil until they are light brown. Drain off oil and reserve onion and garlic. Brush steaks with the oil and salt and pepper to taste. Broil 8 to 12 minutes or until fish flakes easily when tested with a fork.

Mash avocado pulp with equal amount tomato puree. Add reserved onion and garlic, parsley, chili powder and salt and pepper to taste. Spread mixture over fish steaks and serve at once. Serves 6.

FISH STEAKS FLAMBÉ

3 lbs. fish steaks
salt and pepper to taste
2 tbs. butter or margarine, melted

1 tsp. lemon juice
½ cup brandy
½ tsp. grated lemon rind

Season fish with salt and pepper, brush with butter and lemon juice and broil 8 to 10 minutes or until fish flakes easily when tested with a fork. Heat brandy in a small saucepan, but do not boil. Remove steaks from broiler to a preheated serving platter. Add grated lemon rind to brandy, pour over steaks. Flame and serve. Serves 6.

SHELLFISH KABOBS   *Outdoors*

1½ lb. shelled shellfish (scallops, large oysters, jumbo shrimp or lobster chunks)
1 No. 211 can pineapple chunks, drained and liquid reserved
½ cup pineapple juice
2 tbs. lemon juice

½ cup brown sugar
1 tbs. soy sauce
4 tbs. melted butter or oil
1 tsp. ground ginger or to taste
salt and pepper to taste
1 green pepper, par-boiled, seeded, cut in chunks

Wash shellfish by dipping in pan of cold salted water.

Combine pineapple juice and drained liquid with lemon juice, sugar, soy sauce, butter, ginger and salt and pepper. Marinate shellfish in this sauce 30 to 60 minutes, turning 2 or 3 times to be sure all sides are soaked.

Alternate shellfish, pineapple and green pepper chunks on 4 skewers. Baste with marinade and place skewers across outdoor barbecue stand about 4 inches above coals that have burned down to a hot, red-grey and are no longer flaming. Cook 10 to 12 minutes, turning several times and basting with marinade. Use brush or baster to conserve sauce.

Remove as soon as tender. Do not overcook. Serves 4.

IV

Oven Recipes

Stuffings

BREAD STUFFING

For one whole fish or fillets

5 cups soft bread cubes
1½ cups finely chopped
   celery
⅓ cup finely chopped
   onion

¼ cup butter or margarine
½ tsp. salt
½ tsp. poultry seasoning
2 to 3 tbs. milk
1 egg, beaten

Cook celery and onion in butter until tender. Mix salt, poultry seasoning and bread cubes and add to celery-onion mixture. Add milk and egg and use to stuff one whole fish or to spread on fish fillets.

OYSTER DRESSING: Add 1 pint shucked raw oysters, chopped, and substitute strained oyster liquor for the milk.

SHRIMP DRESSING: Add ½ pound raw shrimp, shelled, deveined, washed and chopped.

SOUR CREAM DRESSING: Add ½ cup sour cream.

NOTE: Oyster or shrimp dressing makes enough seafood stuffing for 4- to 5-lb. chicken. Triple recipe for 10- to 15-lb. turkey.

HAWAIIAN STUFFING

2 cups cooked rice
1 egg, beaten
1 cup crushed, drained
   pineapple

2 tbs. lemon juice
2 slices bacon, lightly fried
   and chopped
salt to taste

Combine all ingredients and mix well. Use to stuff whole fish, fillets or steaks.

WILD RICE AND MUSHROOM STUFFING

2½ cups cooked wild rice
1 cup sliced fresh mush-
   rooms
1 medium onion,
   chopped
¼ cup butter or margarine

½ cup canned undiluted
   cream of mushroom
   soup
1 egg, beaten
salt to taste

Lightly sauté mushrooms and onion in butter. When tender combine with all remaining ingredients, mix well and use to stuff whole fish, fillets or steaks.

Baking Whole Fish

1. Baking is an excellent way to cook whole fish weighing two and a half pounds or more. It is important to know the exact cooking weight because this determines oven time. Fish take much less time to bake than meat or poultry.

2. If possible, bake fish with the head on in order to seal in flavor and juices.

3. Rub fish cavity with salt.

4. Line baking pan with aluminum foil to facilitate transfer of fish to serving platter and to lessen cleaning chores. Less grease is needed when foil is used.

5. Place fish on well-greased foil, or in a well-greased pan.

6. Brush fish with melted butter, margarine or salad oil. If preferred, lay three or four strips of bacon over the fish.

7. BAKE IN A MODERATE 350° F. OVEN 8 TO 12 MINUTES PER POUND, OR UNTIL THE FISH FLAKES EASILY WHEN TESTED WITH A FORK.

Many cooks believe in slashing fish diagonally before cooking. But this only hastens cooking time while allowing juices and flavor to escape.

Baste fish with butter or oil as often as you think necessary while baking. For a change, try basting with sour cream, white wine or a little spicy red sauce. Or marinate the fish in French dressing for two hours before baking.

If stuffing is used, allow about one cup per pound of fish. Stuff the salted cavity loosely, close the opening with skewers and lace with kitchen string.

Hard-frozen fish

Follow the same directions but increase baking time to about 14 to 17 minutes per pound.

BASS WITH ANCHOVY BUTTER   *Austria*

4 lbs. bass or halibut	½ cup soft butter
3 anchovy fillets, cut in strips	2 anchovies, rubbed through strainer, or 2
⅓ cup fat	teaspoons anchovy paste

Clean and wash fish. Place anchovy strips diagonally across fish. Melt fat in a foil-lined roasting pan, add fish and bake at 350° F. until it flakes easily, about 30 minutes. Baste frequently with pan juices. Transfer fish to hot serving platter.

Stir butter with anchovy paste and add to the pan juices. Bring to a boil, stir well and pour the sauce over the fish. Serve with boiled potatoes. Serves 6.

BAKED CARP

4- or 5-lb. carp	1 tsp. salt
1 garlic clove, finely minced	⅛ tsp. pepper
½ medium onion, finely minced	½ cup oil
	8 lemon wedges
	8 sprigs parsley

Combine garlic, onion, salt and pepper with oil several hours before baking fish and let them stand at room temperature.

Rub fish inside and out with mixture and place in a well-greased baking dish. Pour remaining oil over fish.

Bake in 350° F. oven 30 to 40 minutes or until fish flakes easily when tested with a fork. If pan becomes too dry, add a little hot water.

Garnish with lemon wedges and parsley and serve. Serves 8.

MACKEREL WITH VEGETABLE SAUCE *Sheepscot Bay*

2 2-lb. mackerel	½ tsp. salt
1 large onion, chopped	1 tbs. chopped parsley
1 large carrot, chopped	¼ tsp. minced or dried thyme
½ green pepper, seeded and chopped	1 bay leaf
¾ cup vinegar	

Combine onion, carrot, green pepper and vinegar in a saucepan and mix thoroughly. Add salt, parsley, thyme, bay leaf and enough water to just cover.

Simmer 20 minutes. Remove bay leaf.

Place mackerel in baking dish lined with well-greased foil and pour sauce over them.

Bake in 400° F. oven about 20 minutes or until fish flakes easily when tested with a fork. Transfer fish to a hot serving platter and serve with its own sauce. Serves 8.

SALT MACKEREL IN SCALLOPED POTATOES

1½ lbs. salt mackerel
 oil
6 medium potatoes, peeled and thinly sliced
 salt and pepper to taste
2 tbs. flour

3 medium onions, sliced and separated into rings
1 cup warm milk
¼ cup light cream, optional

Wash fish and soak at least 24 hours in cold water, changing water several times. Drain, rinse and wipe with absorbent paper. Brush with oil and place in a lightly greased ovenware baking dish.

Arrange potatoes around mackerel and sprinkle with salt and pepper. Dredge with flour and arrange onion rings over fish and potatoes. Add milk and bake in 450° F. oven until potatoes are tender.

Add cream about 10 minutes before removing fish from oven. Serve from baking dish. Serves 4.

POLLOCK WITH CREOLE SAUCE

1 4- to 5-lb. pollock
¼ cup oil or butter or margarine, melted
¾ tsp. salt
½ tsp. pepper
½ cup tomato juice

1 tbs. finely chopped onion
2 cups Creole sauce, page 140
½ cup bread crumbs
3 cups rice, cooked

Rub cavity of fish with oil and season with salt and pepper. Place in a greased ovenware baking dish. Add tomato juice and sprinkle with onion.

Bake in 350° F. oven 25 to 35 minutes or until fish flakes easily when tested with a fork. Baste occasionally.

Pour 1 cup Creole sauce over fish, top with bread crumbs, dot with butter and bake until crumbs are browned.

Mix one cup Creole sauce with rice and arrange around fish. Serve in baking dish. Serves 5 to 6.

POLLOCK KITTERY

1 4-lb. pollock	1 tbs. vinegar
¼ cup butter or margarine	½ tsp. salt
2 egg yolks, lightly beaten	½ tsp. sugar
2 tbs. chopped onion	⅓ tsp. paprika
1 tbs. capers	2 tbs. lemon juice
1 tbs. chopped parsley	

Split and bone pollock. Clean and wipe dry. Rub inside with salt and place, skin side down, on greased foil in baking pan.
Bake 15 minutes in 400° F. oven.

Cream butter, stir in egg yolks, add onion, capers and parsley. Stir in vinegar, salt, sugar, paprika and lemon juice. Spread mixture on fish.

Reduce oven heat to 350° F. and bake fish another 10 to 15 minutes or until it flakes easily when tested with a fork. Transfer to a hot platter and serve. Serves 6.

PORGY IN CHEESE SAUCE

2 2-lb. porgies	¼ cup chopped parsley
½ tsp. salt	¾ cup cracker crumbs
½ tsp. pepper	¾ cup grated mild
¼ cup chopped chives	Cheddar cheese

Wash and wipe cavities dry with absorbent paper or cheesecloth. Rub interiors well with salt and pepper. Sprinkle chives and parsley over bottom of well-greased ovenware baking pan. Arrange fish in pan and cover generously with cracker crumbs and cheese.

Bake in 375° F. oven about 15 minutes, or until fish flakes easily when tested with a fork. Serve in baking pan. Serves 8.

BAKED FRESH SARDINES

3 lbs. fresh sardines
salt to taste
minced fresh or dried
thyme to taste

½ cup olive oil (any oil
flavored with olives can
be substituted)
¼ cup lemon juice

Rub insides of sardines with salt and thyme. Arrange in ovenware baking pan. Blend oil and lemon juice and pour over fish.

Bake in 375° F. oven 10 to 20 minutes or until fish flakes easily when tested with a fork. Serve in baking pan. Serves 6.

FISH SMOTHERED IN TOMATOES

1 4-lb. fish
salt and pepper to taste
½ cup butter or margarine

10 to 12 medium tomatoes,
chopped
1 medium onion, chopped

Rub cavity of fish with salt and pepper and place in an ovenware baking pan. Pour butter over fish and cover with tomatoes and onion. Let stand one hour.

Bake in 350° F. oven about 30 minutes or until fish flakes easily when tested with fork. Serve in baking pan. Serves 8.

MEDITERRANEAN BAKED FISH

1 4-lb. fish
1 tsp. lemon juice
¾ tsp. salt
¾ tsp. pepper
½ cup olive oil (cooking
oil flavored with a little
olive oil can be
substituted)

6 medium tomatoes,
sliced
2 large red Spanish
onions, sliced
5 lemon slices
6 black olives, pitted and
cut in half lengthwise
1 tbs. chopped parsley
½ cup white wine

Rub fish cavity well with lemon juice, salt and pepper. Rub an ovenware baking pan with oil and cover with a layer of half the tomatoes and onions. Lay fish on this bed and top with remaining tomatoes and onions. Add lemon, olives and parsley. Pour remaining oil and wine around fish.

Bake in 350° F. oven 30 to 40 minutes or until fish flakes easily when tested with a fork. Serve in baking pan. Serves 8.

FISH IN INDIVIDUAL FOIL PACKAGES

4 ½-lb. fish	4 tbs. lemon juice
½ cup butter or margarine	marjoram to taste
4 large onion slices	salt and pepper to taste
4 lemon slices	1 tbs. chopped parsley

Rinse and dry fish and rub with 2 tbs. of the butter. Cut foil in 4 pieces large enough to wrap each fish individually and grease foil with 2 tbs. of the butter. Put fish on foil and top each with a slice each of onion and lemon.

Melt remaining butter, add lemon juice, marjoram and salt and pepper. Spoon mixture on fish and fold foil carefully around it. Place in baking pan containing 3 tbs. hot water

Bake about 20 minutes in 350° F. oven. Open foil, garnish with parsley and serve. Serves 4.

PLANKED FISH   *Company Style*

3 or 4 lbs. dressed white-fish or other dressed fish	6 small tomatoes, halved across
1 tsp. salt	2 tbs. chopped basil
dash pepper	3 cups cooked seasoned vegetables (use two
¼ cup melted butter or margarine	kinds—peas, carrots, corn, etc.)
4 cups seasoned mashed potatoes	1 lemon, sliced
	6 sprigs parsley

Sprinkle fish (inside only) with salt and pepper. Brush with butter. Place fish on a well-greased preheated hardwood plank. Bake in a hot oven 400° F. oven 25 to 35 minutes or until fish flakes easily when tested with a fork. Remove from oven.

Pipe a border of hot mashed potatoes around edge of plank. Arrange seasoned tomatoes between fish and potato border. Sprinkle tomatoes with basil.

Place in broiler until potatoes are slightly browned, about 5 minutes. Remove, arrange hot drained vegetables between the tomatoes. Decorate with lemon and parsley, and serve the hot plank on a large platter or tray. Serves 6.

MICKEY MOORE'S SPECIAL BONITO

1 4½-lb. bonito
1 level tbs. seafood
seasoning or to taste
3 large stalks celery,
halved and sliced again
lengthwise
2 tbs. vegetable
shortening

1 tsp. paprika
2 medium onions, sliced
¼-inch thick
3 bay leaves
6 sprigs parsley
1½ cups spiced fruit or 1
can cranberry sauce

Soak fish in cold salted water to cover 15 minutes. Pour off water, scrub cavity, rinse well and soak again for an additional 30 minutes. Drain and thoroughly dry with absorbent paper. Sprinkle cavity with half of the seafood seasoning, stuff loosely with celery and secure opening with skewers.

Make three small diagonal cuts across fish, rub outside with shortening, sprinkle with last half of seafood seasoning and paprika.

Line shallow roasting pan with well-greased aluminum foil and lay fish on a bed made of the onion slices and top with bay leaves.

Preheat oven to 425° F. and bake 10 minutes. Reduce to 375° F. 10 minutes, then reduce heat still further to 350° F. and continue baking 10 to 20 minutes or until fish flakes easily when tested with a fork.

Decorate platter with parsley and serve with spiced fruit or cranberry sauce. Serves 8.

SNAPPER WITH SOUR CREAM STUFFING

1 3- to 4-lb. dressed snapper
  or dressed striped bass
1 tsp. salt
3 to 4 cups sour cream
  stuffing, page 240
3 tbs. oil

paprika to taste
2 tomatoes, sliced
1 lemon, cut into wedges
6 sprigs parsley or watercress

Sprinkle fish cavity with salt. Fill loosely with stuffing. Close opening with skewers and lace with kitchen string. Place fish on a well-greased piece of aluminum foil in a baking pan.

Bake in 350° F. oven 30 to 50 minutes, or until fish flakes easily when tested with a fork. Brush occasionally with oil mixed with paprika. Serve on a heated platter. Garnish with tomatoes, lemon and parsley. Serves 6.

STUFFED SNAPPER IN WINE SAUCE

1 4-lb. dressed snapper
1 cup white wine
  salt and pepper to taste

4 cups stuffing of your
  choice, page 240
4 tbs. butter or margarine
1 lemon, sliced

Sprinkle snapper with 2 tbs. of the wine. Combine salt and pepper and rub into cavity. Stuff loosely and close cavity with wooden picks or skewers and lace with kitchen string. Place fish on greased foil in a baking pan and dot with butter. Add remaining wine to pan and cover with foil.

Bake in 350° F. oven 20 minutes, uncover, baste with wine in pan. Bake about 15 minutes longer, basting every 5 minutes. When fish flakes easily with a fork it is done.

Garnish with lemon and serve. Serves 8.

STUFFED TRIPLETAIL IN SPIKED MILK

1 4-lb. dressed tripletail
salt and pepper to taste
5 cups stuffing of your
choice, page 240
1 cup warm milk

Tabasco to taste
2 tbs. butter or margarine,
melted
1 lemon, sliced

Rinse and dry fish with absorbent paper. Mix salt and pepper and rub into cavity. Stuff with dressing, secure with skewers and place on well-greased foil in a baking pan.

Spike warmed milk with Tabasco and pour around fish. Brush top with melted butter.

Bake 10 minutes in 450° F. oven. Lower heat to 400° F. and bake about 20 minutes more. Baste often, test with a fork until fish flakes easily. Transfer fish to platter, garnish with lemon slices and serve. Serves 8.

VARIATION: Omit Tabasco and spread 4 slices salt pork or bacon over top of fish.

YELLOWTAIL WITH WILD RICE AND MUSHROOM STUFFING

1 7-lb. dressed yellowtail
1½ tsp. salt
1½ tsp. pepper
6 cups wild rice and
mushroom stuffing,
page 240

6 tbs. melted butter or
margarine
4 tbs. chopped parsley
3 tbs. paprika

Wash and wipe fish cavity dry with absorbent paper. Mix salt and pepper and rub into cavity. Stuff fish, secure with skewers and lace with kitchen string. Place on well-greased foil in a baking pan and brush with butter.

Bake in 500° F. oven 10 minutes.

Reduce heat to 350° F. and bake 60 minutes longer or

until fish flakes easily when tested with a fork. Baste occasionally with remaining butter.

Transfer to a warm platter, garnish with parsley, sprinkle with paprika and serve. Serves 10.

FISH STUFFED WITH GARLIC, ONION AND CELERY

1 4-lb. fish	2 garlic cloves, finely
salt and pepper to taste	chopped
juice of 1 lemon	½ cup oil
2 large onions, finely	2 tbs. parsley, finely
chopped	chopped
2 tbs. celery, finely	thyme to taste
chopped	½ cup hot water

Rub cavity of fish with salt, pepper and half of the lemon juice. Let stand 30 minutes.

Fry onions, celery and garlic in oil, until they begin to soften. Add parsley and thyme and stuff fish with mixture. Lay fish on well-greased foil in baking pan and add hot water. Brush top of fish with remaining lemon juice and pour oil from frying pan over it.

Bake in 375° F. oven about 35 minutes or until fish flakes easily when tested with fork. Serves 8.

FISH STUFFED WITH   *Portugal*
SHRIMP CREAM

1 3- to 5-lb. whole fish	1 tbs. lemon juice
4 tbs. butter or margarine,	1 cup cooked shrimp
melted	¼ cup white wine
2 tbs. flour	¼ cup dry crumbs
salt and pepper	2 cups each chopped beets
1 cup milk	and peas, cooked
2 egg yolks, beaten	

Rub cavity of fish with salt. Melt half the butter over low heat, blend in flour, salt, pepper, add milk gradually. Cook, stirring constantly, until thickened. Cool slightly, add a little of the hot sauce to the egg yolks. Then add egg yolks, lemon juice and half the cooked shrimp to the sauce. Stuff fish with this cream and place on greased foil in a long baking dish. Pour any sauce that did not go into cavity around the fish, pour wine and remaining melted butter over the fish and sprinkle with crumbs.

Bake in 350° F. oven about 40 minutes. Add wine if necessary.

Garnish with remaining shrimp, chopped beets and peas. Serves 6 to 8.

Baking Fillets or Steaks

Oven cooking for fillets and steaks simplifies preparation, watching and clean-up. Bake as follows:

1. Sprinkle both sides of the fish with salt and pepper. Place the fish in a well-greased baking dish; or line baking pan with aluminum foil to avoid breaking the cooked fish. Grease foil very lightly.

2. Brush the fish generously with butter seasoned with a little lemon juice and grated onion to taste.

3. Bake in a moderate oven, 350° F. 20 to 25 minutes or until the fish flakes easily when tested with a fork.

Hard-frozen fish

Follow above directions and increase the baking time by 5 to 10 minutes.

Planked fish steaks

Oil a hardwood plank well, place in a cold oven and turn on heat. If you use a metal or glass oven platter, grease lightly before placing in oven. Brush steaks with oil, melted butter or margarine.

Oven poaching fillets or steaks

Fillets or steaks can be poached in liquid in the oven much the same as on top of the stove. Use the same liquids, see poaching instructions, page 184. Bake in 350° F. oven 20 to 25 minutes or until the fish flakes easily when tested with a fork.

Oven-frying fillets

A way of cooking fillets that is highly recommended is to bake them at a high temperature. This is called oven-frying.

A Cornell Extension Bulletin tells you exactly how to oven-fry:

"Baking at a high temperature gives the crisp crust and browned flavor of pan-fried fish yet uses less fat, takes much less attention and causes fewer cooking odors. Since flour, cornmeal and cracker crumbs do not brown well in the oven, use bread for crumbing. Prepare as follows:

1. Dip the fresh or partially thawed fillets into milk that has been heavily salted (1 tsp. salt to ½ cup milk). Then roll the fish in fine, dry bread crumbs that have been mixed with paprika (1 tsp. paprika to 1 cup bread crumbs).

2. Arrange the crumbed fillets, side by side, in a well-greased baking dish.

3. Drizzle a small amount of melted butter or other fat over the fish (about 2 tbs. for each pound of fish).

4. Bake the fish in a very hot oven, 500° F. for 8 to 10 minutes, or until the fish flakes easily when tested with a fork."

OVEN-FRIED OCEAN PERCH FILLETS

2 lbs. ocean perch fillets
1 cup flour
  salt and pepper to taste
1 egg, beaten

¼ cup milk
  fine dry bread crumbs
¼ cup butter or margarine,
  melted

Dredge fillets with seasoned flour. Combine egg with milk. Dip fillets into mixture, roll in bread crumbs and let stand for a few minutes to give bread crumbs a chance to dry.

Place on well-greased aluminum foil in a baking pan. Pour melted butter over the fish.

Bake in 500° F. oven 8 to 10 minutes, or until fish flakes easily when tested with a fork. Serve with or without sauce, see page 106. Serves 6.

VARIATIONS:

1. Eliminate egg, milk, flour and crumbs and use only melted butter.

2. Eliminate egg, milk, flour and crumbs, but spread a sauce on the fillets before oven frying, page 253.

STRIPED BASS IN MUSTARD COAT

2 to 3 lbs. fresh striped bass
  fillets
2 tbs. lemon juice
1 tbs. cold water
1 medium onion, thinly

sliced and separated into
  rings
4 tbs. soft butter or
  margarine
2 tbs. prepared mustard

Wash fillets in cold salted water, changing water two or three times. Drain and sprinkle with lemon juice mixed with cold water. Set aside for 10 minutes.

Line shallow roasting pan with foil and spread with onion rings. Dry fillets thoroughly and lay on onion. Make paste of butter and mustard and spread over entire fish.

Bake in 550° F. oven 10 to 15 minutes or until fish flakes easily when tested with a fork. Serves 6.

BLUEFISH FILLETS WITH TOMATO IN WINE SAUCE

2 2-lb. bluefish fillets, skin on (optional)	1 tsp. salt
	⅛ tsp. pepper
2 medium onions, minced	2 tbs. chopped fresh
1 garlic clove, crushed	parsley
3 tbs. butter or margarine	½ cup white wine
½ tbs. lemon juice	1 cup thick white sauce,
1 cup canned tomatoes, drained	page 123

Wash fish in cold salted water. Dry with absorbent paper.

Sauté onion and garlic lightly in butter. Place in baking pan, forming beds upon which to place the two fillets, skin side down. Squeeze lemon juice over fish. Place drained tomatoes on top of the fillets and season with salt and pepper. Sprinkle with parsley. Pour the wine around the fish.

Cover baking pan with aluminum foil. Make a small set of holes at each end of foil with fork.

Bake in 400° F. oven 20 minutes or until fish flakes easily when tested with a fork. Make white sauce.

Remove fish from baking pan, place on hot platter. Stir liquid from baking pan into white sauce in the top of a double boiler over boiling water, stir until smooth and pour over fish. Serves 8.

COD FILLETS IN SOUR CREAM *Reine Cod—Norway* SAUCE

2 lbs. filleted cod	½ cup crushed rusks or
2 tbs. salt	bread crumbs
1 tbs. vinegar	3 tbs. grated cheese
1 tbs. butter, melted	½ cup thick sour cream
1 egg white, lightly beaten	

Wash fish and rub with salt and vinegar. Allow to stand one hour. Dry well, brush with butter, dip in egg white, then in crumbs and cheese. Place fillets side by side in a well-greased oblong pan and bake in 350° F. oven until golden, about 20 minutes. Add a little boiling water from time to time. Remove fillets to a hot serving dish.

Mix the sour cream with the sauce in the baking pan, heat and serve separately. Serves 6.

FLOUNDER WITH ALMOND SAUCE

2 lbs. flounder fillets
¼ cup butter or margarine
¼ cup lemon juice
2 tsp. paprika

salt and pepper to taste
½ cup slivered blanched almonds

Place fillets in well-greased baking pan. Combine butter, lemon juice, paprika, salt and pepper and pour over fillets. Sprinkle with almonds.

Bake in 350° F. oven 20 to 25 minutes. Push pan under broiler, about three inches from heat unit, and broil 2 to 3 minutes. Serves 6.

VARIATIONS:

1. Roll fillets in seasoned flour before placing in baking pan.
2. Add 1 tbs. grated lemon rind and 2 tbs. chopped chives to sauce.

FLOUNDER FILLETS IN CHEESE SAUCE

2 lbs. flounder fillets, skinned
4 slices lean bacon
1 large onion, thinly sliced
2 large tomatoes, thinly sliced

salt and pepper to taste
1½ tbs. lemon juice
1 11-oz. can Cheddar cheese soup, or same amount very thick cheese sauce

Arrange ingredients in layers in a well-greased casserole in the following order: bacon, onions, tomatoes, flounder fillets seasoned with salt, pepper and lemon juice. Spread the undiluted cheese soup over the fillets.

Bake in 350° F. oven 20 minutes or until fish flakes easily when tested with a fork. Serves 6.

BAKED FLOUNDER IN SHRIMP SOUP

2 lbs. flounder fillets	salt to taste
2 cans frozen shrimp soup	2 tsp. lemon juice

Defrost shrimp soup sufficiently to spread.

Arrange half the fillets in a layer in a well-greased casserole. Sprinkle with salt and half the lemon juice. Spread 1 can shrimp soup over them. Lay the rest of the flounder over the soup. Sprinkle with salt and remaining lemon juice and top with the remaining can of soup.

Bake in 350° F. oven 25 minutes or until fish flakes easily when tested with a fork. Serves 6.

NOTE: Any fish and any soup of your choice can be prepared in this way.

FLOUNDER SOUR CREAM CASSEROLE

2 lbs. flounder fillets, skinned	toasted bread crumbs
1 tbs. lemon juice	3 tbs. sweet pickle relish
salt to taste	6 ripe olives, halved lengthwise and pitted
½ cup sour cream	½ tsp. paprika
½ can undiluted Cheddar cheese soup, or use same amount very thick cheese sauce	¼ tsp. nutmeg

Arrange fillets in a well-greased casserole and sprinkle with lemon juice and salt. Combine cream and cheese soup and spread over fillets. Sprinkle with a layer of bread crumbs.

Decorate top of casserole with diagonal strips of pickle relish, olive halves, paprika and nutmeg.

Bake in 350° F. oven 20 minutes or until fish flakes easily when tested with a fork. Serve in the casserole. Serves 6.

HALIBUT STEAK IN HERB SAUCE

2 lbs. halibut steaks or other fish steaks
1½ cups herb sauce, page 136

1 tbs. butter or margarine, melted
¼ cup dry bread crumbs

Place steaks in a well-greased baking pan. Pour herb sauce over them. Sprinkle with combined butter and crumbs.

Bake in 350° F. oven 25 to 30 minutes or until fish flakes easily when tested with a fork. Serves 6.

HALIBUT STEAKS WITH SPINACH AND WHITE SAUCE

2 lbs. halibut steaks with skin and bone removed
1½ cups white sauce, page 123
¼ tsp. sugar

¼ tsp. Worcestershire paprika to taste
dash nutmeg
1½ cups cooked chopped spinach

Make white sauce and add sugar, Worcestershire, paprika and nutmeg. Combine ½ cup of mixture with chopped spinach and spread in a well-greased baking dish. Lay fish on top of spinach and pour remaining sauce over it.

Bake in 350° F. oven 25 to 30 minutes or until fish flakes easily when tested with a fork. Serves 6.

RED SNAPPER IN ORANGE SAUCE

2 lbs. red snapper steaks
3 tbs. orange juice
1 tbs. grated orange rind
5 tbs. butter or margarine, melted

1 tsp. lemon juice
salt and pepper to taste
dash nutmeg
parsley

Place steaks in a single layer in a well-greased baking pan. Combine remaining ingredients and pour over fish.

Bake in 350° F. oven 25 to 30 minutes or until fish flakes easily when tested with a fork.

Remove to a heated serving platter, pour any sauce remaining in pan over fish and garnish with parsley. Serves 6.

SALMON STEAKS IN SOUR CREAM SAUCE

6 salmon steaks
salt and pepper to taste
½ cup flour
½ cup butter or margarine
½ cup white wine

1 medium onion, chopped
½ green pepper, seeded and finely diced
1 cup sour cream
thyme to taste

Season steaks with salt and pepper, dredge with flour and brown quickly on both sides in half the butter. Place in well-greased baking pan, add wine and cover with lid or aluminum foil.

Bake 10 minutes in 400° F. oven.

While salmon is baking, sauté onion and green pepper in remaining butter. Combine with sour cream and thyme and pour over steaks. Return uncovered pan to oven and bake about 15 minutes longer or until steaks flake easily when tested with a fork.

Serve with sauce from pan. Serves 6.

ED MOORE'S STRIPED BASS SPECIAL

2 7- or 8-lb. striped bass
—cut two fillets from
each fish

2 tbs. lemon juice

2 large onions sliced ¼-
inch thick

2 eggs

2 tbs. water

¾ tbs. fish seasoning

¾ cup dry bread crumbs,
cornmeal or matzo
meal

1¼ cups flour

¾ cup butter or
margarine, melted
freshly chopped
parsley

Soak fillets in cold salted water until free of blood, changing
water often. Add lemon juice to last change and let stand
another 15 minutes.

Line shallow baking pan with well-greased aluminum foil.
Scatter sliced onions over foil.

Beat eggs with water. Stir fish seasoning into crumbs.

Dry fish thoroughly. Dredge with flour, covering both sides
well. Dip only the skinless sides of fillets in beaten egg and
then cover egg with a generous coating of seasoned bread
crumbs. Place fillets skin side down on onion slices.

Bake in preheated 375° F. oven, basting with half the
butter after 5 minutes and with the remaining butter at the
end of 20 minutes. Continue baking another 15 to 20 minutes,
or until fish is white and flaky.

Garnish with parsley. Serves 8.

THE DAN MORRIS SPECIAL

3 lbs. fillets, skinned

1 cup white wine

1½ to 2 pounds white
seedless grapes
salt and pepper to taste

Marinate fish 30 minutes in wine.

Cut grapes in half and spread them in a baking pan. Place
fillets on grape bed and pour wine over them.

Bake in 350° F. oven 20 minutes or until fish flakes easily when tested with a fork.

Baste once or twice with wine from pan. Salt and pepper to taste after cooking. Serves 8.

BAKED FISH ALASKA

2 lbs. fish fillets
1 cup sour cream
½ cup chopped green
  onion tops

salt to taste
⅓ cup grated Parmesan
  cheese
paprika

Place fillets in well-greased baking pan. Combine cream, onion tops, salt and cheese. Spread over fillets.

Bake in 350° F. oven 20 to 25 minutes or until fish flakes easily when tested with a fork.

Sprinkle with paprika and serve. Serves 6.

FILLETS IN SOUR CREAM   *Austria*

1½ lb. white fish fillets,
  skinned and cut into
  small pieces
2 medium onions, finely
  chopped
1½ tbs. butter
  salt and pepper to taste

½ cup sour cream
1½ tbs. capers, chopped
1 tbs. parsley, finely
  chopped
juice and grated rind of
1 lemon

Fry onion in butter, add fish and salt and pepper. Very slowly stir in the sour cream, then the capers, parsley and lemon juice. Add grated lemon rind and stir very gently just until everything is well blended. Pour into a well-greased baking dish.

Bake in 350° F. oven 15 to 20 minutes, or until fish flakes when tested with a fork. Serves 4.

STEAKS WITH TOMATO, ONION, GREEN PEPPER AND OLIVES

4 ½-lb. fish steaks
½ cup oil
4 large onions, finely chopped
6 medium tomatoes, chopped
½ tsp. salt

½ tsp. pepper
¼ cup water or white wine
1 large green pepper, seeded, parboiled 6 to 8 minutes and sliced into rings
4 pitted black olives

Heat oil in skillet and lightly brown onions. Add tomatoes and continue cooking until medium soft.

Place steaks in well-greased baking dish. Cover with tomato and onion mixture, add salt, pepper and wine.

Bake about 15 minutes in 350° F. oven.

Decorate each steak with two green pepper rings with an olive placed in center and bake 10 minutes longer. Serves 4.

STEAKS 'N' SHERRY

6 large fish steaks
salt and pepper to taste
2 garlic cloves, chopped

juice of 2 lemons (less if this is too sour)
1 cup sherry
¼ cup oil

Place steaks in a deep greased baking pan. Sprinkle with salt and pepper. Combine garlic, lemon juice, sherry and oil and pour over fish.

Bake in 400° F. oven 20 minutes or until steaks flake easily when tested with a fork. Serves 6.

SEAFOOD THERMIDOR   *Australia*

4 fish fillets
12 oysters
milk
salt and pepper
¼ lb. mushrooms, sliced

2 tbs. butter or margarine
1½ tbs. flour
¼ cup dry white wine
¼ cup grated cheese

Arrange fish fillets in a buttered baking dish. Clean, shell and drain oysters, reserving the liquor, and arrange them on top of fillets. Strain the oyster liquor and add enough milk to make 1¼ cups. Season with salt and pepper, pour over fish and bake 30 minutes in 300° F. oven.

Cook mushrooms in butter until tender, stir in flour until smooth. Drain liquid from cooked fish and add it very gradually to flour and mushrooms. Stir until thickened, then add wine and cheese and pour over fish.

Brown under hot broiler and serve immediately. Serves 4.

VARIATIONS:

1. Reserve the oysters and put them on top of fillets just before browning under broiler.

2. Reserve the oysters and cook them in the sauce before pouring over fish.

BAKED FILLETS AND STEAKS WITH STUFFING

Don't limit yourself to bread stuffings for baked fillets and steaks. Fillets can be rolled around asparagus, pickles or another kind of fish or shellfish. Flounder or sole stuffed with salmon makes an interesting change, or try herring filled with caviar or with anchovies. Remember when combining two different fish that one of them should have a delicate flavor.

SOLE FILLETS WITH ASPARAGUS IN CELERY SAUCE

2 lbs. sole fillets, skinned
1 tsp. salt
  dash pepper
1 10-oz. pkg. frozen asparagus spears
1 10½-oz. can undiluted celery soup
1 tbs. lemon juice

1 tsp. Worcestershire, or to taste
2 tbs. grated Parmesan cheese
2 tbs. toasted slivered almonds
1 lemon, sliced
  watercress or parsley

Sprinkle both sides of fillets with salt and pepper and let stand.

Cook asparagus according to package directions, cut cooking time by 1 minute and drain well. Place 3 or 4 spears on each piece of fish. Roll fillets around asparagus and place in well-greased baking dish.

Combine celery soup, lemon juice and Worcestershire. Spoon over fish rolls. Sprinkle with cheese and almonds.

Bake in 350° F. oven 25 to 30 minutes or until fish flakes easily when tested with a fork.

Garnish with lemon slices and watercress. Serves 6.

STUFFED COD FILLETS

2 lbs. cod fillets, skinned
2 cups bread stuffing, page 240, or 1 pkg. prepared stuffing
2 tbs. melted butter or margarine
½ tsp. paprika
½ tsp. salt

Spread stuffing in a shallow, well-greased baking pan. Lay fish in a single layer on stuffing. Combine butter, paprika and salt and sprinkle over fish.

Bake in 350° F. oven 30 minutes or until fish flakes easily when tested with a fork. Serves 6.

VARIATION: Add ⅛ cup each, sautéed chopped onions and celery to prepared stuffing.

FISH TURBANS WITH BACON

12 small fish fillets, skinned
1 tsp. salt
dash pepper
1½ cups bread stuffing, page 240, or prepared stuffing
¼ cup melted butter or margarine
4 slices bacon, cut in thirds

Sprinkle fillets on both sides with salt and pepper. Roll them loosely and place them in 12 standard-sized greased muffin tins.

Press bread stuffing into balls and place one ball in center of each rolled fillet. Brush tops with butter and place ⅛ slice bacon over each turban.

Bake in 350° F. oven 25 to 30 minutes or until fish flakes easily when tested with a fork. Serves 6.

STUFFED POLLOCK FILLETS WITH MUSHROOM SAUCE

6 pollock fillets	2 cups soft bread crumbs
1 medium onion, chopped	salt and pepper to taste
1 medium stalk celery, chopped	1½ cups cream of mushroom soup, or creamed mushroom sauce, page 131
1 tbs. chopped parsley	
2 tbs. butter	

Lightly sauté onion, celery and parsley in butter. Add bread crumbs and salt and pepper. Spread over a well-greased baking dish and top with fillets. Pour mushroom soup over the fish.

Bake in 400° F. oven 15 to 20 minutes or until fish flakes easily when tested with a fork. Serves 6.

VARIATION: Add ½ tbs. lemon juice to white sauce, page 123, and substitute for mushroom soup. Garnish with lemon wedges.

STUFFED FILLETS WITH MUSHROOMS

2 lbs. fillets, skinned	1 10½-oz. can mushroom soup, undiluted
1 tsp. salt	6 large mushroom caps, or as many as fillets
pepper to taste	2 tbs. butter or margarine
1½ cups bread stuffing, page 240	

Season fillets with salt and pepper and roll each one around a ball of the bread stuffing. Place in a well-greased baking dish and top with the mushroom soup.

Bake in 350° F. oven 20 to 25 minutes or until fish flakes easily when tested with a fork. Add a little water if fish is getting too dry.

Sauté mushroom caps in butter and place one on top of each rolled fillet. Serves 6.

HERRING WITH ANCHOVIES AND CAVIAR

Olsen's Dream Dish
—Norway

4 fresh herring, filleted
4 fillets of anchovy, finely chopped
2 tbs. Norwegian caviar

½ cup fine crumbs
salt and pepper to taste
1 tbs. cold butter
1 glass sherry

Clean fish. Cover each fillet with a layer of anchovy mixed with caviar. Roll and fasten with wooden picks. Coat with bread crumbs, salt and pepper the fillets and pack tightly together in buttered baking dish. Dot with butter, add sherry and bake 30 minutes in 375° F. oven. Serves 4.

FISH STEAKS WITH OYSTER STUFFING

4 center cut fish steaks, ½-inch thick
2 tbs. lemon juice
salt and pepper to taste

2 to 4 cups oyster stuffing, page 240, depending on size of steaks
6 tbs. melted butter

Place two steaks in well-greased baking dish, cover with lemon juice and sprinkle with salt and pepper. Spread 1 to 2 cups stuffing on each steak, depending on size and top with remaining steaks. Fasten each sandwich with small skewers and brush with melted butter.

Bake in 350° F. oven about 40 minutes or until steaks flake easily. Baste frequently with melted butter. Serves 6 to 8.

NOTE: If any stuffing is left over, spread it on top of the steaks before baking.

VARIATIONS:

1. Substitute for the oyster stuffing any of the stuffings on page 240, and use with either steaks or thick fillets.
2. Add chopped shellfish to plainer stuffings.

FORTY-NINER FILLETS

This recipe grew up with the West where it has fed as few as four and as many as 49 at a sitting. Just allow one fillet per guest and increase other ingredients accordingly.

1 fillet, about ½ lb. per person, cut about ⅜-inch thick	1 slice bacon, chopped, per person
½ dill pickle per person	¼ cup dry white wine per person

Wrap each fillet around the pickle, secure with wooden picks and sprinkle with bacon. Place in greased baking dish, or individual dishes, and pour wine over each pickle roll. Cover dish with aluminum foil and bake in 450° F. oven 10 minutes. Remove foil. Bake 2 minutes longer and serve.

VARIATION: Roll fillet around the ½ pickle, and roll a strip of bacon around the fillet. Secure with wooden picks and bake in 500° F. oven until bacon is brown.

SALMON ROLLED IN FLOUNDER FILLETS

2 lbs. flounder fillets	salt and pepper to taste
1 lb. salmon, cut in chunks	1½ cups shrimp sauce, page 118

Split fillets down the middle lengthwise and cut away line of bone usually left in by fish market. Season fish with salt and pepper. Roll fillets around salmon chunks and pack snugly into well-greased baking dish. Cover with shrimp sauce.

Bake in 350° F. oven 20 to 25 minutes or until fish flakes easily when tested with a fork. Serves 6.

VARIATIONS:

1. Roll different combinations of fish together.
2. Substitute large shrimp or scallops for salmon and cover with white sauce flavored with lemon juice.

Flaked Fish and Shellfish Loaves

Use any flaked or ground fish or shellfish in these recipes or make loaves from some of the fried fish cake mixtures on page 209.

A glass baking dish will let you see the loaf. Remove it from the oven when it is golden brown on all sides. Check to be sure the center is firm. Allow 45 to 60 minutes in an average 2¾-inch-deep baking dish. The shallower the loaf, the more quickly it will bake. If it is too shallow it may dry out before the sides brown. If you like a loaf that is crusty on the outside, turn oven up to 450° F. for the last 10 minutes. If you like a very moist loaf, with only the top browned, set baking dish in a shallow pan of hot water.

HALIBUT LOAF

2 cups cooked halibut or other fish, flaked
1½ cups soft bread cubes
1 tbs. grated green pepper
2 tbs. grated onion
2 tbs. grated or very finely chopped celery
1 tbs. chopped pimiento
¾ cup fish, chicken or meat stock
salt and pepper to taste
2 eggs, beaten
½ cup cream or milk

Combine all ingredients, mix well and press into a 2¾-inch-deep greased loaf pan.

Bake in 350° F. oven 1 hour, or until loaf is firm in the center and golden brown on the outside. Serves 6.

SALMON LOAF   *Ireland*

1½ cups canned or cooked salmon, flaked
½ cup melted butter
2 cups mashed potatoes
1 cup scalded milk
½ medium onion, grated

1 tsp. salt
¾ tsp. pepper
juice of ½ lemon
2 tbs. chopped parsley
3 eggs, beaten

Mix half the melted butter and all other ingredients, except eggs, in a bowl. Stir eggs thoroughly into mixture. Turn into a well-greased 2½-inch-deep baking dish.

Bake about 50 minutes in 350° F. oven, or until loaf is firm and browned on top.

Pour over loaf remaining butter and serve hot or cold. Serves 6.

TUNA LOAF

2 7-oz. cans tuna, drained and flaked, or use canned salmon with bones removed
1 cup soft bread crumbs
½ cup milk or cream
1 egg, lightly beaten

salt and pepper to taste
½ lb. Cheddar cheese, sliced
1 green pepper, par-boiled for 8 minutes, seeded and sliced
chopped pimiento

Combine tuna, bread crumbs, milk, egg, salt and pepper. Place half the mixture in a well-greased 2¾-inch-deep loaf pan. Cover with a layer of sliced Cheddar cheese; add remaining mixture.

Bake in 350° F. oven 25 minutes. Top with a second layer

of sliced cheese and decorate with green pepper and pimiento slices.

Bake 20 minutes longer, or until loaf is firm and cheese a golden brown. Serves 6.

FISH LOAF WITH LOBSTER SAUCE

1 lb. chopped raw fish	4 egg whites, stiffly
2 cups light cream	beaten
2½ cups soft bread crumbs	2 cups lobster sauce,
1 tbs. butter or margarine	page 127, heated
salt and celery salt to	
taste	

Heat cream to scalding, add bread crumbs, butter, salt and celery salt and mix well. Stir fish into mixture. Cook gently until thoroughly heated. Take from heat, cool and fold in egg whites. Pour into a 3-inch-deep casserole set in a shallow pan of water.

Bake in 350° F. oven 60 minutes. Slice and serve covered with lobster sauce. Serves 6.

FRENCH LOAF STUFFED WITH TUNA

2 7-oz. cans tuna, flaked	1 tbs. grated onion
1 loaf French bread	1 cup grated cheese
1 tsp. prepared mustard	2 tbs. chopped sweet
¼ cup butter or margarine,	gherkin or sweet pickle
melted	relish

Slice top off the loaf of bread, remove center leaving a one-inch-thick shell and spread with a mixture of mustard and butter.

Combine onion, cheese, flaked tuna and relish and fill cavity in the bread with the mixture. Put top of loaf back in place, slice part way through at about 1½-inch intervals and wrap in aluminum foil.

Bake in 450° F. oven 30 minutes. Serves 6.

FRENCH LOAF STUFFED WITH OYSTERS: Substitute oysters cooked just until their edges start to curl for the tuna. Eliminate pickle. Add 1 garlic clove, finely minced, to melted butter.

Vegetables with Fish or Shellfish Stuffing

Vegetables baked with a fish or shellfish stuffing can be served as a side dish or as a main course. Hot, cold or sliced and fried, most of them are just as good the second day. Avocados are the only exception. They should be eaten at once.

The stuffings in these recipes can be interchanged, just cook longer for a wide, deep dish; reduce time if the stuffing is in something narrow and shallow. Be sure, of course, that the stuffed vegetable is done through.

Don't stop with the recipes in this section. Some of the stuffing recipes for baked fish and shellfish are suitable for vegetables.

OYSTERS BAKED IN POTATOES

12 shucked oysters, drained	½ tsp. paprika
6 large baking potatoes	butter
½ cup oil	salt and pepper to taste
2 tbs. lemon juice	⅓ cup milk
1 tbs. wine vinegar	½ cup buttered bread
1 tsp. prepared mustard	crumbs
1 tsp. salt	2 tbs. grated cheese

Bake potatoes in their jackets in 450° F. oven about 1 hour or until done.

Combine next 6 ingredients and marinate oysters for one hour, while potatoes bake.

Cut a slice from flat side of potatoes, scoop out and mash pulp with butter, salt and pepper and milk. Refill shells ¾ full with mixture. Press two marinated oysters into each, cover with bread crumbs, top with grated cheese and return to oven. Reduce heat to 350° F. and bake 10 to 15 minutes, or until crumbs are brown. Serves 6.

SARDINES IN BAKED POTATOES   *Portugal*

6 canned boneless
Portuguese sardines
6 large baking potatoes
2 tbs. butter
⅓ cup milk

salt and pepper to taste
2 tbs. melted butter for
brushing
1 cup thick white sauce,
page 123

Bake potatoes in their jackets in 450° F. oven about 1 hour or until soft. Slit lengthwise, scoop out pulp and mash thoroughly with butter, milk and salt and pepper.

Put a sardine into each potato skin and pour white sauce over them. Pipe a border of mashed potato through a bag fitted with a rose tube around each sardine and form a rosette at each end. Brush with butter and brown in a hot oven or under the broiler. Serves 6.

SHRIMP-STUFFED EGGPLANT

1 lb. fresh shrimp, or a 9-
to 10-oz. can shrimp
¾ cup liquor from cooked
or canned shrimp
1 large eggplant
1 cup canned tomato
puree

½ tsp. crushed thyme
salt and pepper to taste
½ medium onion, chopped
1 garlic clove, finely
chopped
⅓ cup butter or margarine
¾ cup dry bread crumbs

Shell and devein shrimp and simmer gently in water to cover until they turn pink, about 3 minutes. Drain and retain liquid.

Cut eggplant in half lengthwise. Scoop out pulp, leaving a ¼-inch-thick shell. Turn shells upside down in a pan of cold water. Chop pulp and combine with shrimp liquor, tomato sauce, thyme, salt and pepper. Simmer about 10 minutes or until eggplant is tender.

Cook onion and garlic in butter until soft, stir into bread crumbs.

Add shrimp to tomato mixture. Fill eggplant shells with alternate layers of mixture and buttered crumbs, topping with crumbs. Bake in 400° F. oven 30 to 40 minutes, or until crumbs are brown. Serves 6.

NOTE: Halved small eggplants can be used for individual servings. Shorten baking time accordingly.

FISH-STUFFED BAKED POTATOES

1 lb. cooked fish, flaked
4 large baking potatoes
1 tbs. butter
2 tbs. minced onion

1 cup hot milk
1 cup grated cheese
salt and pepper to taste

Bake potatoes in their jackets in very hot oven, 450° F. to 500° F., 45 to 60 minutes, or until soft.

Slice off top of each potato. Scoop out insides and mash with butter, onion, hot milk and salt and pepper. Stir in fish, stuff mixture back into shells and sprinkle with cheese.

Bake in 375° F. oven 25 to 30 minutes, or until cheese melts. Serves 4.

STUFFED TOMATOES AND PEPPERS

The red and green colors of this dish are nice during the Christmas season.

2 cups cooked fish or
   shellfish, flaked
6 medium tomatoes
6 medium green peppers
1½ cups bread crumbs or
   cooked rice

2 eggs, beaten
1 small onion, very finely
   chopped
salt and pepper
12 slices Cheddar cheese

Slice tops from tomatoes and peppers and scoop out pulp and seeds. Save tops.

Parboil peppers in water 5 minutes, remove and turn upside down to drain.

Chop tomato pulp, stir in bread crumbs, eggs, onion, flaked fish and salt and pepper. Stuff tomatoes and peppers with mixture and place in baking dish with about ¼ inch hot water.

Bake 20 minutes in 350° F. oven. Remove from oven and place slice of cheese on top of each pepper and tomato. Return pepper tops to tomatoes, and tomato tops to peppers. Return to oven and bake another 15 minutes. Add a little more water to pan if necessary. Serves 6.

LEFTOVERS AND ZUCCHINI

2 or 3 cups leftover cooked fish, flaked	½ cup bread crumbs
6 medium zucchini	3 tbs. chopped parsley
2 medium onions, chopped	½ cup grated Parmesan cheese
¾ tsp. salt	3 cups tomato sauce, page 138
¾ tsp. pepper	

Wash zucchini and place in salted boiling water to cover. Boil 5 to 8 minutes. It should still be firm but slightly softened. Drain, cool and cut in half lengthwise. Scoop out pulp to form pockets in each half. Combine pulp with fish, onions, salt, pepper, bread crumbs, parsley and ¼ cup of the cheese. Blend well and fill zucchini with mixture.

Place in well-greased baking dish. Top with tomato sauce and sprinkle with remaining cheese.

Bake in 350° F. oven 25 to 30 minutes, or until cheese is brown. Serves 6.

Shellfish Baked in Seashells
or Individual Small
Casseroles

No manmade ovenware makes a more satisfactory serving dish for fish than seashells. There is nothing difficult about preparing stuffed shell dishes; do it exactly as if you were using small, individual casseroles.

Grease the insides of shells before filling them. Be careful not to overcook, particularly when using small shells.

STUFFED CLAM SHELLS

1 pt. clams, drained and chopped (save shells)	3 tbs. flour
2 tbs. finely chopped onion	1 egg, beaten
1 medium stalk celery, chopped	1 tsp. salt
1 tbs. chopped parsley	garlic powder to taste
6 tbs. melted butter	1 tsp. lemon juice
	dry bread crumbs

Lightly sauté onion, celery and parsley in 4 tbs. of the melted butter. Blend in flour until smooth, add clams and cook slowly, stirring constantly until thickened. Remove from heat and stir a little of the sauce into the egg. Stir it back into the hot sauce. Add salt, garlic salt and lemon juice. Place in well-greased clam shells or individual casseroles. Blend remaining butter into dry bread crumbs and spread over mixture.

Bake in 400° F. oven 10 minutes or until brown. Serves 4.

VARIATIONS:

1. Add ½ cup chopped sautéed or canned mushrooms.

2. Sprinkle grated cheese over bread crumb topping.
3. Add crushed crisp-fried bacon to mixture.

CRAB MEAT IN SHELLS

1 lb. crab meat, cut in chunks
1 3-oz. can sliced mushrooms, drained and liquid reserved
1 cup thick white sauce, see recipes page 123
¼ cup liquid from mushrooms or thin cream
salt and white pepper to taste
½ cup cooked peas or asparagus tips, cut in small pieces
grated cheese
paprika

Combine all ingredients except cheese and paprika. Fill wellgreased shells or individual casseroles with the mixture. Top with grated cheese and sprinkle with a little paprika.

Bake in 350° F. oven 20 to 25 minutes or until brown. Serves 6.

NOTE: Lobster meat can be used in place of crab meat.

STUFFED LOBSTER

2 1-lb. live lobsters
2 cups soft bread cubes
3 tbs. butter or margarine, melted
onion salt to taste
garlic salt to taste
white pepper to taste
grated cheese
paprika

Follow instructions for killing lobster and preparing for stuffing, page 240.

Combine bread cubes, butter and seasonings and stuff lightly into body cavities and over surface of tail. Sprinkle with grated cheese and paprika.

Bake in 400° F. oven 20 to 25 minutes or until lightly browned. Serves 2.

NOTE: If your prefer a more moist stuffing, stir beaten egg into bread cubes.

STUFFED LOBSTER À LA KING

2 2-lb. boiled lobsters	salt to taste
2 tbs. butter	¼ cup sherry
2 tbs. flour	2 egg yolks
1 cup cream	2 tbs. butter for dotting
1 cup mushrooms	½ cup fine crumbs

Split lobsters, crack claws, remove meat and cut into pieces. Make white sauce of butter, flour and cream, page 123. Add lobster meat, mushrooms, salt and wine. Stir a little of the sauce into the egg yolks. Then stir yolks slowly into the stuffing. Return to shell, sprinkle with crumbs and dot with butter.

Bake in 400° F. oven 15 minutes. Serve with toast and butter. Serves 4.

LOBSTER TAILS WITH DIAVOLO SAUCE *Australia*

4 lobster tails, in shell	1 tbs. chopped parsley
¼ cup olive oil	1 tsp. oregano
2 garlic cloves, finely minced	1 tsp. salt
1 1 lb. 4½-oz. can tomatoes	⅛ tsp. cayenne
	⅛ tsp. pepper

Heat oil in saucepan, add garlic and brown lightly. Add tomatoes, herbs and seasonings. Simmer 30 minutes.

Split lobster tails lengthwise. Remove dark vein. Place in greased casserole and cover with sauce.

Bake in 350° F. oven 20 to 30 minutes. Serves 4.

MUSSELS ON HALF SHELL IN PARSLEY SAUCE

Italy

4 lbs. large mussels
1 large garlic clove, slivered lengthwise
3 tbs. oil
¼ tsp. oregano

salt and pepper to taste
2 cups mussel liquor, strained
10 sprigs fresh Italian parsley, finely chopped

Clean and remove mussels from shells, page 60. Discard half of each shell. Return mussels to remaining shells and arrange in a shallow baking pan.

Heat oil in saucepan, add garlic and cook until reddish brown. Season with oregano, salt and pepper and stir in mussel liquor. Bring to a boil, remove from stove, add chopped parsley and pour sauce over mussels.

Bake in 500° F. oven 15 minutes. Serve with hard Italian whole wheat biscuits or well-toasted Italian or French bread. Serves 6.

MUSSELS ON HALF SHELL IN TOMATO SAUCE

Neapolitan Style
—Italy

4 lbs. large mussels
3 tbs. oil
1 large garlic clove, slivered lengthwise
1 6-oz. can Italian tomato paste

½ cup water
½ cup strained mussel liquor
¼ tsp. oregano
salt and pepper to taste

Clean and remove mussels from shells, page 60. Discard half of each shell. Return mussels to shells and lay in a shallow baking pan.

Heat oil in saucepan. Add garlic and cook until it turns a reddish brown. Add tomato paste, water and mussel liquor. Add oregano and salt and pepper. Simmer 45 minutes.

Pour sauce over mussels in baking pan.

Bake in 500° F. oven 15 minutes. Serve with hard whole wheat Italian biscuits, obtainable in Italian bakeries, or well-toasted Italian or French bread. Serve with wine or beer. Serves 6.

OYSTERS ON THE HALF SHELL I   *In butter*

36 oysters
4 tbs. butter, melted

salt and pepper to taste
lemon wedges

Clean and remove oysters from shells, page 53.

Place oysters in deep half of oyster shell on baking sheet or pan. Brush with melted butter and sprinkle with seasoning.

Bake in 400° F. oven about 10 minutes, or until edges of oysters begin to curl. Serve with lemon wedges. Serves 6.

NOTES:

1. Additional seasonings such as a little grated onion, diced bacon, garlic or cheese may be added.

2. Clams may be placed in a well-greased casserole and prepared in the same way. Serve on French bread or buttered toast.

OYSTERS ON THE HALF SHELL II   *In spicy sauce*

36 oysters
4 slices bacon, diced
1 medium onion, chopped
1 stalk celery, chopped
2 tbs. chopped green
   pepper

1 tbs. frozen, undiluted
   lemonade
2 tbs. catsup
½ tsp. mustard
2 drops Tabasco

Clean and remove oysters from shells, page 53.

Start bacon frying, add onion, celery and green pepper and sauté until tender. Pour off excess bacon fat. Stir in lemonade, catsup, mustard and Tabasco.

Thoroughly clean deep halves of shells and place on a

cookie sheet or shallow baking dish. Return oysters to the half shell and cover with the bacon mixture.

Bake in 350° F. oven about 10 minutes, or until edges of oysters start to curl and sauce is thoroughly heated. Serves 6.

NOTE: This recipe can be prepared in a buttered casserole. Make a layer of the oysters and cover with the bacon mixture.

OYSTERS ON THE HALF SHELL III   *Au gratin*

36 oysters	1 tsp. prepared mustard
2 tbs. minced onion	salt and pepper to taste
2 tbs. butter	½ cup bread crumbs
4 tbs. flour	4 tbs. butter
1 cup rich milk	½ tsp. paprika
½ cup oyster liquor	1 cup grated cheese
1 egg, beaten	

Clean and remove oysters from shells, page 53.

Chop oysters and retain deeper half of shells. Cook onion in 2 tbs. butter in the top of a double boiler, stir in flour and gradually add milk and oyster liquor. Stir until smooth and thickened. Remove from heat, cool slightly, stir in egg, mustard, salt and pepper and oysters.

Fill thoroughly cleaned shells with mixture. Brown crumbs in remaining butter, add paprika and sprinkle over shells. Top with grated cheese and place in a shallow baking pan or sheet.

Bake in 400° F. oven about 10 minutes, or until top is brown. Serves 6.

NOTE: This mixture can be poured over toast in a well-greased casserole, topped with grated cheese and baked.

OYSTERS ON THE HALF SHELL IV   *On rock salt*

36 oysters
  rock salt to almost fill
  baking pan
1 1-lb. can Italian-style
  zucchini in tomato sauce
⅓ cup melted butter or
  margarine

1 cup fine dry bread
  crumbs
1 tbs. dry sherry
6 drops Tabasco
  lemon wedges
  grated cheese

Clean and remove oysters from shells, page 53. Fill baking pan almost to top with rock salt. Inbed thoroughly cleaned deep half of shells in the salt.

Mash zucchini, add melted butter, bread crumbs, sherry and Tabasco. Mix into a paste. Divide half the paste over the shells and place an oyster on top of each. Cover with remaining paste and sprinkle with grated cheese.

Bake in 400° F. oven about 10 minutes, or until edges of oysters start to curl and sauce is thoroughly heated. Serve with lemon wedges. Serves 6.

NOTE: Highly seasoned, finely ground cooked spinach can be used instead of zucchini.

BAKED SCALLOPS IN SHELLS

1 lb. bay scallops; if not
  obtainable, cut sea
  scallops in half
3 tbs. salt
1 3-oz. can sliced mush-
  rooms, drained, or ¼ lb.
  fresh
1 tbs. melted butter or
  margarine

2 cups medium white
  sauce, page 123
  salt and pepper to taste
½ tsp. prepared mustard
3 tbs. grated cheese or
  buttered soft crumbs
  paprika
1 tbs. parsley flakes

Simmer scallops in water to cover 3 to 4 minutes. Add salt for last minute. Drain and remove shell particles.

Sauté mushrooms lightly in butter. Combine with white sauce and scallops. Add salt and pepper and mustard. Divide mixture among 6 well-greased scallop shells or small individual casseroles. Top with grated cheese, sprinkle with paprika and parsley flakes.

Bake in 400° F. oven 10 minutes, or until cheese browns. Serves 6.

NOTE: Lobster and crab recipes can be used for filling scallop shells. Mushroom liquid, clam broth and cream can be combined for a richer white sauce.

Shellfish, Flaked Cooked Fish and Canned Fish in Casserole

CRAB MEAT, SHRIMP, AND FLAKED FISH CASSEROLE

1 cup flaked crab meat	1 tsp. salt
¾ cup cooked shrimp, diced	1½ cups frozen shrimp soup
1 cup cooked fish, flaked	⅓ cup mushroom liquid
3 hard-cooked eggs, sliced	¼ cup cream or evaporated milk, undiluted
1 3-oz. can mushrooms, chopped, liquid reserved	1 cup dry bread crumbs
	¼ cup butter, melted
1 cup American cheese, diced	

Arrange layers of sliced egg, flaked fish, shrimp and crab meat in a buttered casserole. Top with mushrooms and cheese and season with salt. Combine shrimp soup, mushroom liquid and cream and pour over casserole. Top with bread crumbs mixed with melted butter.

Bake in 350° oven 35 to 45 minutes. Serves 6.

SCALLOPED LOBSTER CASSEROLE

3 cups lobster meat, cut in small chunks	5 tbs. butter or margarine, melted
1 cup light cream	onion salt to taste
1 cup milk	salt and pepper to taste
2 eggs, beaten	2 cups dry bread crumbs
	paprika

Mix lobster chunks, cream, milk, eggs, 4 tbs. of the butter and seasonings. Pour into well-greased casserole, top with dry bread crumbs sprinkled with remaining melted butter and paprika.

Bake in 350° F. oven 30 minutes, or until mixture is thoroughly heated and browned on top. Serves 6.

VARIATIONS:

1. For tangy flavor, add a little prepared mustard, lemon juice and a few drops of Worcestershire.
2. Add ½ cup sautéed or canned mushrooms.
3. Substitute cooked shrimp or scallops for lobster.

OYSTER-MUSHROOM CASSEROLE

1½ pts. shucked oysters, liquor reserved	⅓ cup oyster liquor
¼ lb. mushrooms, sliced melted butter	3 cups whipped potatoes (prepared variety can be used)
1 can cream of mushroom soup, undiluted	1 egg white, lightly beaten
⅓ cup milk or cream	

Cook mushrooms in butter in the top of a double boiler over medium heat. Add mushroom soup and milk. Set over simmering water to keep warm.

Simmer oysters in their own liquor until edges begin to curl.

Spread half of whipped potatoes in well-greased casserole. Combine oysters and liquor with mushroom sauce, stir and pour over layer of potatoes in casserole. Top with remaining whipped potatoes, brush with egg white and sprinkle with a little paprika.

Bake in 350° F. oven 20 minutes, or until golden brown. Garnish with parsley and serve. Serves 6.

SCALLOPED OYSTERS IN CASSEROLE

1½ pts. shucked oysters, drained	¼ tsp. Worcestershire
½ cup butter, melted	½ cup cream
2 cups small bread cubes salt and pepper to taste	⅓ cup oyster liquor
	1 tbs. grated cheese

Pour melted butter over bread cubes, mix thoroughly and season with salt and pepper. Place one-third mixture on bottom of a buttered casserole, cover with half the oysters and repeat the layers of bread cubes and oysters. Mix the Worcestershire with the cream and oyster liquor and pour over contents of casserole. Top with remaining buttered bread cubes and sprinkle with grated cheese.

Bake in 350° F. oven 30 minutes or until brown. Serves 6.

ROE-MUSHROOM CASSEROLE

Shad roe is considered a great American delicacy, but that is basically because it is scarce. Shad are fished for and caught both by commercial fishermen and sports fishermen only a few months of the year and in not too many places. However, all female fish have roe and almost all of them compare well with

shad roe. Try cod, bass, flounder roe, but *not* roe of the puffer
family (blowfish, etc.).

3 lbs. roe	½ tsp. salt
36 very large mushroom caps	½ tsp. pepper
	½ cup sherry
¼ cup butter or margarine	1½ cups medium cream
juice of 2 lemons	

Sauté mushroom caps lightly in butter. Lay caps, hollow side
up, in well-greased casserole.

Simmer roe about 10 minutes in boiling water to cover.
Drain, cool and remove the membrane. Combine roe with
lemon juice, salt and pepper and fill each mushroom cap.
Mix sherry and cream and spoon over each cap.

Bake in 375° F. oven about 20 minutes. Serves 6 to 8.

SALMON-POTATO CASSEROLE

2 cups canned salmon, drained and flaked	grated
	¼ tsp. salt
2 cups mashed potatoes	¼ tsp. cayenne
1 cup medium white sauce, hot, page 123	1 cup dry bread crumbs
	4 tbs. butter or margarine, melted
1½ cups American cheese,	

Butter a 2-quart casserole and line bottom with mashed
potatoes.

Make white sauce, page 123, in the top of a double boiler
and add cheese, salt, and cayenne, stirring until cheese is
melted. Pour half over mashed potatoes.

Add salmon to remaining sauce and mix well. Pour over
contents of casserole. Stir melted butter into dry bread
crumbs and sprinkle over sauce. Bake in 350° F. oven 20 to
25 minutes. Serves 6.

SARDINE-POTATO CASSEROLE

2 3¾-oz cans Maine
sardines
2 tbs. chopped onion
2 tbs. butter or mar-
garine, melted
2 cups milk
2 tbs. flour

1 cup grated cheese
2 tbs. Worcestershire
1½ tsp. salt
dash pepper
6 medium potatoes,
cooked and sliced ⅜-
inch thick

Cook onion in butter until tender. Stir milk into flour until smooth. Gradually add to onion and butter and cook over low heat until thickened. Add cheese, Worcestershire and salt and pepper and stir until sauce is smooth. Remove from heat.

Arrange half the potatoes in a well-greased 2-quart casserole. Add all but 6 sardines and cover with the remaining potatoes. Add cheese sauce and garnish with the 6 remaining sardines. Cover and bake in 350° F. oven 15 minutes. Remove cover and bake another 15 to 20 minutes, or until thoroughly heated. Serves 6.

NOTE: Aluminum foil can be used instead of a casserole cover.

PORTUGUESE SARDINE-TOAST CASSEROLE

1 3¾-oz. can Portuguese
sardines
8 slices white bread, crusts
removed
1 cup milk
2 eggs, beaten
¼ cup butter or margarine

1 cup thick white sauce,
page 123
¼ cup grated Parmesan
cheese, or to taste
4 small tomatoes
1 cup canned spinach
puree

Dip bread in milk and then in beaten egg. Fry lightly in butter.

Skin and bone the sardines, mash with a fork, mix with

white sauce and cheese. Spread on the bread, top each slice with a half tomato and place in a well-greased casserole.

Bake in 350° F. oven 10 to 15 minutes. Just before serving, garnish with spinach puree, arranging it in little heaps with a spoon. Serves 4.

NOTE: Potatoes, rice or noodles may be substituted for bread.

SHRIMP-RICE CASSEROLE

1½ cups cooked, shelled and deveined shrimp, broken into pieces	½ cup catsup
	¼ tsp. Tabasco
	1 tsp. Worcestershire
1 cup cream	salt to taste
1 cup milk	½ cup dry crumbs
2 cups cooked rice	5 tbs. butter, melted
1½ tbs. butter	

Combine shrimp, cream and milk in the top of a rinsed double boiler over boiling water. Heat slowly, add cooked rice and stir. When hot, stir in butter, catsup, Tabasco and Worcestershire. Add salt if wanted, but very carefully. Tabasco and Worcestershire already are highly seasoned.

Pour mixture into well-greased casserole. Brown crumbs in butter and sprinkle on top. Bake in 350° F. oven 30 minutes. Serves 4.

NOTE: Cooked lobster meat may be substituted for shrimp.

SHRIMP-CHEESE CASSEROLE

1½ cups small cooked, shelled and deveined shrimp, broken into pieces	removed
	2 cups grated American cheese
	salt and pepper to taste
½ cups butter, melted	3 large eggs
2 cups ½-inch white bread cubes, crusts	2 cups milk

Stir melted butter into bread cubes. Spread ⅓ of cubes in well-greased casserole. Cover with half of shrimp, then half of cheese and sprinkle with salt and pepper. Repeat layers and top with remaining bread cubes. Beat eggs into milk and pour slowly over casserole, covering entire top.

Set casserole in a pan of hot water and bake in 350° F. oven 45 to 60 minutes, or until it is browned on top and sides. Serves 4.

NOTE: Cooked lobster meat or scallops may be substituted for shrimp.

DEVILED TUNA CASSEROLE

2 7-oz. cans tuna	¼ cup flour
1 tbs. grated onion	½ tsp. salt
1 tbs. lemon juice	dash cayenne
2 tbs. chopped parsley	2 cups milk
½ tsp. garlic salt	1 cup soft bread cubes
¼ cup butter or margarine	½ cup crushed potato chips

Drain tuna, break into large pieces, add onion, lemon juice, parsley and garlic salt.

Melt butter, blend in flour, salt and cayenne. Slowly add milk, stirring constantly, and cook until thickened. Fold in bread cubes and tuna mixture. Place in a well-greased casserole and cover with crushed potato chips. Bake in 400° F. oven 15 to 20 minutes. Serves 6.

TUNA, CORN AND MACARONI CASSEROLE

2 7-oz. cans tuna, drained and broken into large pieces	¼ cup butter or margarine
	1 20-oz. can cream-style corn
1 8-oz. pkg. macaroni	¾ cup milk
½ cup chopped onion	¾ tsp. salt
¼ cup chopped green pepper	dash pepper
	paprika

Cook macaroni, as directed on package, drain and set aside. Fry onion and green pepper in butter until tender. Combine with macaroni, tuna, corn, milk, salt and pepper in a well-greased casserole and sprinkle with paprika.

Bake in 350° F. oven 45 to 50 minutes. Serves 6.

SCALLOPED TUNA AND CHEESE CASEROLE

2 7-oz. cans tuna, drained and flaked	¾ cup stuffed olives, sliced
2 cups medium white sauce, page 123	½ small green pepper, seeded and minced
1¾ cups grated American cheese	2 cups soft bread cubes
	¾ cup cornflakes, crushed

Make white sauce in the top of a double boiler over boiling water, add 1¼ cups of the cheese and stir well until melted. Add olives, green pepper and tuna fish.

Alternate layers of bread cubes and tuna mixture in buttered casserole, starting with a bread layer and ending with tuna mix. Top with cornflakes and sprinkle with remaining cheese.

Bake in 350° F. oven 20 minutes. Serves 6.

TUNA-RICE CASSEROLE

1 7-oz. can flaked tuna, drained	2 cups medium white sauce, page 123
½ tsp. paprika	2 cups cooked rice
1 cup grated American cheese	¼ cup dry bread crumbs
	2 to 3 tbs. butter or margarine, melted

Blend paprika and cheese into hot white sauce, stirring well until cheese is melted.

Arrange layers of rice, tuna and sauce in buttered 2-quart casserole. Top with crumbs that have been blended with melted butter. Bake in 350° F. to 375° F. oven 30 minutes. Serves 4.

TUNA-LASAGNE CASSEROLE

2 7-oz cans tuna
1 1 lb. 12-oz. can Italian tomatoes
1 8-oz. can tomato sauce
1 2¼-oz. pkg. spaghetti sauce mix
1 tsp. oregano
1 tsp. sugar
1 garlic clove, finely chopped
1 8-oz. pkg. lasagne
¾ pound ricotta or creamed cottage cheese
½ pound mozzarella cheese, thinly sliced
½ cup grated Parmesan cheese

Combine tomatoes, tomato sauce, spaghetti sauce, oregano, sugar and garlic. Simmer, uncovered, 30 minutes, stirring occasionally.

Drain tuna. Break into large pieces. Add to above mixture. Cook lasagne according to package directions. Place half lasagne in a well-greased baking dish. Cover with layers in this order: one-third the tuna sauce, half the ricotta cheese, half the mozzarella cheese. Add remaining lasagne and repeat the layers. Top with the remaining tuna sauce and sprinkle with Parmesan cheese. Bake in 350° F. oven 30 minutes.

Remove from oven and let stand 15 minutes before serving. Serves 6.

NOTE: The sauce will be improved if you make it a day or two before it is needed.

Fish Pies

Any of the creamed fish casserole recipes in this book can be used for pie filling (substitute cubed, cooked potatoes for bread cubes).

Make the crust from your favorite recipe or a prepared biscuit or pastry mix. If you want a bottom crust, partially cook the shell before filling it.

DEEP-DISH OYSTER PIE

1½ pts. shucked oysters, drained (save liquid)
1 pkg. prepared pie crust or your favorite recipe
1 medium onion, chopped
½ small green pepper, seeded and diced
2 stalks celery, diced
½ cup melted butter
5 tbs. flour
1½ cups milk
½ cup oyster liquor
1 cup diced cooked potato
1 tbs. minced parsley
1 tbs. chopped pimiento
salt and pepper to taste

Prepare pie crust according to package instructions and chill until needed.

In the top of a double boiler over boiling water cook onion, green pepper and celery in butter until tender. Blend flour into the butter mixture. Add milk gradually, stirring constantly, until thickened. Stir in oysters, oyster liquor, potato dice, parsley, pimiento and salt and pepper.

Pour into buttered casserole and top with rolled-out pie crust. Bake in 425° F. oven 15 to 20 minutes, or until crust is nicely browned. Serves 6.

NOTE: Individual oyster pies can be made from this recipe. If bottom crust is added they will have to bake 20 to 25 minutes.

VARIATION:

CLAM PIE: Substitute clams and clam liquor for oysters and oyster liquor in the recipe above.

SEA BASS, SHRIMP AND SCALLOP PIE

1½ lbs. sea bass, cut in chunks	4 cups water
½ lb. boiled shrimp	1 chicken bouillon cube
½ lb. boiled scallops	2 tbs. butter or margarine
1 small onion	1 tbs. chopped onion
1 carrot	2 tbs. flour
1 stalk celery	1 tsp. chopped parsley
salt and pepper to taste	½ recipe your favorite pie crust

Boil onion, carrot and celery with salt and pepper 10 minutes in water. Wrap bass in cheesecloth, add to boiling water and simmer, covered, until tender. Take fish from water, remove skin and bones, place on hot plate and keep warm. Return skin and bones to stock, add bouillon cube and cook 15 minutes longer. Strain stock and reserve.

Melt butter in a skillet, add chopped onion and sauté over low heat until onion is tender. Slowly add flour, stirring until smooth. Blend in 2¼ cups reserved strained fish stock. Add parsley and season with additional salt and pepper to taste.

Alternate layers of fish, shrimp and scallops in deep, well-greased baking dish. Pour the sauce over all and cover with rolled-out pie crust. Cut several vents in crust with a sharp knife.

Bake in 450° F. oven 12 minutes. Reduce heat to 350° F. and bake 20 minutes longer. Serves 8.

INDIVIDUAL TUNA PIES

HERB CRUST:

4 cups soft bread cubes	½ tsp. celery salt
¼ cup oil	¼ tsp. pepper
¼ cup chopped chives	¼ tsp. poultry seasoning
½ tsp. salt	

Combine bread cubes, oil, chives, salt, celery salt, pepper and poultry seasoning. Press firmly into 6 well-greased 10-oz. individual shallow casseroles to form a crust.

Bake in 350° F. oven 15 or 20 minutes or until lightly browned.

FILLING:

2 7-oz. cans tuna	2 cups milk
⅓ cup oil from cans	2 tbs. oil
⅓ cup flour	½ cup dry bread crumbs
¼ tsp. celery salt	¼ cup chopped chives
dash pepper	

Drain tuna, break into large pieces, and reserve oil. Blend flour, celery salt and pepper into tuna oil. Add milk gradually and cook, stirring constantly, until thickened. Add tuna. Place ½ cup tuna filling in each crust-lined casserole. Combine oil and crumbs. Sprinkle over tops of pies.

Bake in 425° F. oven 10 or 15 minutes, or until brown. Sprinkle with chives. Serves 6.

FISH ROLL   *Canada*

CRUST:

2¼ cups sifted flour	⅔ cup cold milk,
3 tsp. baking powder	approximately, or
1 tsp. salt	replace 3 tbs. milk by
4 tbs. shortening	1 beaten egg

Sift flour, baking powder and salt together. Cut in shortening until mixture resembles fine meal. Add milk slowly to make a soft dough. Toss on a floured board and roll out ½-inch thick. Spread fish filling over dough. Roll as for jelly roll. Pinch edges. Prick top with fork in several places. Place on baking sheet. If preferred, dough can be divided and made into two or three rolls.

Bake in 425° oven about 20 minutes or until golden brown.

FILLING:

2 cups cooked fish or shell- 1 tbs. minced onion
fish, flaked   1 tbs. lemon juice
1 tsp. salt

Combine all ingredients and spread over dough.

BAKED FROZEN FISH STICKS

Frozen fish sticks are rebroiled with mayonnaise to make an excellent appetizer or main course.

18 frozen fried fish sticks   1½ tsp. grated lemon rind
⅓ cup mayonnaise   3 tbs. chopped green
⅓ cup sour cream   onion or parsley
¼ tsp. lemon juice

Place frozen fish sticks in a single layer in a well-greased broiler pan.

Bake in 400° F. oven 15 to 20 minutes or until heated through and crisp.

Combine mayonnaise, sour cream, lemon juice and lemon rind and spread over fish sticks. Place in broiler about three inches from heat unit.

Broil two or three minutes or until mayonnaise mixture is lightly browned and bubbling. Garnish with green onion. Serves 6.

V

Buffet, Luncheon and Party Recipes

Fish is perfectly suited to the buffet, snack table, tea, cocktail party or luncheon—whether the luncheon is for hungry children or the most elaborate affair of the year. Because the method of preparation and the ingredients that go into appetizers, sandwiches, salads and seafood molds are so similar and interchangeable, we are putting them together in one section.

Fish Sandwiches

Most Americans have eaten tuna-fish sandwiches, but they overlook the other fish, especially shellfish, that are equally good in open or closed sandwiches. A toasted roll can be stuffed with hot buttered oysters; sliced French bread can be spread with sardines. Any pan- or deep-fried fish or shellfish makes a good sandwich filling. Or take some cold leftover fish, flake it, mix with mayonnaise, tartar sauce or some other combination from Part Two of this book, add a little relish and spread it between two pieces of bread.

Some sandwich fillings can be spread on crackers or on small pieces of lightly toasted bread and served as appetizers and canapés. Others, piled on lettuce leaves, become satisfying salads.

ANCHOVY AND EGG YOLK   *Bull's Eye—Norway*

4 slices bread   just large enough to hold
3 tbs. butter   a raw egg yolk
8 anchovy fillets   4 egg yolks
4 ¼-inch-wide onion rings,   2 tsp. capers
                                  watercress

Cut bread into large rounds with a cutter or drinking glass and spread with butter.

Arrange fillets around the edge of the bread and place an onion ring in the center. Slide a raw egg yolk into the onion ring. Sprinkle with capers. Garnish with watercress and serve as an open sandwich. Serves 4.

SMOKED EEL AND   *Reget Aal og Roraeg—Denmark*
SCRAMBLED EGG

½ skinned smoked eel, cut   2 eggs, scrambled and
  into 16 2-inch pieces   cooled
2 tbs. soft butter   2 tbs. chopped chives
4 slices black bread or
  pumpernickel

Arrange 4 eel pieces, next to each other, on each slice of buttered bread. Cut cold eggs into 4 slices, arrange them on the eel and sprinkle with chives.

NOTE: The eel can be decreased to 2 pieces per open sandwich with the center filled with cold scrambled egg. Scramble 3 eggs and use 2 2-inch pieces of eel for each sandwich.

LOBSTER AND OLIVES

2 cups cooked lobster meat,   1 tsp. capers
  cut in chunks   2 hard-cooked eggs,
2 tbs. chopped black olives   chopped
1 tsp. chopped pimiento   4 to 5 tbs. mayonnaise

Mix all ingredients thoroughly and chill in refrigerator. Serve in a mound on crisp lettuce leaves or use as a filling for tomatoes.

NOTE: Cut recipe in half, mince the lobster and use as a sandwich spread.

SARDINE DELIGHTS   *Portugal*

1 3¾-oz. can boneless
  Portuguese sardines
½ cup butter
1⅓ cups flour
½ cup grated Parmesan

cheese
pinch pepper
2 egg yolks
½ cup thick white sauce,
  page 123

Cut butter into flour, add half the grated cheese, pepper, egg yolks and about ½ tbs. water. Work into a smooth dough and cut into strips 1 inch wide and 2½ inches long. Place on a dry baking sheet and bake in 325° F. oven 12 to 15 minutes.

Pound sardines, mix to a cream with white sauce and stir in remaining cheese. Sandwich the strips of biscuit together in pairs with a filling of the sardine cream and serve hot. Or, for festive occasions, pipe the cream onto each strip. Makes 12.

SHRIMP, HAM, CHEESE AND EGG   *"Land in Sight,"* Smorbrod
                                               —*Norway*

4 pieces large dark bread,
  cut the length of the loaf
4 tbs. soft butter
½ cup cooked shrimp,
  shelled and deveined
½ cup mayonnaise
2 hard-cooked eggs, sliced

1 tomato, sliced
2 tbs. chopped parsley
4 thin slices boiled ham
4 thin slices cheese
4 unpeeled radishes,
  minced

Butter bread and divide each slice into four equal parts. On the first, place shrimp bound with mayonnaise, on the next, place hard-cooked egg slices and tomato sprinkled with parsley, on the next rolls of boiled ham, and on the last, cheese and finely chopped radish. Serve open. Serves 4.

TUNA SUBMARINES

2 7-oz. cans tuna, drained and flaked
3 12-inch submarine rolls cut lengthwise
1 cup chopped celery
2 tbs. chopped sweet pickle
1½ cups mayonnaise, or to taste

2 or 3 tomatoes, cut into 12 slices
1 medium onion, thinly sliced and separated into rings
6 1-oz. slices provolone cheese
6 crisp lettuce leaves
12 black olives
aluminum foil

Mix tuna, celery, pickle and mayonnaise and chill. Spread lower half of rolls with tuna mixture. Top with tomato slices, onion rings, cheese and lettuce. Spread tops of rolls with mayonnaise, invert them to cover sandwiches and secure with cocktail picks through the olives.

Wrap in aluminum foil and refrigerate until needed. When ready to serve cut in half crosswise. Serves 6.

HOT CLAMS

1 can minced clams, drained
1 10½-oz. can clam juice or milk

1 10½-oz. can mushroom soup
4 slices buttered toast
1 tsp. paprika

Add water to drained clam juice to make 1 cup. Add clam juice or milk to mushroom soup and stir until well blended. Heat, add clams, stirring constantly and cook until clams are

hot. Serve on hot buttered toast and sprinkle with paprika.
Serves 4.

COD ROE   *Norway*

8 slices warm fried cod roe   4 slices lemon
3 tbs. soft butter   1 cup mayonnaise
4 slices bread

Place roe on buttered bread, garnish with a slice of lemon,
and pipe a border of mayonnaise around the roe with a
decorating tube. Serves 4.

CROWN PRINCESS MARTHA'S   *Norway*
SPECIAL SANDWICH

4 slices white bread   sauce with 1 tsp. finely
3 tbs. soft butter   chopped dill, page 124
1 lb. freshly boiled cod   1 cup cooked shrimp,
   roe   shelled, deveined and
½ cup thick béchamel   diced

Cut roe into small pieces less than ½ inch thick. Fry lightly
in butter and place piping hot on a slice of buttered bread.
Pour warm dill sauce over it and sprinkle with shrimp.
Serves 4.

GRANDMA KLEIN'S OYSTER SANDWICHES

1½ pts. select shucked   2 eggs, beaten
   oysters, liquor reserved   salt and pepper to taste
2 cups sifted flour   6 or 12 slices bread
¼ tbs. baking powder   4 to 8 tbs. soft butter
2 cups milk

Sift flour and baking powder together. Add milk and mix
thoroughly. Add egg slowly, stirring until batter is smooth,
season to taste.

Warm oyster liquor, add oysters to it and leave over heat just long enough to warm but not cook them. Remove oysters and dry on absorbent paper. Roll in batter and fry in deep hot fat at 350° F.–375° F. 3 to 5 minutes, or until lightly browned.

Remove from oil, drain on absorbent paper and serve as filling for open or closed sandwiches with tartar sauce or catsup. Serves 6.

ENGLISH MUFFIN FISH PIZZA

4 English muffins, broken in half with a fork
8 slices Cheddar cheese
2 tomatoes, cut into 8 slices

tuna chunks, small cooked shrimps or oysters
4 strips bacon, cut in half

Cover muffins with cheese slices. Lay one slice of tomato on cheese and top this with several pieces of fish and a piece of bacon.

Arrange muffin halves on broiler pan and place 3 inches from heat unit. Broil until cheese melts and bacon browns. Serves 4.

TO SERVE AS HOT APPETIZERS: Halve again the hot muffin halves.

VARIATIONS:

1. Use slices of lightly toasted bread instead of muffins.
2. Add canned mushroom caps, drained.
3. Make with prepared pizza dough and bake instead of broil.

FISHBURGERS

Use basic recipe for fish or shellfish cakes. Shape into flat round patties and fry until light golden brown on both sides.

Serve with toasted hamburger rolls. A slice of cheese can

be placed on top of open-faced fishburgers and toasted under broiler until cheese melts. Fishburgers also can be served with tartar sauce or any sauce of your choice from Part Two.

QUICK HOT-LUNCH FISHBURGERS

18 sticks cut from leftover fish (frozen fish sticks can be substituted)

⅓ cup mayonnaise or salad dressing

2 tbs. sweet pickle relish

¼ cup melted butter or margarine

3 rolls, split, buttered and toasted

Combine mayonnaise and relish. Chill 15 minutes.

Brush fish sticks with melted butter. Arrange on a greased baking sheet in a single layer and bake in 400° F. oven 15 to 20 minutes, or until heated through and crisp.

Place three fish sticks on each roll and top with relish sauce. Serves 6.

Dishes, Dips and Spreads
for Entertaining

FLAKED COD PLATTER   *Italy*

2 lbs. boiled cod fish, flaked

¼ cup olive oil

1 garlic clove, finely chopped

juice of 1 lemon

salt and pepper to taste

2 tbs. Italian parsley, chopped

Mix oil, garlic, lemon juice, salt and pepper and spread over flaked fish on platter. Garnish with parsley, chill and serve cold.

SMOKED MUSSELS IN ONION BOATS

1 or 2 large red onions   1 3¾-oz. can smoked
                                              mussels

Quarter onions and separate layers, slice each layer into
several boat-shaped wedges.

Place one mussel and a little of the oil in which it was
canned in each onion boat.

NOTE: Rolled stuffed anchovies may be substituted for smoked
mussels.

TUNA SPREAD WITH CRANBERRY STARS

2 6½- or 7-oz. cans tuna,   ½ cup mayonnaise
  finely flaked   2 tbs. sweet relish, well
3 1-lb. cans jellied   drained
  cranberry sauce   ½ tsp. salt
¾ cup finely chopped   dash pepper
  celery   crackers or Melba
1¼ tbs. grated onion   toast rounds

Chill cranberry sauce until it is very firm and can be removed in one piece. Combine all ingredients except crackers
and cranberry sauce. Mix well and spread on crackers.

Cut cranberry into slices a little over ⅛-inch thick and
make stars and other shapes with miniature cookie cutters.
Use only one can of sauce at a time, leaving others in refrigerator to stay cold and firm. Decorate tops of tuna salad
with cranberry cutouts.

Serve immediately. Makes 50 to 60.

FISH-STUFFED EGGS

1 lb. cooked fish or shellfish, flaked
18 hard-cooked eggs
⅔ cup cream of shrimp or
mushroom soup

1 tsp. mustard
1 tsp. catsup
1 tsp. chopped pimiento
2 tbs. minced parsley
paprika

Cut eggs in half lengthwise and remove yolks. Mash yolks
and combine with soup, mustard, catsup and pimiento. Pile
mixture into egg white cavities and sprinkle with parsley and
paprika. Makes 36.

SALAD: Slice a large tomato for wedges without cutting through
at the bottom. Set stuffed egg half in center and open out tomato
wedges like petals. Serve on crisp, cupped lettuce leaf. Garnish
with mayonnaise.

SLICED STUFFED PEPPERS

3 large green peppers
1 cup flaked fish or shellfish
1 tbs. grated onion
1 egg, beaten
½ cup bread crumbs
2 tbs. sour cream or

undiluted canned shrimp
or mushroom soup
salt and pepper to taste
sliced Cheddar cheese to
cover toast
24 toast rounds or stale
bread cut in circles

Slice tops from green peppers, remove seeds and parboil in
salted water until just beginning to soften, 5 to 8 minutes.
Remove from water and invert to drain.

Combine next six ingredients and stuff peppers with mixture. Bake in 350° F. oven 25 to 30 minutes, or until peppers
are tender.

Chill stuffed peppers in refrigerator. (They can be cooked the day before you need them.) Slice crosswise in half-inch slices. Place a slice of cheese on each toast round and top with circle of the stuffed pepper. Place in hot oven or under broiler until cheese melts and stuffed pepper heats. Makes 24.

VARIATIONS:

1. Place stuffed pepper rounds on full slices of bread topped with cheese; heat and serve for luncheons.
2. Open parboiled peppers by slicing down one side from top to bottom. Lay flat and spread with fish-stuffing mixture. Roll up like jelly roll. Cook, chill, slice and use as above.

ROLY POLYS   *Canada*

1½ cups flaked fish	¼ cup chopped pineapple
¼ lb. pimiento cheese	¾ cup grated coconut,
¼ cup chopped almonds	chopped nuts or
¼ cup chopped gherkins	crushed cornflakes

Mix flaked fish and cheese and divide into two parts. To one part add chopped almonds; to the other add gherkins and pineapple. Shape into small balls and roll in grated coconut, chopped nuts or crushed cornflakes.

Serve with cocktails or as evening refreshment.

SARDINE AND CHOPPED EGG   *Portugal*
SPREAD OR DIP

1 3¾-oz. can boneless Portuguese sardines	4 tbs. mayonnaise
2 hard-cooked eggs, chopped	pepper to taste

Drain sardines and mash. Stir into chopped egg and mayonnaise. Season with salt and pepper.

SARDINE-TOMATO APPETIZERS   *Portugal*

6 small tomatoes, sliced in   scooped out
   half   1 tbs. finely chopped
6 small tomatoes with tops   parsley
   sliced off and centers

Top tomato slices and stuff cavities of scooped-out tomatoes
with sardine and chopped egg spread, page 304. Sprinkle
with chopped parsley. Makes 18.

MINCED CLAMS WITH CREAM CHEESE
DIP OR SPREAD

1 7-oz. can minced clams,   salt to taste
   drain and reserve liquor   1 tsp. Worcestershire
2 3-oz. pkgs. cream cheese   pinch garlic salt
1 tbs. lemon juice   chips or Melba toast
   onion salt to taste

Blend enough of the clam liquid into cheese to give desired
consistency. Should be softer for dip than for spread. Add
lemon juice, minced clams, onion salt, salt, Worcestershire
and garlic salt.

VARIATIONS:

1. Add chopped parsley.
2. Add finely grated onion.
3. Add a few drops Tabasco sauce.
4. Combine with cottage cheese, pineapple and place on lettuce.
5. Combine with cottage cheese to fill tomato.

SARDINE DIP OR SPREAD

1 3¾-oz. can boneless   1 8-oz. pkg. cream cheese
   sardines, finely flaked   mayonnaise
                                salt and pepper to taste

Combine sardines and cheese. Mix and mash together, adding mayonnaise to give the desired consistency. It should be softer for a dip than for a spread.

VARIATIONS:

1. Add grated onion.
2. Add 2 tbs. finely chopped cucumber.

TUNA AND AVOCADO DIP OR SPREAD

1 7-oz. can tuna, flaked and drained
2 medium avocados
2 tbs. lemon juice
3 tbs. mayonnaise, or as needed

½ tsp. Worcestershire
onion salt to taste
garlic salt to taste
salt and pepper to taste
corn chips, crackers or bread

Peel and halve avocados, remove seeds and sprinkle with lemon juice. Mash with remaining ingredients.

Spread can be chilled before serving, but the avocado will be nicer if eaten at once. Lemon juice helps prevent discoloration.

VARIATION: Mound on lettuce leaves for salad or fill tomatoes.

OYSTERS IN POTATO HALVES

24 oysters, shucked and drained
12 small baking potatoes, not more than 2 inches long
½ cup melted butter
1 tbs. grated onion
⅛ tsp. garlic salt
juice of ½ lemon

1 tsp. prepared mustard
salt and pepper to taste
2 tbs. butter
salt and pepper to taste
¼ cup milk, or to taste
¾ cup dry bread crumbs
6 tbs. melted butter
¼ cup grated cheese (optional)

Bake potatoes in 450° F. oven 30 minutes. Combine melted butter, grated onion, garlic salt, lemon juice, mustard, salt and pepper. Add oysters and marinate.

When potatoes are baked, cut in half lengthwise, scoop out pulp and mash with butter, salt, pepper and milk until fluffy. Refill potato shells and press an oyster into each half. Brown crumbs in butter, add paprika and sprinkle over oysters. Add grated cheese and return to oven. Reduce heat to 350° F. and bake until crumbs are darker brown and oysters are heated through. Makes 24.

NOTE: The potatoes may be placed under broiler to brown.

OYSTERS IN MUSHROOM CAPS

24 oysters, shucked and drained	1 cup hot whipped potatoes
24 mushroom caps about 1½ inches in diameter	3 tbs. melted butter
2 tbs. butter	¾ cup catsup
	paprika

Sauté mushroom caps lightly in butter. Arrange them, top down, in buttered broiler pan and divide whipped potatoes over mushroom cavities. Make small indentation in center of potatoes, fill with melted butter.

Dip oysters in catsup and lay one on top of each mushroom. Sprinkle with paprika.

Broil about 3 inches from heat unit until oysters start to curl at edges. Makes 24.

OYSTER PUFFS

1 8-oz. can oysters, drained and chopped	1 cup flour, sifted before measuring
½ tsp. sugar	4 eggs
1 cup milk	1 cup cocktail sauce of your choice
¼ cup butter or margarine	

Drain oysters well and chop them.

Add butter and sugar to milk in saucepan and stir over medium heat until mixture boils. Lower heat, add flour all at once and beat vigorously until mixture leaves the side of pan. Remove from heat. Add eggs, one egg at a time, beating thoroughly after each addition.

Add chopped oysters to the batter and mix well. Drop mixture by teaspoonfuls into deep fat 350°–375° 5 to 6 minutes or until brown. Drain on absorbent paper. Serve on wooden picks with cocktail sauce. Makes 50 to 60.

OYSTERS WRAPPED IN BACON

1 pt. select oysters, shucked and drained	barbecue sauce, page 112 (optional)
	12 slices bacon, cut in half

Dip each oyster in barbecue sauce, roll in bacon slice and fasten with wooden picks. Place rolls on rack in shallow baking pan.

Bake in preheated 450° F. oven about 3 minutes on each side, or until bacon is crisp. If rolls are to be served as an appetizer, place picks so they will not rest in bacon drippings. Makes about 24.

OYSTER KABOBS

1 qt. select shucked oysters	6 slices bacon, cut in thirds
¼ cup oil	3 tomatoes, cut in thick slices
1 tsp. salt	
½ tsp. Worcestershire	18 mushroom caps
2 tbs. catsup	2 green peppers, seeded and cut in chunks
3 tbs. lemon juice	

Marinate oysters 20 minutes in a sauce made by combining oil, salt, Worcestershire, catsup and lemon juice.

String oysters, vegetables and bacon alternately on skewers leaving enough space at both ends to place skewers across a shallow baking dish. Brush with sauce in which oysters were marinated, and baste with remaining sauce during cooking. Use brush or baster to conserve sauce.

Bake in very hot 500° F. oven about 20 minutes or until bacon is crisp. Serves 6.

VARIATIONS:

1. Marinating is not necessary. This kabob can be made without the sauce and all you need is a sprinkling of pepper, salt and paprika.
2. Scallops, large shrimp and chunks of lobster can be substituted for oysters.
3. Green pepper and mushrooms can be precooked for 5 minutes if you like them tender.
4. Substitute large black olives for one of vegetables.

OUTDOOR BARBECUE: Place skewers across outdoor barbecue grill about 4 inches above coals that have burned down to hot, red-grey and are no longer flaming. Cook 3 to 5 minutes or until edges of oysters start to curl and bacon is crisp. Baste with marinade while cooking.

SALMON KABOBS *Oven or outdoor barbecue*

2 lbs. salmon steaks, cut into 1-inch cubes	¼ cup vinegar
	¼ cup brown sugar
1 cup catsup	2 tsp. salt
⅓ cup salad oil	8 drops Tabasco

Combine catsup, oil, vinegar, sugar, salt and Tabasco. Pour sauce over fish and marinate for 1½ hours. Turn every 20 minutes.

Remove fish from marinade and string on 6 skewers. Place skewers across a baking pan. Baste with sauce. Bake in a 375° F. oven for 20 minutes. Baste once during baking with remaining sauce. Serves 6.

OUTDOOR BARBECUE: Cut 6 sheets of aluminum foil large enough to cover kabobs. Place skewers in center of sheets, and baste with a little sauce. Wrap and place on charcoal grill for 10 minutes, rotating occasionally.

Unwrap and continue barbecuing for a few minutes more until fish flakes easily when tested with a fork.

NOTE: Large shrimp, oysters, scallops and chunks of lobster meat can be prepared this way. Do not overcook.

FISH TIDBITS

½ lb. cooked fish or shellfish, ground
1 tbs. grated cheese
1 tbs. grated onion

2 tbs. soft butter or
margarine
1 egg yolk, well beaten
1 tsp. lemon juice
2 or 3 drops Tabasco

Mix cheese and onion with butter. Add egg yolk, lemon juice and Tabasco, thoroughly blend and combine with ground fish. Arrange by teaspoonfuls on well-greased cookie sheet.

Bake in 400° F. oven about 5 minutes, or until lightly brown. Makes 36.

SHRIMP PIES INEZ

¾ cup cooked shellfish,
flaked and mashed
2 tbs. condensed frozen
shrimp soup (mayon-
naise or sour cream can
be substituted)
1 tbs. grated onion
1 tbs. grated celery
1 tbs. grated cheese

½ tsp. lemon juice
salt to taste
36 tiny cooked shrimp or
chunks of shrimp
2 10-oz. pkgs. pie crust mix
paprika
onion salt to taste
cookie cutter, 2 to 2½
inches in diameter

Mix first seven ingredients and crush to a paste. Cover a cookie sheet or shallow pan with wax paper. Place mix in 36 rounds on paper. Press one tiny shrimp or chunk of shrimp into center of each dab. Put in freezer until frozen solid. (Use ice-cube trays if you have no freezer.)

Prepare pie crust according to package instructions. Roll dough as thin as you can and cut into 72 small circles, 2 to 2½ inches in diameter.

Place a frozen round in centers of 36 circles and cover with the other 36. Pinch edges together, prick tops with fork, spread little pies on cookie sheet and place in freezer. When pie crusts are firm, remove and cut excess dough from outer edges with cookie cutter.

Sprinkle tops of pies with paprika and onion salt and bake in 450° F. oven. When crusts start to brown, reduce heat to 350° F. and continue baking about 10 minutes or until pies are lightly browned. Makes 36.

NOTE: *To prepare ahead of time:* Make as above, wrap pies in wax paper and place in freezer until time to cook and serve. These pies are so small that they need only a few minutes extra time in the oven to defrost. They hold their shape better when baked frozen.

The secret of success in making these appetizers is to work only with very cold ingredients. Otherwise they are too hard to handle and do not turn out well.

PETITE SALMON ROLLS

1 cup canned salmon (or smoked fish) flaked and mashed

2 tbs. condensed mushroom soup (mayonnaise or sour cream can be substituted)

1 tbs. grated onion

1 tbs. grated celery

1 tbs. grated cheese

½ tsp. lemon juice
salt to taste

1 10-oz. pkg. pie crust mix
paprika

Mix first seven ingredients. Crush to a paste, divide into three parts and place in refrigerator.

Prepare pie crust according to package instructions. Divide into three parts and roll into three balls. Roll each into a circle, as thin as possible. Spread each circle with a third of the salmon paste and cut in 16 wedge-shaped pieces. Starting with wide end of wedges, roll each jelly-roll fashion. Sprinkle with paprika, arrange on baking sheet and bake in 450° F. oven until rolls start to brown. Reduce heat to 350° F. and continue baking about 15 minutes or until the rolls are lightly browned. Check to be sure they do not burn. Makes 48.

PICKLED HERRINGS

Haugesund Silt—Norway

2 large pickled herrings
2 tbs. oil
2 tbs. vinegar
3 tbs. sugar
1 tsp. pepper
1 small onion, finely chopped

1 pickled beet, finely chopped
ample supplies of finely chopped parsley

Rinse herrings and soak in water to cover 12 hours in refrigerator. Cut into diagonal pieces, one inch long, and place on a flat dish so that the herring looks all of a piece. Stir together oil, vinegar, sugar, and pepper, pour over herrings, refrigerate three hours. Decorate with onion, beet strips and parsley. Serve with freshly boiled potatoes and a large bowl of whipped sour cream.

MARINATED PICKLED HERRING

Silt—Norway

3 pickled herrings
3 tbs. tomato paste
2 minced onions
12 bay leaves

2 tbs. sugar
4 tbs. vinegar
1 tbs. water

Soak herrings 6 hours in cold water. Cut in small pieces. Blend remaining ingredients and marinate herring in mixture. Allow to stand in refrigerator 48 hours before serving.

NOTE: Use glass dish for marinating.

QUEENSLAND LOBSTER COCKTAIL   *Australia*

3 lobster tails
juice of 1½ lemons
2½ tsp. Worcestershire
6 tbs. tomato chili sauce

6 tbs. liquid lobster was cooked in
½ cup heavy cream, whipped

Simmer lobster tails, page 69, adding the lemon juice to water. Cool lobster and refrigerate 2 hours in same liquid. Drain lobster and cut into chunks. Combine Worcestershire, chili sauce and 6 tbs. liquid drained from lobster. Fold in whipped cream and lobster chunks.

Serve in fish cocktail glasses garnished with watercress and lemon wedges. Serves 6.

MACKEREL   *Norrkoping—Sweden*

2 lbs. mackerel
1 tbs. salt
1½ tbs. vinegar
8 peppercorns
juice of ½ lemon
1 medium onion, sliced
6 tbs. mayonnaise
5 tbs. very heavy cream

1¾ tbs. dried or fresh dill, chopped
1½ tbs. chopped parsley
1½ tbs. chopped chives
3 hard-cooked eggs, sliced
2 large tomatoes, sliced

Wash and clean mackerel, place in pot, in water to cover. Add salt, vinegar, peppercorns, lemon juice, onion and bring to a boil. Reduce heat immediately and simmer 15 to 20 minutes or until meat comes freely from bones. Let cool in stock overnight, in a glass dish.

Remove fish from stock and place on serving platter.

Fold mayonnaise into whipped cream and spread over cold mackerel. Sprinkle with dill, parsley and chives and arrange a border of egg slices and tomatoes around it. Serve with small boiled potatoes.

MARINATED OYSTERS

24 oysters, shucked
6 medium onions, sliced
1½ cups vinegar

2 tsp. chili powder, or to taste
1½ tsp. salt

Mix onions, vinegar, chili powder and salt in glass container.

Place oysters in separate dish, cover with boiling water and let stand 3 minutes. Drain oysters and add to vinegar mixture. Cover tightly and store in refrigerator at least 12 hours.

Serve cold. If oysters are removed from marinade, be sure to include onions in serving.

NOTE: Always marinate in a glass container, do not use metal.

MARINATED SHRIMP   *Ecuador*

30 large shrimp, about 2 lbs.
   juice of 8 lemons
   juice of 2 oranges
3 red Spanish onions, sliced
   Tabasco to taste

salt to taste
3 garlic cloves, finely chopped
   white pepper to taste
1 tbs. olive oil
   catsup

Simmer shrimp in water to cover until shells become pink, about 5 minutes. Shell, clean and devein.

Combine lemon and orange juice with sliced onions, hot sauce and salt. Add shrimp and marinate in refrigerator, in glass container, at least 5 hours.

When ready to serve, mix in garlic, pepper and olive oil and add catsup to color. Serve with French or Italian bread or korn-parchis (available in most delicacy shops) and beer. Makes 30.

RAW OYSTERS

See Shelling and Cleaning Oysters, page 53.

SPICY, HOT OYSTER COCKTAIL

48 shucked oysters
oyster liquor, strained
through cheesecloth
½ cup butter
1 cup catsup
2 tbs. Worcestershire
1 tbs. Tabasco

1 cup chili sauce
1 tsp. lemon juice
1 cup finely chopped
celery
1 onion, finely chopped
1 garlic clove, crushed
(optional)

Remove any bits of broken shell from oysters, put in their own liquor and store in refrigerator until ready to serve.

Rub butter over bottom and sides of large pot. Add all other ingredients except oysters. When almost ready to serve cocktail, heat sauce just to a simmering point, do not boil. Turn off heat and add only as many oysters (in a strainer basket) as you are going to serve right then. Leave the oysters in the heated sauce just long enough to heat through. Reheat sauce before adding more oysters.

Serve at once on wooden picks. Or on shredded lettuce in cocktail glasses with lemon wedges. Serves 8 to 12.

Salads

HALIBUT AND SHRIMP SALAD   *Denmark*

1½ lbs. halibut, poached
and flaked
3 jars or cans tiny Danish
or Greenland shrimp
juice of half a lemon

1 tbs. minced dill
2 hard-cooked eggs,
chopped
salt and pepper to taste
mayonnaise to bind

Drain brine from shrimp, sprinkle with lemon juice and chill. Combine halibut with shrimp (retaining a few for garnish), dill and hard-cooked eggs and season to taste with salt, pepper, lemon juice and enough mayonnaise to bind well. Chill salad before serving.

Arrange on lettuce leaves with sliced cucumbers and sprinkle with extra shrimp. This salad is at its best when chilled five or six hours. Serves 6.

NORWEGIAN HERRING SALAD

2 pickled herrings	1 cup thick sour cream
2 boiled potatoes, peeled and diced	1 tbs. sugar
2 apples, cored and diced	4 pickled red beets, diced
1 small pickled cucumber	2 tbs. minced parsley
1 tbs. minced onion	2 hard-cooked eggs, cut in wedges
2 tbs. vinegar	

Soak herring in water to cover for 12 hours. Drain and dice herrings, combine with potatoes, apples and cucumber. Add onion and vinegar. Whip cream with sugar. Stir into herring mixture and let stand 1 hour in a cool place. Mix in half the beets, put into bowl, decorate with wedges of hard-cooked eggs, remaining beets and minced parsley. Serves 6.

NOTE: Add beets just before serving if you do not want them to tint the salad red.

SOUTH PACIFIC LOBSTER SALAD   *Australia*

6 lobster tails	1 cucumber, thinly sliced
½ head of lettuce, shredded	1 medium onion, thinly sliced
2 cups cooked, mixed, diced carrots, green beans and peas	1 cup ripe olives
salt and pepper	3 tomatoes, peeled and quartered
1 cup mayonnaise (about) capers to taste	1 avocado, peeled and sliced at last moment
1 canned pimiento, sliced	1 cup carrot curls

Boil lobster tails, cool and remove meat from shell, discarding dark vein. Reserve several large chunks. Chop remaining meat finely and combine with shredded lettuce, mixed vegetables and seasonings. Bind with some mayonnaise and pile into shells. Top with chunks of lobster meat and coat with mayonnaise.

Garnish with capers and pimiento strips. Arrange tails on platter and surrounded with cucumber, onion rings, olives, tomatoes, avocado and carrot curls.

Chill well and serve with additional mayonnaise. Serves 6.

SARDINE SALAD I   *with apples*

3 3¾-oz. cans boned sardines, drained

2 red apples, ripe but firm, diced

1 large stalk crisp celery, diced

¼ cup slivered toasted almonds

½ cup sour cream, or to taste

Chill all ingredients. Cut sardines into large pieces.

Combine all other ingredients and stir with sour cream. Gently add sardine chunks, being careful not to break them.

Serve on lettuce. Serves 6.

SARDINE SALAD II   *with cabbage*

3 3¾-oz. cans boned sardines, drained and chilled

½ small head of cabbage

1 small onion, finely chopped

2 hard-cooked eggs, chopped

¼ cup chopped parsley vinegar to taste sugar to taste

½ cup heavy cream

Cut cabbage in three wedges and soak in cold salted water for about one hour. Drain, wipe as dry as possible and continue draining in a sieve in the refrigerator until needed.

Break sardines into large pieces and mix with onion, egg and parsley.

Shred cabbage very finely and combine with sardine mixture.

Mix a little vinegar and sugar into the heavy cream, testing as you go, to make a dressing. Stir into salad and serve. Serves 6.

MOLDED SHRIMP AND SCALLOP SALAD

¼ lb. cooked shrimp, shelled and deveined
¼ lb. cooked scallops, cut in quarters
1½ tsp. lemon juice
1 tsp. sugar
4 sections orange, skinned, cut in half and dried on absorbent paper
4 sections grapefruit, skinned, cut in half and dried on absorbent paper
½ cup mayonnaise
1 3-oz. pkg. cream cheese
½ cup chopped blanched almonds, toasted
½ cup seedless grapes
½ cup heavy cream, whipped

Sprinkle lemon juice on shrimp and scallops, toss lightly and drain off any excess. Sprinkle sugar over orange and grapefruit sections. Blend mayonnaise into cream cheese and add shellfish, almonds and fruit.

Combine whipped cream with fruit and shellfish mixture, pour into freezer dish or ice-cube trays and let it get almost firm. Stir twice while it is soft. Return to freezer and chill until firm.

Unmold, slice and serve on bed of lettuce. Serves 6.

NOTE: Use only very ripe fruit.

VARIATION: Make in individual round molds and serve on top

of a circle of colored gelatin, on a pineapple slice, a large peach half or avocado slices.

SHRIMP PINEAPPLE SALAD

1 lb. large fresh shrimp, cooked, shelled, deveined and chilled, or 3 4½-oz. cans shrimp	1 avocado
	2 large oranges
	1 tbs. lemon juice
	½ cup mayonnaise
1 large ripe pineapple	¼ cup medium cream

Place prepared shrimp in refrigerator for ½ to ¾ of an hour or drain canned shrimp and cover with ice. Allow to stand 10 minutes and drain.

Cut pineapple in half lengthwise; remove core and meat. Save shell for serving. Cube pineapple meat. Peel and section oranges. Peel and slice avocado; sprinkle with lemon juice to prevent discoloration. Combine mayonnaise and cream.

Fill shells with orange, pineapple and avocado slices. Top with chilled shrimp and mayonnaise dressing. Serves 6.

VARIATIONS:

1. Add green or purple grapes or cherries for color.
2. If you cannot purchase fresh pineapple, same recipe does well with pineapple chunks, well drained, and placed in refrigerator. This will be a little sweeter.

FISH AND VEGETABLE SALAD

½ to 1 lb. cooked fish or shellfish, chopped	½ cup diced cucumber
	½ tsp. lemon juice
1 small onion, finely chopped	salt and pepper to taste
	½ to 1 cup mayonnaise
2 stalks celery, chopped	lettuce
1 pimiento, chopped	

Combine fish, onion, celery, pimiento and cucumber in salad bowl. Add lemon juice and salt and pepper to mayonnaise and stir into salad. Serve at once on lettuce leaves. Serves 4 to 6.

VARIATIONS:

1. Add ribbons of green pepper.
2. Add sliced, hard-cooked eggs.
3. Add sliced radishes.
4. Add ¼ tsp. minced dill.
5. Serve with a Louis dressing, page 120, instead of mayonnaise and lemon juice.

LOUIS SALAD

1 lb. crab meat, lobster meat or salmon, cooked and cut into chunks	2 or 3 hard-cooked eggs, sliced
1 head lettuce	1 cucumber, sliced
	Louis dressing, page 120

Shred lettuce, place in a bowl and top with chunks of seafood. Surround with egg and cucumber slices and cover entire salad with Louis dressing. Serves 6.

VARIATIONS:

1. Add tomato wedges.
2. Substitute plain mayonnaise or any other dressing.

Seafood molds

Use one or more of these suggestions to make and remove your seafood aspic from its mold:
1. Rinse mold with cold water just before pouring in gelatin.
2. Press aluminum foil into rectangular mold, lift out chilled

gelatin and peel off foil. Quilted foil leaves a nice design on the surface of the gelatin.

3. Rub mold with unseasoned oil. Add cooled gelatin after it has begun to set, but is still liquid enough to pour.

4. Line a rinsed mold with a layer of plain gelatin before adding gelatin containing seafood, fruit or vegetables. Do this by pouring gelatin into the mold and revolving the mold until all sides are coated. Chill and repeat until an even layer of gelatin is obtained. Use this method for making decorative arrangements inside the mold.

5. Dip mold briefly in hot water to within ½ inch of the top or warm it with towels wrung out of hot water. Invert a serving platter on the mold, invert both and shake or tap the mold gently until the aspic slides onto the platter.

6. Most important, unless you are experienced and very skillful, choose a simple rectangular or round form without indentations. Any amount of decorating can be added after it is removed from the mold (see list of garnishes, page 325). The colors of the gelatin and fish are often very attractive. Try a pale lemon gelatin with pink shrimp, or a brilliant red gelatin encasing chunks of white lobster.

To Glaze With Gelatin or Aspic: Lay fish on serving tray. Spoon cool, but liquid gelatin or aspic over it, letting each layer of liquid set in the refrigerator before applying the next one. Set the pan of liquid gelatin in warm water if it becomes too firm to flow.

For Firmer Aspics: Cut down on the liquid or increase gelatin.

For Richer Flavored Gelatin: Substitute fruit juice or bouillon for some of the water.

To Chill More Quickly: Use chilled instead of cool liquid. Ice cubes can be added, but be sure they do not increase quantity of liquid.

To Make Your Own Gelatin: Liquid in which fish bones and skin are cooked forms a jelly when chilled. Scandinavians cook the fish in a spicy stock and leave it to set in its own jelly. The fish is garnished and served on the "cold table." Jewish gefilte fish is prepared in much the same way, except that the fish is ground.

CARP IN JELLY

Karpfen in gelée—Austria

4 lbs. carp, cut into 1-inch
steaks (do not remove
skin and bones, they
make the jelly)
2 cups julienne carrots

and celery root
1 small onion, thinly
sliced
10 peppercorns
½ cup vinegar

Boil the vegetables, onion and peppercorns, in vinegar and
3 to 4 cups salted water until almost tender. Add fish and
more water if necessary to completely cover. Cook gently
15 minutes more. Arrange fish in serving dish. Remove skin
and bones. Pour fish stock with vegetables over fish, chill
until set. Serves 7 to 8.

NOTE: Any other fish can be prepared this way.

SALMON IN ASPIC

Netherlands

2 center cut salmon steaks
3 envelopes gelatin
(unflavored)
3 chicken bouillon cubes
3 tbs. lemon juice
salt and pepper

mayonnaise
2 pkgs. frozen peas
6 hard-cooked eggs, halved
and stuffed, page 303
parsley
1 lemon, thinly sliced

Soften gelatin in 6 tbs. cold water. Dissolve bouillon cubes
in 3 cups boiling water, add lemon juice, salt and pepper.
Take from heat, add softened gelatin and stir until dissolved.
Set aside to cool.

Wash salmon and boil in salted water to cover, taking care
that slices remain whole. Allow to cool quickly in stock.
Remove skin and bones from fish without disturbing its
shape and arrange in center of large shallow platter. Brush
salmon with liquid aspic and chill. Repeat brushing until

salmon is heavily glazed. Pipe mayonnaise on center and around edges of each salmon steak. Chill.

Pour ¼-inch-layer of aspic in 12 muffin tins that have been rinsed with cold water. When set, place small mounds of cooked peas in center of each tin, then fill with aspic and chill. Unmold and make a border of the jellied peas around the salmon, alternating with the halved stuffed eggs. Garnish with mayonnaise, parsley and wedges of lemon. Serves 6.

NOTE: A traditional accompaniment is cucumber salad, and more stuffed eggs. See next two recipes.

TUNA OR SALMON MOLD

2 7-oz. cans tuna or 1 16-oz. can salmon, drained and broken into pieces
2 tbs. unflavored gelatin
2 pkgs. instant chicken bouillon powder (or 2 cubes chicken bouillon)
⅔ cup sour cream or mayonnaise
2 hard-cooked eggs, chopped
½ cup chopped celery
¼ cup cooked peas
½ cup ripe olives, chopped lettuce leaves or finely shredded cabbage
2 tomatoes, peeled and cut into wedges mayonnaise or French dressing

Soften gelatin in ½ cup cold water for 5 minutes. Dissolve bouillon powder in 1½ cups boiling water, take from heat, add gelatin and stir until dissolved. Set aside to cool. Chill to the consistency of unbeaten egg white, stir in canned fish, sour cream or mayonnaise, chopped eggs, celery, peas and olives. Pour into a rinsed 2-quart mold and chill until firm.

Unmold on lettuce leaves, pipe with mayonnaise and garnish with tomato wedges. Serves 6.

VARIATION: Add finely grated onion.

SEAFOOD MOUSSE

2 cups canned or cooked fish or shellfish, drained and flaked
1 pkg. lemon gelatin
1 cup boiling water
½ cup cold water
2 tbs. lemon juice
¼ tsp. salt
½ cup mayonnaise or salad dressing
2 tbs. catsup
½ cup chopped celery
2 tbs. stuffed olives, sliced
lettuce leaves or finely shredded cabbage

Dissolve gelatin in boiling water. Add cold water, lemon juice and salt. Chill until consistency of unbeaten egg white. Combine mayonnaise, catsup, celery and olives. Add flaked fish and combine into gelatin. Pour into mold that has been rinsed with cold water. Chill until firm.

Unmold on lettuce leaves. Serves 6.

VARIATIONS:

1. Substitute 1 envelope unflavored gelatin for lemon gelatin.
2. Substitute 1 tsp. prepared mustard and grated onion for catsup.
3. Add ½ to ¾ cup heavy cream, whipped.
4. Add 2 tbs. chopped sweet pickle, drained.

VI

Garnishes

The plainest of dishes can be made more appealing by the simple addition of one or two garnishes. Cut a thin cross section from the end of a green pepper, add some thin circles of a cross-cut carrot and lay them on a fish or float them in a bowl of soup. The garnishes that go with fish start with lemon slices, or wedges, and parsley. Here is a list of them and suggested ways of preparing them. Keep them simple so that they don't cover up or detract from the fish aspic. Pour fruit-flavored gelatin or tomato aspic ¼ inch thick, unmold and cut into decorative shapes. Reduce the liquid to make firmer mold. Replace some of liquid with fruit juice for richer color and flavor.

* BEETS: cooked whole, sliced or pickled. The juice can be used to flavor and color mayonnaise.

CABBAGE: finely shredded with knife, and spun around to make a nest, or grated.

CAPERS

* CARROTS: sticks, curls, shredded or grated.

CELERY: tops, hearts, sticks, curls. An inside celery stalk is often beautifully shaped and can be used as a garnish just as it is.

* CRANBERRY: and other fruit jelly that can be chilled and sliced. Cranberries cooked whole.

* Designs can be cut from these foods with cookie cutters or a knife.

CUCUMBERS: sliced or sticks. Leave skin on for more color and nutrition. Score sides before slicing.

DILL: powdered, chopped, sprigs.

FRUIT (canned or fresh): spiced, sliced, whole or cut in pieces.

* GREEN PEPPERS: strips or rings.

GRAPEFRUIT SECTIONS: peeled.

* HARD-COOKED EGGS: slices, wedges, riced, chopped, crushed yolk can be mixed with mayonnaise for added color.

LEMONS: slices, wedges, grated rind, lemon shells filled with mayonnaise or salad dressing.

LETTUCE: crisp leaves, torn (tear with fingers), shredded.

MAYONNAISE: serve separately or pipe over fish as garnish.

MUSHROOM: caps and filled caps.

* NOODLES AND PASTA: cooked. Your supermarket has many interesting and beautiful shapes—wagon wheels, shells, bows, green noodles.

ONIONS: sliced, rings or pickled pearls.

ORANGE: sliced, peeled sections, grated peel, shells filled with sauces.

PAPRIKA: sprinkle sparingly.

PARSLEY: sprigs, chopped and dried flakes.

* POTATO: boiled and sliced. Mashed for borders, chips.

* Designs can be cut from these foods with cookie cutters or a knife.

* PICKLES: whole, sliced, relish.

RADISHES: slices, whole, flowers.

SHELLFISH: tiny shrimp.

SOUR CREAM: whipped.

PASTA ALPHABETS: cooked. Use for lettering for children.

SPINACH: pureed for borders. Juice can be used to flavor and color mayonnaise.

TOMATOES: sliced, wedges, small ones whole or filled.

WATERCRESS: sprigs or chopped.

* Designs can be cut from these foods with cookie cutters or a knife.

Index